Business Relationships with East Asia

This collection of articles analyses the business environment in East Asia with reference to trade and FDI flows within the region and between East Asia and Europe. Focusing on the two-way flow of management ideas, investment and technology, this study highlights the way in which both sides can benefit. Neither Europe nor East Asia behaves as a homogenous entity but, within each, important cultural and economic differences affect the success and failure of business ventures.

Jim Slater is Director of the Graduate Centre for Business Administration, The Birmingham Business School, University of Birmingham. **Roger Strange** is Head of Management Centre, King's College London.

Routledge Advances in Asia-Pacific Business

Business Relationships with East Asia

The European Experience

Edited by Jim Slater and Roger Strange

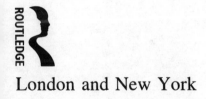

London and New York

First published 1997
by Routledge
11 New Fetter Lane, London EC4P 4EE

Simultaneously published in the USA and Canada
by Routledge
29 West 35th Street, New York, NY 10001

© 1997 Jim Slater and Roger Strange

Typeset in Times by
J&L Composition Ltd, Filey, North Yorkshire

Printed and bound in Great Britain by
Mackays of Chatham PLC, Chatham, Kent

British Library Cataloguing in Publication Data

A catalogue record for this book is available from the British Library

Library of Congress Cataloging in Publication Data

A catalogue record for this book has been requested

ISBN   0–415–13705–5

Contents

Figures

Tables

Contributors

Nigel Campbell is Senior Lecturer in Strategic Management at the Manchester Business School.

Chen Changzheng is former Chief of Section of the Planning and Economic Commission, Jiangsu Province, People's Republic of China.

Jocelyn Chen is Lecturer at the School of Management and Finance, University of Nottingham.

Robert Hine is Senior Lecturer in Economics at the University of Nottingham.

Yeon Hak Kim is Senior Researcher at the Management Research Laboratory, Korea Telecom Research Centre, Seoul.

Wolfgang Klenner is Professor at the Faculty of East Asian Studies, University of Bochum.

Yi-Cheng Liu is a Ph.D. student at the Management Centre, King's College, London.

Sid Lowe is Lecturer at the Management Centre, King's College, London.

Corrado Molteni is Adjunct Professor at the Institute of Economic and Social Studies for East Asia, Luigi Bocconi University, Milan.

Sang-Kun Nam is Director of the International Affairs Department at the Korea Chamber of Commerce and Industry.

Weihwa Pan is Researcher at the Centre for Research in Industrial Strategy, University of Birmingham Business School.

David Parker is Senior Lecturer at the Centre for Research in Industrial Strategy, University of Birmingham Business School.

Gordon Robinson is Senior Lecturer at the University of Central England Business School.

Jim Slater is Director of the Graduate Centre for Business Administration, The School of Business, at the University of Birmingham.

Roger Strange is Senior Lecturer in Economics and Head of the Management Centre at King's College, London.

Yong Gu Suh is Lecturer at Templeton College, Oxford.

Peter Wright is Lecturer in Economics at the University of Nottingham.

Xiaohong Wu is a Ph.D. student at the Management Centre, King's College, London.

1 Introduction

Jim Slater

A widespread implicit belief in both Europe and East Asia is that the 'other' region is homogeneous. Visitors are often dismayed to discover that both are equally diverse linguistically, culturally and economically. This diversity complicates business decision-making and increases the need for accurate intelligence. The authors' hope is that this book will assist in the requisite environmental scanning. The emphasis here is on conditions in East Asia, rather than on Europe. None of the studies is specifically concerned with Japan. Even though roughly one-third of the papers presented at the conference in Birmingham, which forms the basis of this collection, were concerned with Japan, it was felt that Japan is already heavily researched, but that there is relatively little easily available information on other, faster-growing East Asian economies. The scale and pace of change in these countries is unprecedented as technology transfer, globalization and liberalization have undammed their commercial energies. However, though the 'Region' exists as a geographical entity it is no more homogenous in national or business/organizational culture than is Europe. There are, for example, clear differences in industrial organization: the Chaebol of Korea and the Japanese sogoshosha differ in concept and management style and contrast with the networking of relatively small Taiwanese firms. The physical distance between Singapore and Tokyo is similar to that between Europe and the USA, but the cultural distance is probably considerably greater. Economic development also varies considerably among Asian countries: what these countries have in common is the ability to generate and cope with change at a rate outside contemporary experience elsewhere. A summary of the development status of the relevant countries is shown in Table 1.1 below.

Within Europe there are, of course, also wide differences between countries though within narrower geographic limits. The southern countries of the EU are less developed than the north, whilst the difference in development between the EU and the former Soviet Eastern European countries is even more marked. Because of these differences and because of liberalization, there are, within and between both these regions, considerable opportunities for trade and, particularly, investment. Whilst regionalism

Table 1.1 Economic development status among Asian countries

	Country	Development status
NIE 'Dragons'	Singapore	Developed*
	South Korea	Mature NIE/Developed
	Taiwan	Mature NIE/Developed
	Hong Kong	Mature NIE
ASEAN	Thailand	Young/Mature NIE
'Tigers'	Indonesia	Developing
	Malaysia	Developing/Young NIE
	Philippines	Young NIE
	China	Young NIE
	Vietnam	Low income Developing
	Cambodia	Low income Developing
	Laos	Low income Developing
	Myanmar	Low income Developing

* Singapore's official status as 'developed' is subject to some ambiguity. The Organisation for Economic Cooperation and Development (OECD) puts Singapore in the category of advanced developing nations no longer eligible for aid. However, its living standards are ahead of Britain.
Source: Adapted from Nomura Research Institute. Classification is based on current trade structure.

may have lessened internal trade barriers, it has also raised external ones. Trade barriers and frictions are likely to stimulate Foreign Direct Investment (FDI), an alternative to exporting, as a means of circumvention. Globalization and liberalization of firms and national economies, tied to emerging regionalism, have, in fact, provided the foundations for an enormous growth in FDI. Statistically, FDI figures are subject to varying degrees of over- or under-reporting, as well as to unpredictable innaccuracies due to problems of reporting and data collection. However, the main trends and rough magnitudes seem incontestable. Between Asia and Europe, in both directions, and within Asia, this type of commercial activity is growing rapidly and at a much faster rate than conventional trade. Most of this book, therefore, is concerned with investment and direct linkages rather than with trade *per se*.

Much of the growth in Asian FDI has been driven by China's liberalization and opening-up to the outside world, particularly as a result of policies aimed at investment-led growth. Table 1.2 shows outward FDI figures for some of the main Asian investors. Between the mid-1980s and 1990s the total volume of outward investment increased by orders of magnitude. Absolute values of investment to the major destinations increased but the share of the US as a recipient declined in favour of the Asian countries, including China, and Europe. Only Singapore's pattern is different, arising from a very large decline in Malaysia's share of Singaporean FDI (from over 50% to less than 25% between 1985

Table 1.2 Destinations of outward investment – selected Asian origins (US$ m.)

		East Asia		Europe		North America		China	
Japan[1]	1985	460	(19.6)[2]	323	(13.7)	1,223	(52)	22	(0.9)
	1993	3,659	(32.9)	2,041	(18.3)	4,146	(37.2)	1,377	(12.4)
Taiwan	1985	4.2	(10.2)	0.9	(2.2)	35.8	(86.7)	–	–
	1992	(369.9)	(32.7)	292.8	(25.8)	202.2	(17.8)	247	(21.8)
Singapore[3]	1985	1,663.5	(73.7)	90.3	(4.0)	65.5	(2.9)	58.7	(2.6)
	1993	5,541.3	(42.3)	93.4	(11.4)	1,375.5	(10.5)	379.9	(2.9)

[1] Figures for Japan are Manufacturing only.
[2] Figures in parentheses are percentages.
[3] $ m. Singapore.

Note: The above figures and those in Table 1.3 are collected from a variety of sources and are not comparable in absolute terms. However, they are indicative of changes in magnitude over time.

Table 1.3 Inward FDI in selected Asian destinations (US$ m.)
(% share in brackets)

Singapore

Year	USA		Japan		Europe		East Asia		Others	
1985	4,659.6	(23)	2,937.6	(14.5)	7,414.8	(36.6)	4,153.1	(20.5)	1,073.7	(5.3)
1992	9,639	(17)	13,211	(23.3)	16,386	(28.9)	6,861	(12.1)	10,603	(18.7)

South Korea

Year	USA		Japan		Europe		East Asia	
1962–71 Total	120.324	(45)	98.017	(37)	20.732	(8)	6.398	(2.4)
1993	340.669	(33)	285.943	(27)	307.424	(29)	105.640	(10)

China[4]

Year	HK/Macau		Japan		Other East Asian		USA		Europe	
1984	747.53	(53)	224.58	(16)	8.51[6]	(0.6)	256.25	(18)	143.69[5]	(10)
1993	17,275	(63)	1,324	(5)	3,513[6]	(13)	2,063	(7)	418[7]	(1.5)

[4] Implemented.
[5] UK, West Germany, France, Italy.
[6] Taiwan (US$3,139 m.) and South Korea only.
[7] UK, West Germany, France.

and 1993). It is fairly clear that massive shifts in FDI can occur over relatively short periods of time. The boom in FDI into Europe in the early 1990s may have been induced by implementation of the Single Market and anticipatory fears of a Regional fortress. In the last two or three years there are indications of increasingly large switches into China despite Tiananmen.

Table 1.3 shows the magnitude and origins of FDI into Singapore, Korea and China. It shows clearly the massive increase in intra-regional FDI in less than a decade and, again, a decline in the US share. Both Table 1.2 and 1.3 confirm that there has been a significant increase in FDI, especially within the East Asia region, that Europe–East Asia investment is highly active in both directions and that this is growing.

Investment patterns are neither simple nor unidirectional. For example, between Hong Kong and China, capital is moving in both directions. Investment from Hong Kong to China is primarily in the traditional mature manufacturing sectors to take advantage of lower labour and land costs. Most of the manufacturing companies who have moved have closed their plants in Hong Kong. Increasingly, service firms are moving not only for cost advantage but also as support services following their mainly manu-facturing clients. Investment from China to Hong Kong is primarily in the trade and financial services sectors: either to help emerging Chinese multinationals to engage with the world economy or to provide a back-door for domestic capital to realize packages of benefits designed for foreign investors (sometimes known as round-trip investment). By far the greatest proportion of inward investment to China is from 'overseas' Chinese in Hong Kong, Macau and Taiwan, primarily a consequence of geographical and cultural proximity.

The complexity of FDI patterns reflects the different circumstances and objectives of firms. Analysts have identified a range of motivators, or determinants of FDI, none of which stands unique as a touchstone for understanding investment behaviour. Rather, the importance and relative ranking of these factors will vary from firm to firm, from time to time and from place to place. Most simply, in Porter's (1990) terminology, firms may adopt strategies in order to gain:

- *Cost advantage*. In this case firms seek to locate where production costs are low. Output may be exported, or re-exported in the case of semi-manufactures. Gaining cost advantage through relocation reinforces the product lifecycle view of FDI whereby firms transfer production to take advantage of growing demand in developing country markets for pro-ducts which have matured in domestic and other developed markets. The process is seen on an accelerated scale within East Asia as firms move capital within the region and climb up the 'development ladder': e.g. from Japan to the NIEs, from the NIEs to ASEAN countries, and from ASEAN to China, Vietnam, etc. This is known as *flying geese* investment.
- *Differentiation advantage*. Here companies seek access to specialist

production factors, skill and expertise. Typically, this may be undertaken to facilitate technology transfer and is particularly likely to be accompanied by partnership or takeover arrangements with local firms. Examples include South Korean firms in Europe and even US firms in Taiwan (see Jocelyn Chen, chapter 4). In Singapore, government policy is active in encouraging centres of excellence, for example in silicon wafer technology, to attract incomers as well as to benefit domestic firms.

The actual decision to undertake FDI along the lines of the two generic strategies above may be precipitated by changes in socio-economic, political or legal conditions which can in turn be differentiated as 'push' or 'pull' factors. 'Push' factors typically describe increasingly adverse domestic conditions, such as tight labour markets (skill shortages, job-hopping and high wage costs), disadvantageous exchange rates, regulation and political instability. Economic 'push' factors are, especially in Asia, in business eyes often the unanticipated consequence of collective success. 'Pull' factors, conversely, result from increased attractiveness elsewhere. Examples are favourable changes in market proximity and growth, fiscal incentives, political risk, access to marketing channels, technology and information. Significant pull factors have emerged as a consequence of regionalization: firms try to realize the benefits of locating facilities within trading blocs rather than attempt to surmount rising trade barriers. There may be disadvantages of location, of course, which need to be measured against the pull factors. In Eastern Europe, Asian and Western firms are trading off the long-term potential for market growth, proximity and favoured access to EU markets and low labour costs against relatively short-term problems of skill deficiencies, motivation and infrastructure. Clearly, in the judgement of some firms such as the South Korean Daewoo (investments in automobiles in Poland and Romania, electronics in the Czech Republic), the net outcome is positive.

The important point is that different types of FDI occur simultaneously, ultimately according to the judgement of the investing companies' strategic leaders. Even within organizations, Strategic Business Units may undertake different forms of FDI at the same time. Three chapters in this book describe and attempt to analyse particular instances of FDI activity. Jocelyn Chen (chapter 4) uses developments of product/industry life cycle theory to analyse the international alliance behaviour of Taiwanese firms. Development involves technology transfer through inward investment in the early stages, moving through outward technology transfer to the newly industrializing economies (NIEs), then ASEAN countries in the mature stage. Ultimately 're-birth' follows with mutually beneficial partnerships based on advanced R&D and technological development. An example is the recent TI-ACER joint venture, an association between two major leading-edge technological innovators, one American, one Taiwanese. Nam and Slater (chapter 3) research the motives of Korean firms investing in Europe: 'pull' factors seem important in Europe as a destination, but results seem to confirm the views of Saad (1995) that local fiscal incentives are neither a necessary nor sufficient inducement to undertake investment *per se*, though they do seem to influence the choice of actual destination. Corrado Molteni (chapter 5) looks at the non-equity linkages between Italian and ASEAN firms. His concern is with medium-sized rather than large multinational enterprises. This sector, he argues, offers good potential synergies between the Italian firms, experienced in outsourcing and networking, and the ASEAN firms, successful in generating cash and with the requisite managerial expertise in the Asian regions.

Two chapters comment on the impact of Asian growth on Europe. Gordon Robinson (chapter 6) fears that the preoccupation of the EU with local and internal issues and the blindness of EU firms with regard to Asia Pacific development are likely to presage a disastrous hiatus in global strategy. The strength of the Asian economies is easily shown. On a PPP basis, in 1995 the developing countries excluding Eastern Europe and the former Soviet Union, accounted for 40.1% of GDP, the Developed Countries 54.6%. Figure 1.2 indicates four Asian economies in the top ten, eleven in the 32 countries' GDP shown. The rankings in Table 1.4 show the concentration of much of the world's foreign exchange reserves in Asia Pacific. This distribution derives, of course, from the global trading success of the Asia Pacific countries. Success, however, may come at a price, and Robert Hine and Peter Wright (chapter 2), in the only study in this book emphasizing trade rather than investment, examine the impact of imports on the UK economy. Focusing on price/cost margins in a range of manufacturing sectors and further disaggregating by origin of imports, they find differences in the competitive pressures generated by Asian Pacific NIEs

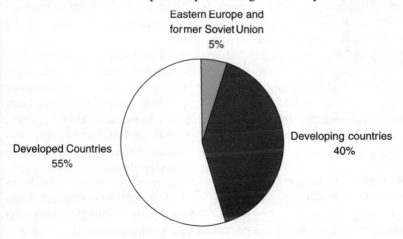

Figure 1.1 Gross domestic product (GDP) at purchasing power parity (PPP)
Source: International Monetary Fund (IMF).

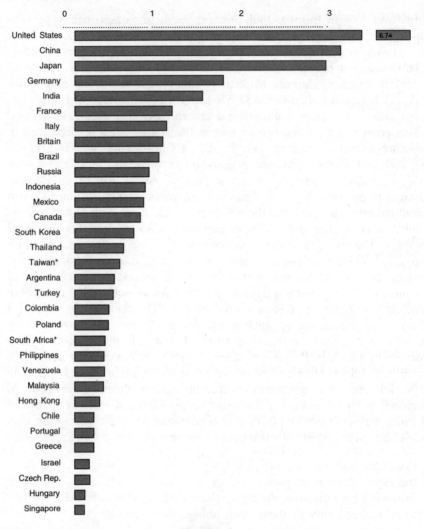

Figure 1.2 Rankings of world GDP at PPP. Scaling based on US$ trn.
Source: World Bank. (Not strictly to scale.) Adapted from *The Economist*,
2 February 1996.
* Estimate.

and European competitors. Whilst there are also differences within these
regions, the 'disciplinary' effect of Asian competition is more marked.
Two warnings are offered: one that defensive tactics of European survivors
may minimize the benefits to consumers of the single market; the other is
that the winds of competition may yet be felt in other sectors as the NIEs
upgrade into more sophisticated products and markets.

If then, a passive response to East Asian dynamism is likely to lead to

Table 1.4 Foreign exchange reserves (US$ bn)

Country	Latest		Year ago
Japan	182.1	Nov	125.4
Taiwan	90.6	Sep	91.6
Germany	84.2	Nov	82.8
United States	75.2	Oct	67.1
China	71.4	Sep	41.2
Singapore	66.9*	Sep	56.5*
Hong Kong	54.6	Sep	49.3**
Brazil	47.4	Oct	41.1
Britain	41.9	Aug	40.2
Thailand	35.2	Nov	28.8
Holland	34.5	Nov	34.4
Switzerland	34.4	Nov	32.3
Spain	34.2	Nov	41.6
Italy	33.4	Oct	29.5
South Korea	32.1	Oct	23.7
France	27.2	Sep	25.0
Malaysia	24.8	Aug	30.7

* Includes gold.
** December 1994.
Source: Adapted from *The Economist*, 27 January 1996.

problems, what then of the opportunities for those firms with a proactive attitude? Japan is notoriously difficult for Western firms to penetrate, either by export or direct investment. However, both South Korea and China appear to be inviting foreign firms to contribute to investment-led growth. Sang-Kun Nam (chapter 8) details legislative changes in South Korea and suggests opportunities for potential investors. Chen Changzheng (chapter 12), Weihwa Pan and David Parker (chapter 13) and Xiaohong Wu and Roger Strange (chapter 14) undertake similar studies for China. In view of the rapid changes in policy and of the speed of industrial restructuring following liberalization, the high value of this level of information is likely to be realized only by those firms able to move quickly.

As companies do begin to globalize they may face unfamiliar problems. For example, South Korean firms have extended their territory more rapidly, some would say less cautiously, than most. Yeon Hak Kim and Nigel Campbell (chapter 11) stress the organizational control processes and styles in Korean corporate internationalization. They propose a theoretical framework which aims to distinguish between and evaluate the effectiveness of forms of MNC control in the context of major Korean corporations. Whilst the Chaebol structure is specific to Korea, its actual form differs in evolution and adaptation between major players. The differences are seen to contribute directly to performance over time and, although the absolute success of these organizations is indisputable, there are substantial differences in relative performance. Two other types of managerial problem associated with globalization are investigated by Wolfgang Klenner (chapter 7) and Yong Gu Suh (chapter 10). Klenner looks at the case for standard globalized products against that for products tailored to local tastes and conditions. The arguments, in similar dimensions, spill over into choice of production and marketing techniques and location. Pointing to the relative underrepresentation of European enterprises in Asian markets compared with Asian enterprises in Europe, he concludes that the competitive advantage of the Asian firms is flexibility based upon good local intelligence and that the sustainability of this advantage is considerably aided by their being first-movers. In other words, there is no single answer to the original question, but a heavy-handed blunt-instrument approach is unlikely to succeed in new markets. Suh looks at the problem of brand degradation as the 'made in' label changes from the original country of manufacture. Again, there are no fixed rules: quality signals conveyed by brands can overcome consumers' suspicions regarding transplants, but only if sufficiently strong and confirmed by their experience. Reputations change and complacency with regard to quality in the search for lower cost is unlikely to engender long-term consumer confidence.

Sid Lowe (chapter 9) is concerned with the cultural environment into which firms might venture. Using Hong Kong as a paradigm, his approach concerns the more philosophical foundations of culture rather than pure organizational form. The consonance between business and national cultures is seen as of prime significance to inter- rather than intra-business relationships. The implications for the adoption and transplant of Western management theories and practices are significant.

The production and manufacturing industries provide the basis for most of the chapters in this book. The service industries are clearly of major importance to Hong Kong and Singapore as they approach a stage of development where manufacturing is being or has been exported through FDI within the region and the home territories increasingly become operations bases. Yi-Cheng Liu and Roger Strange offer analysis of Taiwan's aspirations to develop Taipei as a major financial centre (chapter 15). As there is competition from various other governments to promote their capital cities as regional alternatives to the existing centres of Hong Kong, Singapore and Tokyo, the chapter identifies the necessary prerequisites and provides a ranking of twelve possible alternative sites in the region. The chapter concludes with recommendations as to policy measures aimed at improving Taipei's ranking.

Foreign Direct Investment clearly emerges from the researches in this book as central to the problems and opportunities associated with Europe–Asia business relationships. Within Asia China is both representative of and a focus for many of the significant changes in investment activity. With its investment-led growth strategy, China is making a clear statement about export-only trade relations. Within China, the pattern of investment seems to be spreading, from Guangdong, Shanghai and the coastal zones, along the Yangtze River and into the interior provinces in a manner parallel to the 'flying geese' pattern of FDI in the whole region. Intra-regional FDI, through the opening of China and the developing countries, based largely on 'push' factors may have diverted a considerable amount of Asian FDI away from Europe. For example, in February 1996, South Korea's LG Group announced a US$5 billion investment programme in Malaysia, Vietnam, Indonesia and India in line with its selection of Asia as its primary strategic target. Western Europe cannot rely on an influx of Asian capital as great as might have been expected in the mid- to late 1980s, but there are signs that Eastern Europe is becoming a strong candidate. However, there remain considerable opportunities for, particularly, alliances between European and Asian businesses in both regions.

In the concluding chapter, Roger Strange moves the spotlight from business to political activity in the East Asian region and offers a critique, based on a 1993 World Bank report, of the growth miracle. None of the other chapters deals with the 'politics' of the East Asian experience, although these are, of course, of major concern to industrial economists and strategists. There is really a dual question here: first, to what extent have national government policies contributed to the success of the 'High and Performing East Asian Economies' (HPEACs) or to what extent can other factors be considered responsible? Second, what opportunities or threats do regional political groupings offer? With regard to the first, the debate is likely to last a long time as no academic methodologies seem able usefully to make a clear distinction – if, indeed, there is one to be made. There is some evidence that the second, characterized by a current instability in the groupings (e.g. the efforts to articulate a specifically ASEAN lobby within APEC, known as EAEC) are more concerned with strategic power groupings than with investment and trade. Strange's optimism lies in the anticipation of business as the source of initiatives, particularly in the form of alliances between European firms and their counterparts in Taiwan, Hong Kong, Singapore and Korea. Ultimately, it is firms who trade and invest: an oft-heard remark in these countries is 'where business leads, politics follows'.

BIBLIOGRAPHY

Lee, K. (1993) *New East Asian Economic Development: Interacting Capitalism and Socialism*, New York: M.E. Sharpe, Inc.

Nomura Research Institute and Institute of Southeast Asian Studies (1995) *The New Wave of Foreign Direct Investment in Asia*, Singapore: Institute of Southeast Asian Studies.

Porter, M.E. (1990) *The Competitive Advantage of Nations*, New York: The Free Press.

Saad, I. (1995) 'Foreign Direct Investment, Structural Change, and Deregulation in Indonesia', *The New Wave of Foreign Direct Investment in Asia*, Singapore: Institute of Southeast Asian Studies.

Wade, R. (1990) *Governing the Market*. Princeton: Princeton University Press.

2 Europe and the Orient Express – the impact of East Asian trade on European economies

Robert Hine and Peter Wright

INTRODUCTION[1]

The performance of the East Asian economies over the last thirty years has been truly remarkable – Woronoff's (1986) term, the 'miracle economies', conveys their extraordinary growth record which since the 1960s has surpassed that of any other region. The dynamism of the East Asian economies is clearly of interest to all those concerned with the economic improvement of the Third World, both as an inspiration as to what can be achieved in a relatively short period of time and as a guide to what policies may be most conducive to rapid economic and social development. The 'Orient Express' also has important implications for the already industrialized economies, including the UK. It generates rapidly growing export opportunities, but also poses a strong challenge. European industry will be subjected to serious competitive pressure in trying to match the quality and performance of the dynamic, efficient and innovative East Asian firms. The response to this trade challenge and the associated growth of foreign direct investment in Europe by East Asian firms will have a powerful influence on the future evolution of the European economy.

This chapter begins with some general observations about the growth of the East Asian economies, drawing particularly on the World Bank's recent report *The East Asian Miracle* (1994) and Chowdhury and Islam (1993). Next, the trade policies and performances of the East Asian countries are outlined, noting particularly the considerable differences within the group. In the following sections two empirical analyses are made. The first examines the factors which influence the pattern of trade between Europe and East Asia, taking the particular case of the UK. The second empirical analysis assesses the impact on UK price-cost margins of competition from the Asian countries: do high levels of import penetration from East Asia depress margins in UK industry and, if so, is this a general feature or is it export-country specific? The final section draws some conclusions.

'THE ORIENT EXPRESS'

The extraordinarily rapid growth of the East Asian economy is largely attributable to China and eight other high-performing economies (HPEs): Japan; the Four Tigers – Hong Kong, the Republic of Korea, Singapore and Taiwan; and the Three Dragons – the newly industrializing economies of Indonesia, Malaysia and Thailand. In the quarter century from 1960, real per capita incomes increased more than fourfold in Japan and the Four Tigers and more than doubled in the Three Dragons. All of the countries were among the twenty fastest growing economies in the world during this period, and six of the top seven places were occupied by East Asian economies. Moreover the benefits of fast economic growth have been widely shared within the East Asian economies. Income distributions have become less unequal – according to the World Bank the eight high-performing East Asian countries are the only ones to combine high growth and declining income inequality. Other indicators point to the diffusion of benefits – life expectancy, for example, advanced from 56 to 71 years between 1960 and 1990. The United Nation's Human Development Index, which combines purchasing power, life expectancy and literacy shows a high level of well-being in each of the eight HPEs, except for Indonesia (Chowdhury and Islam 1993: 5).

The crucial issue for economists in particular is how the spectacular growth of China and the other East Asian countries was achieved. Considering first the eight HPEs, according to the World Bank (1994), the key elements in their success were:

- a high rate of investment sustained by high levels of domestic financial savings
- a fast expansion of production and productivity in agriculture
- declining population growth
- a well-educated labour force
- an efficient public administration.

Put this way there seems little miraculous in the East Asian countries' superior economic performance – they got the basics right which resulted in a rapid accumulation of physical and human capital. However, there is a continuing debate as to the role played by governments in the economic success of the eight HPEs in East Asia. The World Bank points to a sound development policy in which there was:

- unusually good macro-economic management which provided a stable economic framework
- improvements in the banking system to encourage savings
- education policies which focused particularly on technical and vocational aspects
- agricultural policies to foster greater productivity

- an attempt to keep price distortions within bounds, and
- openness to foreign ideas and technology.

Government intervention was clearly substantial and designed to promote selected industries. But it is difficult to determine how far that intervention contributed to the success of the East Asian economies. As Chowdhury and Islam (1993) remark, the economics literature seems to be caught in the cross-currents of two competing paradigms. The neoclassical view suggests that the crucial role was played by a market-friendly approach which concentrated on 'getting prices right' especially through trade and financial liberalization. Reforms in these areas were reinforced by prudent macro-economic management and a well-functioning labour market. The revisionist view – the statist 'counter-revolution' (Chowdhury and Islam, p. 246) – emphasizes the interaction between policies and the underlying political process. It is claimed that a common institutional feature of the East Asian countries, and in particular the Four Tigers is the 'strong developmental state' (ibid.), relatively immune from interest group pressures. Thus governments were able to lead the market in critical ways 'without the corresponding burden of government failure' (ibid.). In this view, markets do not always guide investment to those industries which would generate the highest growth, and there is scope for selective government intervention which in certain circumstances deliberately 'gets prices wrong'. Both Chowdhury and Islam (1993) and the World Bank (1994) concur that neither an extreme neoclassical nor a strong revisionist view is supported by the available evidence which points instead to a more eclectic view.

China is inevitably a special case. Yet in a number of respects there are important parallels with recent economic growth spurt in the HPEs, notably the fast productivity growth in agriculture in the years following the launch of the Open Door Policy in 1978, and the restrained growth of population. Lardy (1994: 22) argues that the similarities between China and the HPEs suggest that the former's growth in the 1980s and early 1990s was not an anomaly. However, he also notes a number of differences which strain the analogy, such as the shortage of arable land which may constrain future productivity growth in Chinese agriculture, severe weaknesses in China's banking system, the greater dependence of Chinese exports on foreign capital rather than a broad base of domestic industry, and the wide gap between rural and urban standards of living. Clearly, too, the roles of government and public ownership have been much more pervasive in China than in the HPEs. Hence recent economic progress owes much to the *reduced* role of government through marketization and the 'shift towards more flexible and entrepreneurial state involvement in the economy' (Howell 1991: 131) rather than to astute government intervention.

EAST ASIAN TRADE POLICIES

The outstanding growth performance of the East Asian economies has been based on a strong encouragement of manufacturing exports. This represented a turnaround from policies which, except in the case of Hong Kong, were historically strongly biased towards import substitution and against exports. The movement away from import substitution took place earlier in East Asia than in most developing countries and was typically a response to a foreign exchange constraint (World Bank 1994): export promotion was seen as a means of relieving this constraint. Japan shifted to a pro-export regime coupled with moderate protection of the domestic market in the 1950s and a similar change took place in the Four Tigers in the late 1960s. Policy re-orientation in the Three Dragons came in the 1980s in the form of a gradual liberalization of imports and institutional support for exporters. China's Open Door Policy on foreign trade, borrowing and investment was initiated in 1978.

Within East Asia trade regimes differ considerably, though a common feature is support for export expansion. Hong Kong followed an export-oriented growth strategy through a free-trade regime virtually from the beginning. By contrast Japan, Korea and Taiwan have combined export promotion and import protection – in this way, offsetting subsidies have kept incentives largely equal between export- and import-competing industries. The pro-export regime has included automatic access to credit for exporters, duty-free imports for exporters and suppliers, and tax incentives. Macro-economic stability also contributed to export growth particularly through the maintenance of competitive exchange rates. Import protection has combined tariffs, import quotas and other non-tariff barriers (NTBs). The liberalization of formal import quotas was largely accomplished in Japan by the early 1960s, in Taiwan by the early 1970s and in Korea in the mid-1980s. Other NTBs have been slower to disappear. Because of its sustained and large trade surpluses Japan has come under pressure over the last decade to improve access for imports through dismantling NTBs. But critics have argued that the changes made have had little substance, and the US has made strong efforts to secure quantitative commitments on import access, notably for semiconductors and auto components. Taiwan's NTBs included a 'hidden list' of products that officially could be imported but which Taiwanese firms were encouraged to procure from domestic suppliers (Wade 1989). Taiwan also had high levels of tariff until recently (e.g. 75% for motor cars) but a significant reduction in tariffs took place in the 1980s (Herderschee 1995). Korea has also progressively cut import tariffs from initially high levels which included an effective protection rate of 71% for heavy and chemical industries in 1978 (Young *et al.* 1982); the average tariff on manufactured products was scheduled to fall to 6.2% in 1993, but agricultural protection remains substantial.

In the 1980s, the Three Dragons – Indonesia, Thailand and Malaysia –

deployed a wide variety of export incentives while also reducing barriers to imports. In the case of Thailand, although nominal rates of protection for manufactured products in the mid-1980s were moderate (22% and 25% for capital and consumer goods), effective rates were estimated to be much higher (Herderschee 1995). However, cuts in import protection in the 1980s, by reducing the profitability of production for the domestic market, encouraged the expansion of exports. Indeed, import liberalization may have had a greater impact on export growth than did Thailand's extensive range of export incentives. The latter included offsets on customs duties on imported components, subsidised credits and tax concessions and holidays (ibid.). Indonesia's progress in shifting from an import regime based on non-tariff barriers to one based on tariffs was recognized in the 1994 GATT review of its trade policies, but it was also observed that the average level of tariffs remained relatively high at 20%, and that tariff escalation[2] and tariff dispersion had tended to increase and import surcharges were often used (*GATT Focus* December 1994: 7). Malaysia's average nominal tariff at 15% is lower, but again tariff escalation is high and tariff peaks of over 50% are found in some sectors (*GATT Focus* August 1993: 11).

The trade regime in China was transformed during the 1980s. Under the import substitution regime in the 1950s, foreign trade was heavily controlled by the state. A relatively small number of specialized state foreign trade corporations handled external trade, the quantities of which were specified in detail in the state plans. During the 1980s, controls were decentralized through the creation of many new trade corporations; trade according to the plan gave way to a reliance on import and export licensing, and the active use of tariffs and taxes as trade instruments. Exports were stimulated through modifications to the stringent system of foreign exchange control, and through measures such as export credits, cheap domestic currency loans, and subsidised transport, storage and insurance. Industries such as those producing machinery and electronic equipment were targeted for special export encouragement (Lardy 1992).

THE RISE OF EAST ASIA IN WORLD TRADE

Although import barriers remain substantial in the East Asian countries, participation in world markets rather than import substitution is the main focus of trade policies. Pro-export policies are reflected in the region's dynamic export performance which in turn has underpinned the overall rapid economic growth. East Asia's export expansion has greatly outpaced that of other regions, leading to a rising share of world exports. Thus the share of the Four Tigers in world exports of manufactures which was only 1.6% in 1965 rose to 5.4% in 1980 and 8.8% in 1989 (Chowdhury and Islam 1993: 73). This increased penetration of world markets has continued in the last decade: between 1984 and 1993 the share of Japan and the Four Tigers rose from 16% to 21% of world exports, while China doubled its share from 1.5% to 3% (see Figure 2.1). Since 1980 each of the Four Tigers have recorded a *volume* growth in their exports of over 10% a year (Table 2.1).

Among the Four Tigers, export performance over the last decade has varied with Korea and Taiwan increasing their share of world trade in the second half of the 1980s and then stabilizing at around 3% each, while Singapore recorded a steady expansion throughout the period, and

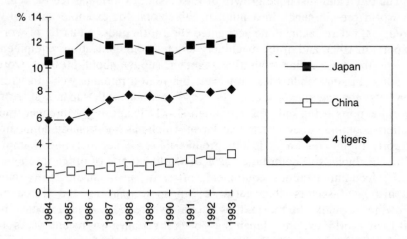

Figure 2.1 East Asian shares of world exports 1984–93
Source: Eurostat, *External Trade Statistics*.

Table 2.1 Growth of East Asian trade 1980–93

	1993	1993	Average Annual % Change 1980–93			
	Value $billion exports	Value $billion imports	Value exports	Volume exports	Value imports	Volume imports
Japan	362	242	8	4	4	5
Taiwan	85	77	12	10	11	12
Korea	82	84	13	11	11	11
Hong Kong	135	142	16	15	15	14
(domestic)	29	35	7	3	6	–
(re-exports)	107		25	–		
Singapore	74	85	11	12	14	12
(domestic)	47	58	11	–	9	–
(re-exports)	27		11	–		
Malaysia	47	46	10	–	12	12
Thailand	37	46	14	14	13	11
Indonesia	37	28	4	5	8	5
China	92	104	13	13	14	12

Source: GATT (1994) table II.56.

Hong Kong's share remained stable. (The figures for Singapore and Hong Kong do not include re-exports.) The economies of the Four Tigers are now highly trade-oriented. The annual value of exports from Hong Kong and Singapore exceeds their GDP, and exports have risen as a share of GDP in Korea from less than 10% in 1965 to about 50% by the late 1980s, and in Taiwan from less than 20% to approaching 60% over the same period (Chowdhury and Islam 1993: 74).

The rapid and sustained growth of East Asian exports has led the region to world pre-eminence in a number of sectors, for example automotive products, where Japan alone accounted for a little under a quarter of world exports in 1993, and office machinery and telecommunications equipment, where the East Asian countries together supply about 50% of world exports. In some industries, however, the region remains weak in world markets: the chemicals sector is a case in point with Japan's share of world exports being only 6.2%, though slowly increasing. Moreover trade patterns continue to evolve so that Japan which has traditionally dominated exports in the region is losing ground in some sectors. For example, although Japan still contributes 22% of world exports of office machinery and telecommunications equipment, often in the technologically most sophisticated sectors, the shares of Singapore, Taiwan and Korea are growing strongly. In the textiles sector, where East Asia accounts for 30% of world exports, Japan has been overtaken in recent years by Korea, Taiwan and China. The re-structuring of Japanese exports has proceeded furthest in the clothing sector where the country is no longer in the top 15 of world exporters; the Tigers remain important suppliers but with a falling share of world trade and production has shifted to the Three Dragons and to China, whose share of world exports rose from 4% in 1980 to 13.9% in 1993. Part of the changing pattern of exports from Japan reflects the development of foreign direct investment (FDI), especially in neighbouring East Asian countries where labour-intensive processes can be carried out more cheaply. Trade with Europe and the US is also affected by the establishment there of Japanese transplant factories especially in the automotive industry. Taiwanese and Korean firms are also beginning to undertake FDI on a substantial scale.

East Asia, except for Hong Kong and Japan, has a growing share of world imports as well as of exports, despite the often high import barriers (Figure 2.2). Rising incomes, the need for imported components and materials and, in recent years especially, liberalization of import regimes have all contributed to the buoyant growth of imports. As Hill and Phillips (1993) show, economic liberalization and rising outward-orientation have resulted in import penetration ratios in the East Asian countries (excluding Japan) which are on the whole much higher than those of the industrial countries. Moreover, whereas the ratios reached a plateau in the industrial countries in the 1980s, in East Asia (again excluding Japan) they generally increased. The exceptions are Korea where the ratio was stable, Malaysia

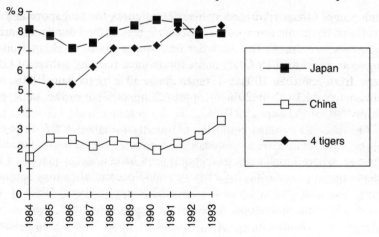

Figure 2.2 East Asian shares of world imports 1984–93
Source: Eurostat, *External Trade Statistics*.

where the decline was from an exceptionally high level, and Indonesia where the expansion of petroleum refining capacity displaced imports. As Table 2.1 shows, China, the Four Tigers and the Three Dragons have achieved similar growth rates of imports and exports and have balanced exports and imports overall.

By contrast, Japan's import performance has been less buoyant: the country's share of world imports has remained around 8% whereas its share of world exports reached 12% in the early 1990s (Figures 1 and 2). The resulting export surplus has been a source of controversy with the US and the EU. Unlike other industrialized countries, Japan has a relatively low propensity to consume imported manufactured goods, but the impact on this of Japanese trade barriers is hotly contested: 'Few issues in international economics are more contentious than the allegedly closed nature of the Japanese market' (Lawrence 1991). Japan's low imports may be explained on the one hand by the country's distance (physically and culturally) from its trading partners and on the other hand by extensive non-tariff trade barriers. The recent appreciation of the yen may in time influence the balance of exports and imports, though in the past Japanese manufacturers have managed to offset the effect of a rising yen on their export volumes through increased efficiency and outsourcing of labour-intensive parts of the production process.

EAST ASIA'S TRADE WITH THE EUROPEAN UNION

The dynamic export performance of Japan and the other East Asian countries has caused problems for European producers and this is reflected in the development of EU trade policies towards them. Japan has been a special case for a number of reasons. First, Japan has led the economic

development of East Asia and therefore the challenge to European producers from Japan occurred earlier. Second, the size of Japan's industrial
economy sets it apart from the other East Asian countries: this is reflected
in trade shares. Japan alone accounts for about a half of East Asia's exports
to the EU (Table 2.2). Third, Japan has had a persistently large trade
surplus with the EU, supplying 10% of EU imports but providing a market
for only 5% of EU exports (Table 2.3). By contrast, trade between the EU
and the other East Asian countries is broadly in balance. Of course, in a
multilateral world a trade imbalance with one partner should not be a
matter of economic concern provided that there is a broad balance overall
in the medium term, as has been the case with the EU. However, concern in
the EU has arisen because increased import penetration without a corresponding growth in exports is seen as aggravating the already severe
problem of unemployment. Also, Japan's export success in the R&D
intensive industries is seen as posing a threat to the creation of new
manufacturing employment in Europe. Consequently, EU trade policy
has aimed at reducing the trade imbalance with Japan, in the first place
through increasing EU penetration of the Japanese market. A series of
initiatives over the last decade to dismantle Japanese non-tariff trade
barriers has however achieved relatively little success and, alarmed at
the growth of Japan's share of EU imports from about 1% in 1960 to
10% by 1986, the EU took a series of national and common actions in the
1980s to restrict Japanese exports. These included a number of voluntary
export restraints on Japanese machine tools, cars, video recorders, colour
TVs and forklift trucks. The Japanese export challenge has also been

Table 2.2 EU imports from the East Asian countries (ECU m.)

	Extra-EU total	Japan	China	Four Tigers	Korea	Hong Kong	Taiwan	Singapore
1958	24,126	258	164	180	2	97	7	74
1960	28,999	397	236	247	3	156	11	77
1965	40,826	798	292	398	15	339	44	
1970	61,823	2,090	349	949	61	620	145	123
1975	132,932	5,599	696	3,126	635	1,404	707	380
1984	390,640	25,668	3,323	14,158	2,945	5,172	3,875	2,166
1985	406,418	28,586	3,936	14,280	3,352	4,819	3,997	2,112
1986	334,564	33,215	4,223	16,333	4,312	5,300	4,702	2,019
1987	340,058	34,757	5,239	20,460	5,959	5,507	6,626	2,368
1988	387,891	41,618	7,005	24,617	7,240	6,317	8,067	2,993
1989	446,717	46,337	9,149	26,667	6,953	6,432	9,259	4,023
1990	462,720	46,224	10,603	26,326	6,557	5,916	9,159	4,694
1991	493,990	51,818	14,973	30,516	7,843	6,401	11,052	5,220
1992	487,730	51,511	16,781	29,700	7,430	5,908	10,713	5,649
1993	485,975	47,649	19,538	31,150	7,735	6,590	10,398	6,427

Source: Eurostat, *External Trade Statistics*.

Table 2.3 EU exports to the East Asian countries (ECU m.)

	Extra-EU total	Japan	China	Four Tigers	Korea	Hong Kong	Taiwan	Singapore
1958	21,742	211	384	350	57	142	17	134
1960	25,554	313	332	431	66	199	21	145
1965	33,492	531	306	396	37	326	33	
1970	54,178	1,426	461	1,125	155	533	117	320
1975	118,530	2,345	1,173	2,320	487	723	419	691
1984	350,859	9,364	3,765	11,667	2,242	3,981	1,957	3,487
1985	378,651	10,475	7,180	13,417	2,763	4,551	2,291	3,812
1986	341,934	11,399	6,533	12,637	3,062	4,229	2,463	2,883
1987	339,338	13,618	5,533	15,052	3,663	4,777	3,418	3,194
1988	362,910	17,020	5,802	19,691	4,392	6,772	4,460	4,067
1989	413,010	21,130	6,369	22,922	5,207	7,023	5,206	5,486
1990	419,814	22,721	5,318	23,269	6,061	6,602	4,917	5,689
1991	423,497	22,155	5,605	25,677	7,087	7,395	5,511	5,684
1992	435,660	20,507	6,848	27,613	6,232	8,784	6,246	6,351
1993	482,588	22,573	11,302	34,017	7,552	11,299	7,573	7,593

Source: Eurostat, *External Trade Statistics*.

blunted by numerous anti-dumping actions. These measures have played a role in the decision by a growing number of Japanese firms to establish production facilities in Europe, and the stabilization of the Japanese share of EU imports since 1986 (Figure 2.3). But the EU–Japan trade imbalance remains, since the growth during the 1980s in the share of EU exports destined for Japan has not been maintained in the first part of the 1990s (Figure 2.4).

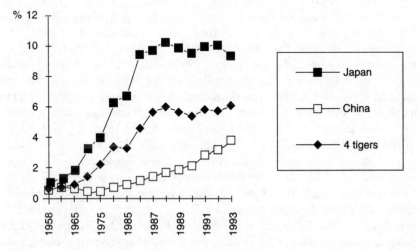

Figure 2.3 East Asian shares of EU imports 1958–93
Source: Eurostat, *External Trade Statistics*.

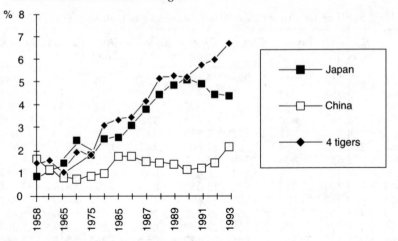

Figure 2.4 East Asian shares of EU exports 1958–93
Source: Eurostat, *External Trade Statistics.*

Trade relations with the other East Asian countries have followed a different course. Since 1971 the EU has offered tariff preferences on manufactured goods imported from developing countries as an encouragement to their economic development. Most of the East Asian countries benefited from this arrangement. However, as their manufactured exports took off, so the EU introduced ceilings on tariff-free treatment of particular items, ostensibly to benefit other newly industrializing countries but also in response to complaints from European manufacturers about low-cost competition. Furthermore, clothing and textiles exports from East Asia have been kept under strict quantitative control through the Multi Fibre Arrangement. These restrictions have contributed to a stabilization in the Four Tigers' overall share of the EU import market at 6% since 1987 (Figure 2.3). Among the Four Tigers, Taiwan and especially Singapore have continued to increase their shares of the EU market, but Hong Kong and Korea have lost ground since the late 1980s (Figure 2.5). China's penetration of the EU market has occurred since the mid-1980s, and has now reached about 4%. At the same time, East Asia is an increasingly important market for Europe's exporters. In particular, there has been a steady expansion in the share of EU exports going to the Four Tigers from 2% in the mid-1970s to 7% in 1993. This expansion has been rather evenly spread among the four countries (Figure 2.6 and Table 2.3).

As a result of the Uruguay Round negotiations in the GATT/WTO, the Common Customs Tariff of the EU will be further reduced, to the benefit of Japan and products from other East Asian countries which do not fully benefit from the Generalized System of Preferences. Voluntary export restraints will be phased out. Furthermore, the MultiFibre Agreement will be gradually dismantled which should stimulate exports from the low-wage economies in the region, but may weaken the position of higher-cost

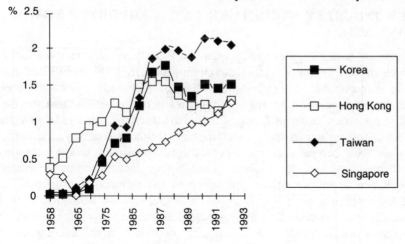

Figure 2.5 The Four Tigers' shares of EU imports 1958–93
Source: Eurostat, *External Trade Statistics*.

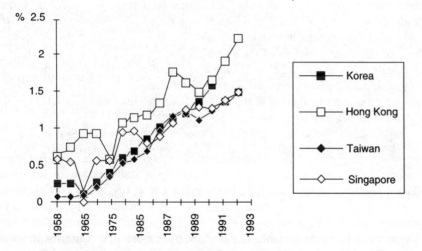

Figure 2.6 The Four Tigers' shares of EU exports 1958–93
Source: Eurostat, *External Trade Statistics*.

producers whose access to the EU market has been protected by the quota system on clothing and textiles. At the same time, East Asian producers may face tougher competition from EU firms as a result of the Single Market programme and the expansion of EU membership, as well as more favourable access for central European and Mediterranean producers. Anti-dumping measures have been used to blunt the competitive challenge from East Asian firms over the last decade and this will be a continuing feature of EU trade policies. Partly in response to this, foreign direct investment by East Asian firms in the EU is likely to expand allowing them to replace exports with local production.

THE INDUSTRY STRUCTURE OF UK IMPORTS FROM EAST ASIA

In a recent paper Buigues and Jacquemin (1994) have examined the factors which drive EU imports from developing countries in general and East Asia in particular. They argue that part of this trade reflects different patterns of specialization among industries between the EU and the East Asian countries. In terms of the standard Heckscher-Ohlin model of international trade, inter-industry specialization of this kind occurs as countries exploit their comparative advantage according to their relative resource endowments. Thus, for example, developing countries with a relative abundance of labour should specialize in the production of goods like clothing which require a large input of labour relative to capital in their manufacture. Exports of clothing would then be exchanged for imports of goods in whose production developing countries enjoy a comparative disadvantage, such as technologically sophisticated machinery.

In addition to trade driven by inter-industry specialization of the type described above, much of today's international trade – including some trade between the EU and East Asia – is based on specialization *within* industries (intra-industry trade). It involves the exchange between countries of different varieties of the same product in order to meet consumers' demands for a wide range of choice and manufacturers' requirements for highly specialized components and inputs. Access to international markets allows producers to reconcile the demands for product differentiation with the need to achieve economies of scale in production.

Buigues and Jacquemin estimate a model of EU trade with developing countries in general and the East Asian countries in particular, of the following form:

$$\log I_{LYC}/I_{TOT} = a + b_1 \log K/L + b_2 \log Qual + b_3 \log Dem + b_4 \log Sca + e_i$$
(1)

where the dependent variable is the share of low-income countries in total extra-EU imports in 1992. Two variables are intended to pick up determinants of inter-industry trade. The first is the ratio between physical capital and labour (K/L). This measure of capital intensity is computed as gross fixed capital formation per employee over the period 1985–90. The second is described as an index of the qualification of the labour force (Qual), measured by the share of non-manual workers in the total of employees.

With regard to intra-industry trade conducted in an imperfectly competitive environment, the variable employed is a measure of economies of scale (Sca) relevant to monopolistic competition. It is defined as the average size of enterprise, measured by the number of employees per enterprise. It is also argued that a further factor driving the pattern of international trade is the growth of demand (Dem) measured by the annual growth of intra-EU demand between 1982 and 1992.

Table 2.4 Buigues and Jacquemin's results for the low-wage economies' shares of EU imports by industry, 1992

	Coefficient	T-statistic	
Constant	−0.07	0.06	
K/L$_i$	−0.88	2.82	
Qual$_i$	−0.07	0.11	
Dem$_i$	1.10	2.00	R^2 0.22
Sca$_i$	−0.44	2.18	F 4.7

Source: Buigues and Jacquemin (1994).

The analysis uses data at the 3 digit industry level (n = 74) and the equation is estimated in double logarithmic form.

The results are summarized in Table 2.4. They suggest that the East Asian countries are weak in industries where capital labour ratios are high and where economies of scale (proxied by the average size of enterprise in the EU) are pronounced. These findings are in line with the results computed for all developing countries and suggest that the East Asian countries are continuing to exploit their comparative advantage as relatively low-wage countries. Where the East Asian countries are distinctive compared with developing countries is in their high import shares in the fast growing industries, measured in relation to the growth in EU demand over the previous decade. Also, and unlike developing countries in general, the East Asian countries do not show a tendency to concentrate on exports to the EU which have a high content of manual relative to non-manual labour. These findings suggest that competition from the East Asian countries is in the process of transition, and that the EU will increasingly face competition from the region in areas where EU exporters have traditionally been strong.

The Buigues and Jacquemin analysis of East Asian import shares relates to the EU as a whole. How closely does this reflect the situation in the UK? UK manufactured imports from the East Asian countries were valued at £13,707 million in 1991, or 31.6% of total non-EU imports. Japan's share was 14.8%, the Four Tigers 12.2% , the Three Dragons 4.1% and China 0.5%. Table 2.5 illustrates the industry pattern of these imports, ranking products in order of the value of imports from each of the three sources. In value terms Japanese exports to the UK are dominated by motor vehicles and electrical and electronic products. The latter are also important in the Four Tigers' exports to the UK, along with clothing and footwear. The Three Dragons' principal exports include electronic products together with more traditional processed primary products such as fats and oils. Table 2.6 provides a different perspective in ranking imports from the East Asian countries according to their share of UK imports. This focuses attention on the performance of the East Asian countries in relation to other suppliers and is the basis for the empirical work presented below which applies the

Table 2.5 Top ten industries by *value* of UK imports from East Asian countries, 1991 (Standard Industrial Classification (SIC) 4 digit)

Rank	Japan	Four Tigers	Three Dragons
1	motor vehicles	computers	electronic components
2	electronic components	hosiery	footwear
3	computers	electronic consumer goods	electronic consumer goods
4	electronic consumer goods	electronic components	hosiery
5	photographic equipment	photographic equipment	wood products
6	motor vehicle parts	toys & games	fish processing
7	radios	footwear	vegetable oils processing
8	basic electrical equipment	clothes (womens')	saw milling
9	machine tools	clothes (outerwear)	clothes (outer)
10	telecomms components	leather goods	textile weaving

Source: OECD, *Commodity Trade Statistics for the UK*, 1991.

Buigues and Jacquemin approach to UK data. The following equation was estimated:

$$\log I_{EA}/I_{TOT} = a + b_1 \log K/L + b_2 \log Qual + b_3 \log Dem + b_4 \log Sca + e_i \tag{2}$$

where I_{EA} = imports from East Asia and I_{TOT} = total imports from non-EU countries, in 1991. The definitions of the other variables were as follows:

K/L_i = the average ratio of capital investment per employee over the five year period 1986 to 1990 in each industry
$Qual_i$ = the ratio of manual workers to total workers in industry i in 1991
Dem_i = the growth in UK apparent consumption from 1986 to 1991 for the products of industry i
Sca_i = the average number of employees per enterprise in industry i in 1991.

It is expected that for Japan the signs on the capital-labour and scale coefficients will be positive, and that on the labour quality variable negative, reflecting Japan's developed industrial status. For the low income countries the opposite signs are expected. Regarding the consumption growth variable, a positive sign is expected for the Tigers.

Because of the presence of zero import shares for a number of industries, particularly in the case of the Dragons, the equation was estimated using the Tobit procedure. Estimates were made for each of the countries sepa-

Table 2.6 Top ten industries by *share* of East Asian countries in UK imports, 1991 (SIC 4 digit)

Rank	Japan	Four Tigers	Three Dragons
1	motor cycles	cycles	oils & fats treatment
2	radios	clocks	wood products
3	musical instruments	leather goods	sawmilling
4	weighing machinery	men's shirts	fish processing
5	office machinery	weatherproof outerwear	carpentry
6	optical instruments	gloves	gloves
7	electronic consumer goods	toys & games	electronic components
8	telephone equipment	sports goods	oils & fats processing
9	industrial electrical equipment	jeans	weatherproof outerwear
10	machine tools	utensils	footwear

Source: OECD, *Commodity Trade Statistics for the UK*, 1991.

rately and for the Tiger and the Dragon groups. The results are given in Tables 2.7, 2.8 and 2.9. They confirm the role of both inter- and intra-industry factors in driving East Asian exports to the UK and point also to important differences among the East Asian countries.

The distinctive feature that emerges from the regression results about *Japan*'s exports to the UK is their strength in industries where there is a high proportion of non-manual workers in the labour force, reflecting their technological sophistication. The coefficients on the scale and consumption growth variables are both positive, but not significantly so. Unexpectedly, however, Japan though a high-income capital-rich country does not have a high share of UK imports in industries which are capital-intensive, indeed the coefficient on the capital–labour variable is significantly negative. One

Table 2.7 Regression results for UK import shares by industry, 1991

	Japan		Tigers		Dragons		China	
Constant	0.208	(4.491) ***	0.237	(0.503) ***	−0.863	(−2.995) ***	−0.036	−1.511
K/L_i	−0.460	−2.885 ***	−0.861	−5.290 ***	0.238	2.431 ***	−0.160	−1.907 *
$Qual_i$	−0.893	(−4.986) ***	0.320	(1.775) *	0.359	(3.247) ***	0.011	1.239
Dem_i	0.205	(0.790)	0.868	(3.235) ***	−0.101	(−0.632)	0.009	0.685
Sca_i	0.097	(0.841)	−0.183	(−1.571)	−0.235	(−3.337) ***	−0.014	−2.363 **
InL	92.85		92.09		143.16		149.38	
n	183		183		183		183	

Notes: Significance tests *** 99%; ** 95%; * 90%. T-statistics in parentheses.
Source: OECD, *Commodity Trade Statistics for the UK*, 1991.

Table 2.8 Regression results for Dragons' shares of UK imports by industry, 1991

	Indonesia		Malaysia		Thailand	
Constant	−0.859	(−3.952) ∗∗∗	−0.782	(−3.150) ∗∗∗	−0.323	(−2.297) ∗∗
K/L$_i$	0.075	(1.173)	0.188	(2.310) ∗∗	−0.002	(−0.041)
Qual$_i$	0.284	(3.495) ∗∗∗	0.083	(0.873)	0.183	(3.383) ∗∗∗
Dem$_i$	0.067	(0.618)	−0.018	(−0.131)	0.051	(0.666)
Sca$_i$	−0.120	(−2.523) ∗∗∗	−0.171	(−2.791) ∗∗∗	−0.057	(−1.709) ∗
InL	73.53		106.84		193.83	
n	183		183		183	

Note: T-statistics in parentheses.

Table 2.9 Regression results for Tigers' shares of UK imports by industry, 1991

	Hong Kong		Singapore		South Korea		Taiwan	
Constant	−0.148	(−0.446)	0.114	(0.901)	−0.086	(−0.504)	−0.304	(−1.126)
K/L$_i$	−0.476	(−4.179) ∗∗∗	−0.072	(−1.660)	−0.178	(−2.992) ∗∗∗	−0.310	(−3.385) ∗∗∗
Qual$_i$	0.205	(1.643)	−0.134	(−2.764) ∗∗∗	0.089	(1.351)	0.114	(1.151)
Dem$_i$	0.335	(1.764) ∗∗∗	0.062	(0.861)	0.235	(2.403) ∗∗∗	0.648	(4.230) ∗∗∗
Sca$_i$	−0.147	(−1.800)∗	−0.017	(−0.542)	−0.021	(−0.485)	−0.077	(−1.168)
InL	140.35		228.67		184.65		162.48	
n	183		183		183		183	

Note: T-statistics in parenthesis

possible explanation is that the pattern of capital intensities among Japanese industries is different from that used in the analysis which is derived from UK data. In the latter, the capital intensive industries are concentrated in the chemicals and non-metallic minerals processing (e.g. glassware) industries. These are industries in which Japanese and other East Asian firms have been less successful in increasing market share at the expense of established suppliers from other non-EU developed countries such as Switzerland. In the newer industries such as electronics, the problem of overcoming entry barriers has been less acute.

The results for the *Four Tigers* support only in part the findings of Buigues and Jacquemin for the EU. We also find that exports from these countries to the UK are significantly lower in industries where capital/labour ratios are high; they are lower too where the average size of enterprise in the UK is large, though not significantly so. Unlike Japan, they have a strong concentration on industries with strong demand growth in the UK. Our findings differ from those of Buigues and Jacquemin in suggesting that Tigers exports are still concentrated on manual labour intensive industries. However, within the Tigers group there is some variation and in particular the results for Singapore suggest that its position is more similar to that of Japan than to the other Tigers.

The results for the *Dragons* are consistent with their generally lower level of economic development, except for the capital–labour variable. The Dragons' most competitive export industries are relatively capital-intensive, especially those concerned with the processing of primary products. This reflects also the increasingly international nature of the capital market, with much Japanese investment in the region to develop raw material supplies. In other respects, the results for the Dragons are as expected: the industries with high shares of the UK import market tend to be small scale and have a high proportion of manual workers. There is no concentration yet on high growth industries, and indeed in the case of Thailand slow growth industries are more pronounced. The results for China are broadly similar to those for the Dragons – a concentration on small-scale industries with a high proportion of manual workers in the labour force. Unlike the Dragons however China does not have high market shares in capital-intensive industries, which is consistent with its low endowment of capital and its greater isolation from international capital markets.

THE IMPACT OF TRADE FROM EAST ASIA ON INDUSTRY PRICE COST MARGINS IN THE UNITED KINGDOM

As mentioned previously, one of the areas in which the impact of trade from East Asia may be felt in the domestic economy is on the profit margins of United Kingdom firms. Indeed it is this effect which ostensibly leads to the call from manufacturers for voluntary export restraints, anti-dumping measures and quantitative controls on imports. We therefore examine this contention in the following section.

The theoretical link between import penetration and the price cost margin may be illustrated using the model of Hansson (1992). This is a development of the Urata's (1984) conjectural variation model. Suppose that there are k domestic firms producing a homogeneous good then the profit function of firm i ($i = 1 \ldots k$) is given by

$$\pi_i = pq_i - c_iq_i - F_i$$

where:

π = profit
p = price
q = output

F = fixed cost
c = constant marginal cost.

The price level faced by each firm is determined by the inverse demand function.

$$p = p(q) = p(q_d + q_{m1} + q_{m2})$$

where

$$q_d = \sum_{i=1}^{k} q_i$$

q_d = quantity produced by domestic firms
q_{mn} = quantity imported from country group n ($n = 1, 2$)
q = total quantity demanded.

Hansson (1992) shows that, if it is assumed that firms maximize profits, then the industry level price-cost margin can be derived by aggregating across firms to give:

$$PCM = \frac{\pi + F}{R} = (1 - M_1 - M_2)[(1 - \alpha)H + \alpha]\eta^{-1} + (\varphi_1 M_1 + \varphi_2 M_2)\eta^{-1}$$

where:
H = Herfindahl index of domestic producer concentration
M_n = Share of imports in consumption originating from country n
η = Elasticity of demand
α = Conjectural variation parameter (home demand)
ϕ_n = Conjectural variation parameter (foreign demand).

This model is a relatively simple extension of conventional oligopoly models. The size of the price-cost margin depends positively on the degree of concentration amongst domestic producers (H), negatively on the price elasticity of demand (η), and on the conjectures that the firm has regarding the likely response of other firms. In the above framework α and φ_n indicate the extent of implicit collusion between home and foreign producers respectively. If $\alpha = \varphi_n = 1$ then the firms perfectly collude in order to increase profits. Conversely, if $\alpha = \varphi_n = 0$ then Cournot conjectures prevail and each firm believes that other firms will not respond if they alter their own behaviour.

Within the above framework imports of different origins may have differential impacts on price cost margins for a number of reasons. If products are differentiated in some way then the trade between two countries is likely to be of an intra-industry form. That is, rather than each country specializing in products for which they possess a relative advantage, the countries maintain a diversified industrial structure and develop a two-way trade in products of slightly different specifications. If this is the case, then the disciplinary effects of imports will be reduced. This argument is of importance since evidence suggests that European integration is associated with a complementarity in production which leads to the development of intra-industry trading patterns. In addition, there is evidence that horizontal and vertical agreements have developed between firms in the EC which act to reduce competition. Thus firms within the EC may more effectively collude with each other to maintain price-cost margins than they do with firms outside the EC. Finally, barriers to trade may exist which temper competitive pressures from some regions more than others. These may be either natural, such as differences in preferences, language and income or artificial as is the case with tariffs and voluntary export restraints.

In order to make operational the preceding arguments regarding the differential influence of trade on price cost margins, the following equation will be estimated.

$$PCM_i = \beta_0 + \beta_1 CR5_i = \beta_3 IMI_{i,1} + \beta_4 IMI_{i,2} + \ldots + \varepsilon_i$$

where:

PCM_i = price cost margin[3] industry i
$CR5_i$ = 5 firm concentration ratio[4] industry i
$IMI_{i,j}$ = import intensity[5] industry i from country group j.

It is a common finding in the industrial organization literature that the share of imports in consumption has a depressing effect on the price cost margin. Of those authors who have looked at the effect of imports from different countries of origin, Hansson (1992) examines the impact of trade on Swedish price cost margins and finds that Japan and the Asian NICs have a greater disciplinary effect than do the European Community countries. Jacquemin and Sapir (1991) study the effect of imports on a pooled sample consisting of France, Germany, Italy and the United Kingdom and find that imports constrain profitability, but only extra EC imports exert a statistically significant effect on the price-cost margins.

The major innovation in this study is the use of a much more disaggregated trade breakdown than has previously been possible to examine the impact of trade competition on price-cost margins in the United Kingdom. The data which will be used in this study is 4 digit industry data taken from the Report of the Census of Production summary tables for 1983, 1988 and 1991. Imports and exports are categorized on the same basis and by country of origin/destination. The results of this analysis are presented in Table 2.10 and, as can be seen, the results presented largely concur with what would be expected from the previous discussion. Imports from outside the EC and OECD have a statistically significant disciplinary impact on price-cost margins, as do imports from Japan and the Asian NICs. This result is also consistent across the three years which have been studied. EC trade, and OECD trade in general, has a negative but statistically insignificant impact on margins.

A weakness of the previous analysis is that it has implicitly assumed that the country sub-divisions used form homogeneous sub-groupings. Therefore, in

Table 2.10 The disciplining effects of imports from different origins

	1983	1983	1983	1983	1988	1988	1988	1988	1993	1993	1993	1993
Constant	0.41 (18.89)	0.41 (18.970)	0.41 (19.092)	0.41 (18.819)	0.42 (21.143)	0.42 (21.191)	0.42 (21.546)	0.42 (21.312)	0.37 (17.618)	0.37 (17.591)	0.37 (17.525)	0.37 (17.478)
Five firm concentration	0.0018 (3.832)	0.0017 (3.866)	0.0017 (3.732)	0.0017 (3.722)	0.0020 (4.954)	0.0019 (4.768)	0.0019 (4.734)	0.0019 (4.605)	0.0019 (4.504)	0.0018 (4.307)	0.0018 (4.391)	0.0018 (4.273)
Total import intensity	−0.15 (−3.763)				−0.096 (−2.522)				−0.11 (−2.831)			
NICs and Japan		−0.49 (−4.429)				−0.33 (−3.522)				−0.30 (−2.435)		
Other		−0.06 (−1.278)				−0.019 (−0.399)				−0.065 (−1.339)		
OECD			−0.049 (−0.913)				0.026 (0.504)				−0.080 (−1.440)	
non-OECD			−0.40 (−4.121)				−0.325 (−4.283)				−0.17 (−2.027)	
EC				−0.076 (−0.952)				0.060 (0.827)				−0.033 (−0.395)
non-EC				−0.22 (−2.913)				−0.23 (−3.514)				−0.17 (−2.542)
R^2	0.14	0.19	0.18	0.14	0.15	0.18	0.20	0.18	0.14	0.16	0.15	0.15
$\bar{R}^2$	0.13	0.17	0.16	0.13	0.14	0.17	0.19	0.16	0.13	0.14	0.13	0.13
F	13.10	12.86	11.73	9.11	14.47	12.48	14.25	12.01	13.54	9.98	9.22	9.42
N	168	168	168	168	172	172	172	172	163	163	163	163

Note: T-statistics in parentheses.
Source: OECD, *Commodity Trade Statistics for the UK*, 1991.

Table 2.11 The disciplining effects of imports from Europe

	1983	1983	1988	1988	1991	1991
Constant	0.41 (18.819)		0.42 (21.312)	0.42 (23.355)	0.37 (17.478)	0.36 (18.149)
Five firm concentration	0.0017 (3.722)		0.0019 (4.605)	0.0014 (3.716)	0.0018 (4.273)	0.0014 (3.363)
non-EC	−0.22 (−2.913)	−0.16 (−2.285)	−0.23 (−3.514)	−0.14 (−2.238)	−0.17 (−2.542)	−0.14 (−2.183)
EC	−0.076 (−0.952)		0.06 (0.827)		−0.033 (−0.395)	
France		0.54 (1.468)		0.80 (2.631)		0.62 (1.794)
Germany		−0.59 (−2.740)		−0.36 (−2.079)		−0.48 (−2.283)
Italy		−1.00 (−2.841)		−1.05 (−2.045)		−0.60 (−1.527)
Spain		1.50 (1.236)		1.26 (1.003)		−017 (−0.129)
Ireland		1.56 (2.415)		0.96 (1.757)		1.06 (1.998)
Benelux		0.26 (1.272)		0.45 (2.376)		0.42 (1.796)
Denmark						
Portugal/Greece		−1.24 (−3.356)		−1.01 (−3.452)		−0.67 (−1.759)
R^2	0.14	0.30	0.18	0.35	0.15	0.26
$\bar{R}^2$	0.13	0.26	0.16	0.31	0.13	0.22
F	9.11	7.40	12.01	9.73	9.42	6.15
N	168	168	172	172	163	163

Note: T-statistics in parentheses.
Source: OECD, Commodity Trade Statistics for the UK, 1991.

Table 2.12 The disciplining effects of imports from Japan and the NICs

	1983	1983	1988	1988	1991	1991
Constant	0.41 (18.970)	0.40 (17.979)	0.42 (21.191)	0.41 (20.328)	0.37 (17.591)	0.36 (17.342)
Five firm concentration	0.0017 (3.866)	0.0018 (3.895)	0.0020 (4.768)	0.0020 (4.778)	0.0018 (4.307)	0.0020 (4.749)
non-NICs non-Japan	-0.061 (-1.278)	-0.062 (-1.301)	-0.19 (-0.399)	-0.018 (-0.386)	-0.065 (-1.339)	-0.051 (-1.072)
NICs and Japan	-0.50 (-4.429)		-0.33 (-3.522)		-0.30 (-2.435)	
Japan		-0.56 (-3.816)		-0.39 (-2.928)		-0.86 (-3.507)
NICs		-0.36 (-1.553)		-0.25 (1.680)		-0.004 (0.024)
R^2	0.19	0.19	0.18	0.18	0.16	0.20
$\bar{R}^2$	0.17	0.17	0.17	0.16	0.14	0.17
F	12.86	9.73	12.48	9.45	9.98	5.67
N	168	168	172	172	163	163

Note: T-statistics in parentheses.
Source: OECD, Commodity Trade Statistics for the UK, 1991.

contrast to previous analyses it was decided to investigate this hypothesis by breaking down the country groups into their constituent components. The results of this analysis may be seen in Tables 2.11 and 2.12. As can be seen, imports from different parts of the EC have very different effects on the price-cost margin depending on their country of origin. German and Italian imports act in a disciplinary fashion, as do those from Portugal and Greece. In contrast, increasing import penetration from France, Ireland and the Benelux countries appears to raise price-cost margins. It is hypothesized that the proximity and the similar industrial structure of these Northern Countries may mean that increased import penetration is associated with increased intra-industry trade and collusion between firms in these countries and the United Kingdom (Germany is rather the exception to this rule).

The assertion that trade from East Asia is uniformly disciplinary is also open to some contention. Table 2.10 shows the effect of splitting the disciplinary impact of trade from East Asia into that deriving from Japan and that deriving from the Asian NICs. It indicates that the disciplinary effect on price cost margins primarily derives from imports originating from Japan. Although trade from the Asian NICs does appear to depress margins, the effect is not statistically significant at conventional levels. Quite why this is so is uncertain. It is certainly the case that many of the sectors in which the NICs now compete have been subject to intense competition for a number of decades, often initially from Japan. Many of these sectors have now downsized dramatically (e.g. clothing, textiles, motorcycles) and, by finding highly specialized niches, have recovered their profit margins. Such dynamic effects cannot be measured within the static framework adopted however. This would seem to indicate that the 'threat' from the Asian NICs is overstated since they tend to specialize in sectors which have long since become marginalized in the United Kingdom. It is only if they begin to compete in more technologically sophisticated sectors that the effect of import competition from this region on price-cost margins will be felt.

So, what are the policy implications of the above analysis? As Hansson (1992) and Jacquemin and Sapir (1991) argue, there is some evidence that the formation of the European single market may lead to mergers and collusive activity as firms adopt strategies to maintain their profit margins. If this is the case then the welfare of consumers will be reduced and the hoped for benefits of the single market may not be fully felt. Viewed in this light, increased import competition from East Asia should be welcomed as it acts as a disciplinary device which will prevent the abuse of market power by domestic oligopolies. However, the use of more disaggregated data suggests that the lowering of trade barriers within the EC is in fact likely to be more effective in lowering price-cost margins than previously thought, as long as mergers and collusive behaviour between firms in the EC may be avoided, since the Southern European Countries in particular have a strongly disciplinary effect on behaviour. This effect is likely to be larger than that derived from lowering trade barriers with the NICs as they appear to specialize in sectors which are already fairly marginal in the United Kingdom.

CONCLUSIONS

The East Asian countries have been dramatically successful in achieving a high and sustained rate of economic growth. This has been based on a growing integration into world trade with rapidly rising shares of world exports and imports. The empirical analysis presented in this chapter suggests that the factors that drive East Asian trade with the UK are far from uniform across countries in the region. At one end of the spectrum, Japanese and Singaporean export industries are human-, but not physical-capital intensive; at the other end, China and the three Dragons have a comparative advantage in small-scale, manual-labour-intensive industries; the Tigers, except for Singapore, occupy an intermediate position on labour quality and firm size, but are distinct in their strong presence in industries experiencing a rapid growth in consumption in the UK market. The prospects are for a continued move upmarket in the Dragons and Tigers towards technologically more sophisticated products, if only to escape the potentially huge competition from China in labour-intensive industries. Whilst this chapter has concentrated on the very real competitive challenge from the East Asian economies for UK industry, it should be emphasized that through its fast-growing appetite for imports and its burgeoning foreign direct investment the Orient Express is also a potentially important source of dynamism and re-invigoration for the UK economy.

NOTES

1 The authors gratefully acknowledge the financial assistance of the Economic and Social Research Council through the Asia Pacific programme in undertaking the empirical work on which this chapter draws. Helpful comments on an earlier draft have also been received from Dr Jim Slater and from David Greenaway.
2 The tendency for nominal tariffs to increase with the degree of processing of a product so that the effective protection on value-added on finished goods is understated by the nominal tariff.
3 The price-cost margin is defined as:
PCM = (value-added-operative wage bill)/value-added
and corresponds to the measure used by Hansson (1992) and Conyon and Machin (1989).
4 The five firm concentration ratio is used as a proxy for the Herfindahl index suggested by theory.

5 $IMI_{i,j} = \dfrac{\text{Imports from country j in industry i}}{\text{apparent consumption industry i}}$

$= \dfrac{\text{imports from country j in industry i}}{\text{(sales value industry i + imports industry i − exports industry i)}}$

BIBLIOGRAPHY

Buigues, P.A. and Jacquemin, A. (1994) 'Les pays à bas salaires et les échanges commerciaux avec l'Union Européenne', Discussion Paper 9419 Department of Economic Sciences, Catholic University of Louvain.
Chowdhury, A. and Islam, I. (1993) *The Newly Industrialising Economies of East Asia,* London: Routledge.
Conyon, M. and Machin, S. (1989) 'Profit Determination in UK Manufacturing', Warwick Economic Research Papers, no. 330, October, University of Warwick.
GATT (1994) *International Trade: Trends and Statistics 1994,* Geneva.
Hansson, P. (1992) 'The Discipline of Imports: the Case of Sweden', *Scandinavian Journal of Economics,* 94(4): 589–97.
Herderschee, H. (1995) *Incentives for Exports, a Case Study of Taiwan and Thailand 1952–87,* Aldershot: Avebury.
Hill, H. and Phillips, P. (1993) 'Trade is a Two-way Exchange: Rising Import Penetration in East Asia's Export Economies', *The World Economy,* 16/6: 687–97.
Hong, W. (1992) 'Trade Policies in Korea', ch. 20 in D. Salvatore (ed.) *National Trade Policies,* Amsterdam: North Holland.
Howell, J. (1991) 'The Impact of the Open Door Policy on the Chinese State', ch. 5 in G. White (ed.) *The Chinese State in the Era of Economic Reform,* London: Macmillan.
Jacquemin, A. and Sapir, A. (1991) 'Competition and Imports in the European Market', ch. 5 in A. Venables and L.A. Winters (eds), *European Integration: trade and industry,* Cambridge: Cambridge University Press.
Lardy, N.R. (1992) *Foreign Trade and Economic Reform in China 1978–1990,* Cambridge: Cambridge University Press.
—— (1994) *China in the World Economy,* Washington DC: Institute for International Economics.
Lawrence, R.Z. (1991) 'How Open is Japan?', ch. 1 in P. Krugman (ed.) *Trade With Japan: Has the Door Opened Wider?,* Chicago: University of Chicago Press.
Urata, S. (1984) 'Price Cost Margins in an Oligopolistic Market', *Economic Letters,* 15: 139–44.
Wade, R. (1989) *Export Promotion and Import Controls in a Successful East Asian Trading Economy,* Trade Policy Division, World Bank, Washington DC (mimeo) (cited by Herderschee, op. cit.).
World Bank (1994) *The East Asian Miracle – Economic Growth and Public Policy,* New York: Oxford University Press.
Woronoff, J. (1986) *Asia's Miracle Economies: Korea, Japan, Taiwan, Singapore and Hong Kong,* New York: M.E. Sharp.
Young, S. (1982) *The Basic Role of Industrial Policy and a Reform Proposal of Industrial Incentives.* Seoul: KDI Press (cited by W. Hong op. cit.).

3 Korean investment in Europe: motives and choices

Sang-Kun Nam and Jim Slater

INTRODUCTION

Korea is not alone as a country whose rapid growth and spectacular success as a trading nation has created a set of consequent domestic problems characterized by, among others, increasing cost of labour and other factors of production, including imports, trade frictions associated with a persistent trade surplus, a shortage of capacity, and a relatively low investment in R&D. Regional development has increased the cost of success and Korean and other East Asian businesses have been and are looking to Foreign Direct Investment as a means of re-establishing international competitiveness. One trend has involved the attempt to regain a cost advantage through FDI in developing countries, ('push' factors) particularly in the Asia Pacific region. This trend is fairly typical of traditional, declining industries towards the tail end of the life-cycle in domestic markets. The other involves establishing production facilities close to or in major markets previously served by exports. This is mainly a response to increased trade frictions associated with Regionalism ('pull' factors). In this chapter we examine the motives of Korean businesses investing in Europe and attempt to identify reasons for choice of location. A survey of Korean businesses with subsidiaries in Europe provides the data for most of this study. Of necessity, the survey was undertaken after the location decision was made, but the intention was to identify the *ex ante* factors.

KOREA'S INVESTMENT IN EUROPE

In 1992, in terms of EU trade, Korea was the twentieth largest export destination and thirteenth largest import origin, accounting for 1.8% of the EU's imports and 0.8% of the EU's exports. Relatively speaking, the EU is rather more important to Korea, accounting for 11% of Korean imports and over 12% of exports in the same year. Before the eighties, Korea's overseas investment total was negligible, but began to be significant after the 1982–3 oil crisis. However, it was not until 1986 that overseas investment began the rapid growth that has continued to the present. It was also during 1986 that Korea's first Trade Surplus was realized. The major reasons for FDI are: cost advantage; security of raw material supplies; circumvention of trade barriers; consolidation and expansion of overseas markets; technology transfer; and access to different sources of finance. From 1985 the cumulative overseas investment total rose from $476 million to $7,266 million by the end of 1993. Over the same period the number of projects rose from 443 to 3,513. Table 3.1 indicates the regional breakdown.

Specifically in Europe, Korean (cumulative) FDI increased from $41 million in 1988 to $789.1 million in 1993. Europe's share, at 11%, is modest compared to South East Asia at 44% and North America at 33%.

However, Korea's investment in Europe is expected to increase greatly in the years to come in order to make in-roads into the integrated expanded European market. In particular, Korea's investment in the UK increased to $15.9 million in 1993, up by 52.3% compared with 1991. Of the EU total, 29.6% of cumulative investment, amounting to $534 million, was directed to the UK. As of July 1994, ten Korean manufacturers had located and invested in the UK, and some fifteen Korean financial institutions had maintained their European headquarters in the UK.

Table 3.2 shows the breakdown of Korean FDI by European country. Note that the figures include not only the European Union, but also the European Free Trade Association (EFTA). The Central and East European countries also include the Central Asian Republics of Kazakhstan and Uzbekhistan.

Whilst the general economic factors motivating FDI are well-documented (e.g. Dunning), this chapter uses survey data to examine the priorities of Korean businesses who have actually made the investment decision and are engaged in implementation. The survey also investigates attitudes to and expectations of global change, particularly with respect to European regional integration.

Table 3.1 Outward investment from Korea by destination
(On approval basis, unit: US$1,000)

Regions	1991	1992	1993	Share (%)
South East Asia	1,875,106	2,325,099	3,200,601	(44.04)
Middle East	287,177	164,709	105,169	(1.45)
Europe	372,603	489,257	789,195	(10.86)
(the EU)	*246,173*	*380,086*	*534,038*	*(7.3)*
North America	1,979,432	2,098,189	2,373,328	(32.67)
Latin America	209,848	255,013	266,367	(3.66)
Africa	111,420	107,353	183,928	(2.54)
Oceania	231,802	332,298	347,608	(4.78)
TOTAL	5,067,388	5,771,918	7,266,196	(100.0)

Source: The Bank of Korea.

Table 3.2 Cumulative investment of Korea in Europe by country
(on approval basis, unit: US$1,000)

Countries	1991		1992		1993	
EU	246,173	(128)	386,086	(141)	534,038	(146)
France	22,488	(15)	72,927	(17)	106,200	(19)
Italy	5,864	(11)	10,828	(12)	15,881	(12)
Germany	55,612	(49)	86,324	(53)	172,927	(54)
Netherlands	1,459	(7)	9,399	(10)	10,169	(13)
Belgium	6,293	(3)	6,797	(3)	6,797	(3)
Denmark	6	(1)	6	(1)	–	
UK	104,638	(32)	137,266	(34)	159,442	(35)
Portugal	17,499	(2)	14,344	(2)	24,144	(2)
Ireland	25,000	(3)	24,870	(3)	24,870	(3)
Spain	7,314	(5)	17,325	(6)	13,608	(5)
EFTA	4	(1)	922	(2)	1,174	(2)
Norway	4	(1)	422	(1)	206	(1)
Sweden	–		500	(1)	968	(1)
CEEC*	71,068	(22)	51,566	(36)	199,657	(64)
Russia	20,526	(15)	25,504	(20)	29,349	(39)
Poland	679	(2)	559	(2)	6,359	(4)
Hungary	49,363	(4)	12,044	(5)	15,238	(7)
Czech	–		10,780	(1)	11,780	(2)
Romania	500	(1)	500	(1)	500	(1)
Kazakhstan	–		2,179	(7)	5,941	(7)
Uzbekistan	–		–		130,490	(4)
Others	55,358	(9)	56,683	(11)	54,326	(10)
TOTAL	372,603	(160)	489,257	(190)	789,195	(222)

( ): Number of Projects.
* Central and East European Countries.
Source: The Bank of Korea.

SURVEY RESULTS

In the survey, Korean companies investing in Europe were questioned, and 43 subsidiaries from 31 companies responded. The survey was designed to identify the motivation for Korea's investment in Europe, and to analyse the views of Korean businessmen on the effects of the Uruguay Round (UR) and of possible further European integration (the EU with Central and Eastern Europe). A major purpose of the research, not reproduced here, was to review Korean business strategies in response to these global trends and suggest strategies for the future.

The likely determinants of FDI have been listed above. In the case of Korea trade frictions and other aspects of European integration have been reported as 'pull' factors influencing Korean businessmen. The latter, according to informal sources, are keenly aware that bilateral trade relations with Europe have been particularly contentious in recent years and express concerns about the negative effects of the European Union. These include protectionist actions against Korea such as anti-dumping measures, countervailing duties, and quantitative restrictions. Furthermore, suspension of the General System of Preferences (GSP), requirements of local content, and European standardization are becoming major concerns. Conversely, European concerns include openness and access to financial markets in Korea to European business and protection of EU copyrights and intellectual property rights.

This chapter aims to test the relative importance of the hypothesized motivating factors to Korean investors. The major motivators are displayed and ranked according to the survey outcome in Table 3.3.

The most important are 'expansion of European market share' and 'circumvention of trade barriers'. These factors provide a basis not only for understanding and accessing current strategies, but also for helping design future Korean strategies in Europe.

These results tend to confirm that the major motivators were 'pull' factors rather than the 'push' associated with declining competitive advantage at home. 'Fortress Europe' appears to have attracted FDI as a means of overcoming anticipated trade frictions.

FACTORS IN THE SELECTION OF LOCATION (CHOICE OF HOST COUNTRY)

The location decision is well explored in micro-economic theory: factors, such as land, labour and transportation costs; raw material, labour quality, technology (particularly where joint ventures are concerned) and cost and availability of intermediate inputs are likely to be significant. Evidently,

Table 3.3 Determinant factors for investment in Europe

Determinant factors	Rank*
Expansion of internal market share in Europe	4.6
Circumvention of trade barriers imposed by European countries	3.9
Bridge role to facilitate exports to Eastern Europe	3.0
High production costs due to increasing wages at home	1.7
Establishment of channels of acquiring high-technology	3.2
Easier access to raw materials, parts and components	2.0
Favourable conditions of financing	2.7
High productivity	–
Others†	4.6

* Ranked on a scale 1–5, 1 being least important.
† Collection of market information, Establishment of sales networks to extend after sales services to European customers, etc.

from the point of view of economic policy, we may wish to investigate the significance of the array of subsidies and tax concessions available in many areas. Table 3.4 shows the results.

The generalized economic (market) variables appear to be less significant than the policy ensemble. Infrastructure and incentives collectively outrank other factors, with geographical advantage in terms of proximity to third countries' markets in second place. From the comments in the open section of the questionnaire it was clear that 'favourable investment climate' included political and social stability and that 'Geographical advantage' included not only other countries in the EU but also the potential for the host country as a stepping stone into the adjacent emergent markets of Eastern Europe. An aspect of this is investigated below. It seems reasonably clear that whilst advancing into the EU is seen as a strategic move, actual location may be chosen on a fairly short-term balance-sheet basis. The principal strategic factors are the opportunities provided by stability, favourable infrastructure and expected growth of the large internal market.

FAVOURED LOCATIONS (PARTICULAR HOST COUNTRIES) FOR FDI

Having examined the strategic factors influencing Korean investors, we now turn to the execution of the decision and examine the reasons given for the actual choices made. These should be consistent with the relative importance of the factors examined above. Korea has invested $172.9 million in Germany, $159.4 million in the UK and $106.2 million in France as of 1993, accounting for 21.8%, 20.2% and 13.2% of Korea's investment in Europe, respectively.

Among the European countries invested in, it turns out that the UK is the favourite even though cumulative investment to date has favoured Germany. The deciding advantages seem to be language and access to financial markets, outweighing the pure locational advantages of Germany. Whilst

Table 3.4 Criteria for selection of location within Europe

Criteria	Rank*
Favourable investment climate in terms of infrastructure, government incentives, etc.	4.6
Advantage of production costs	3.4
Geographical advantage to third countries	4.0
Advanced technology	3.2
Easier access to raw material, parts and components	2.2
Favourable conditions of financing	3.5
Others*	4.6

* Diversification of sales network, strategic alliances in Europe, expectation of growing market, etc.

Table 3.5 Favoured countries for investment in Europe

Countries	Reasons	Rank (3.0)
UK	Language (English), easier access to financing, high productivity, incentives such as grants, etc.	2.8
Germany	Well-established infrastructure, biggest market in Europe, geographical advantages to Eastern Europe, etc.	2.7
France	Favourable investment incentives, good location in Europe	2.5
Spain	Low wage, high growth market potential, etc.	2.5

Spain's significant cost advantage was the main reason given by those businesses choosing Spain, low-input cost advantage was not the dominant concern for the majority of firms investing in Europe.

DRAWBACKS OF BUSINESS CONDITIONS IN EUROPE

So far we have concentrated on the perceived benefits of Europe as a destination for FDI. However, the questionnaire was also designed to shed light on the difficulties perceived by Korean firms, in both trade and FDI terms. In particular, the sample of firms was asked to make comparisons with other trading blocs. Figure 3.1 shows the result.

Clearly Europe is seen as a 'difficult' trading partner. Two-thirds of firms perceived that barriers to trade are equal to or significantly higher than other regions. In addition to formal trade barriers, the survey revealed other handicapping aspects of doing business with (and in) Europe. The most frequently cited are shown in Table 3.6, below.

PAN-EUROPEAN INTEGRATION

Emerging from the survey is a profile of investors taking a strategic view, based on the societal environment, of the decision to invest in Europe and

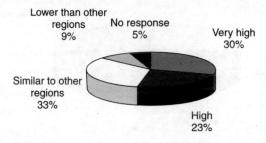

Figure 3.1 Views of European trade barriers relative to other regions
Note: Very high (13); High (10); Similar to other regions (14); Lower than other regions (4); No response (2). Figure in brackets indicate number of respondents.

Table 3.6 Drawbacks of trading in and with Europe

Drawback elements

– Lack of accumulated business information on European market
– Lack of expertise and experience in European markets
– High levels of wages
– Economic recession and unstable exchange rates of major European currencies
– Anti-dumping, quotas, and GSP suspension
– High tariff rates
– Limitation of business activities of foreign firms and discriminatory policies
  towards foreign firms
– High local content
– Excessive requirements for security management and standardization
– High market entry barriers and intense competition
– Others*

---

* Racism, bureaucratism, differences of languages and culture.

taking a tactical view of actual location based upon task environment factors. We were interested to pursue the long-term strategic perspectives and in consequence the survey attempted to capture the awareness and expectations of a changing European political and economic structure. Views were, therefore, elicited on the extent and likelihood of pan-European integration, that is, of the unification of the whole of Europe for

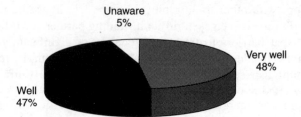

Figure 3.2 Awareness of pan-European integration
Note: Very well (21); Well (20); Unaware (2).

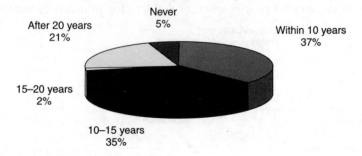

Figure 3.3 Expected timescale for integration
Note: Within 10 years (16); 10–15 years (15); 15–20 years (1); After 20 years (9); Never (2).

trading purposes, including the former European Soviet Republics. Figure 3.2 indicates 95% are (or claim to be) aware of the potential for a greatly expanded EU and Figure 3.3 summarizes the respondents' forecasts of the time scale.

A total of 37% think the integration process will be completed within 10 years and 35% think between 10 and 15 years. However, integration is not expected to be completed for at least 20 years by 21%. Of the respondents 4.7% expect full integration will never be achieved. This implies that pan-European integration is being anticipated by a sizeable majority of Korean companies and that the prerequisites for the development of appropriate strategies are in place.

EFFECTS OF PAN-EUROPEAN INTEGRATION ON KOREA

Over half the respondents expected that integration would have negative effects on Korea, while only 16% of them thought that Korea would benefit. Their expectations of and anxieties about the effects of the completion of integration stem from the factors summarized in the Table 3.7.

Clearly, the wider integration of Europe is viewed on balance as being more of a threat than an opportunity.

TREND OF WORLD TRADE AFTER PAN-EUROPEAN INTEGRATION

To this question, 77% of respondents forecast that Regionalism after pan-European integration would be the predominant feature of world trade and only 7% anticipated a move towards global free trade in the years ahead. Only one respondent anticipated no change in the world trading environment. There was, therefore, a clear majority anticipating a trend towards a world divided into major trading blocs.

Table 3.7 Positive and negative aspects of integration

Positive aspects	Negative aspects
– Increased demand through market expansion and growth	– High standardization of quality and high level of local content
– Favourable investment climate for foreign investors	– Rise of regionalism and protectionism
	– Increased competitive intensity
	– Discriminatory trade policies towards non-member countries

CONCLUSION

Not surprisingly, Korean firms investing in Europe seemed primarily motivated by 'pull' factors in terms of the decision to locate in Europe. One might expect 'push' factors to be more significant with regard to FDI undertaken in developing countries such as those in East Asia (China, Indonesia, Philippines, Myanmar, Vietnam, etc.). The strategic decisions of Korean firms seem consistent with a fairly consensual view of long-term environmental trends. Perhaps of more interest, and certainly of interest to policy-makers, is the importance attached to factors such as infrastructure and incentives in determining the final location. Whilst local policy instruments may be effective in securing FDI, there is a danger that, if the overall inward level of FDI is relatively unaffected, intra-regional competition for inward FDI may serve only a distributional function laying the foundations for problems of efficiency in the future.

BIBLIOGRAPHY

Bhagwati, C. (1987) *International Trade*, Cambridge, Mass.: Massachusetts Institute of Technology (MIT) Press.

Boddewyn, J.J. (1983) 'Foreign and Domestic Divestment and Investment Decisions', *Journal of International Business Studies*, Vol. XIV(3), Winter: 25–35.

Bollard, A. (1992) 'Regionalism and the Pacific Rim', *Journal of Common Market Studies*, 30, June.

Calvet, A.L. (1981) 'A Synthesis of Foreign Direct Investment Theories and Theories of the Multinational Firm', *Journal of International Business Studies*, Spring–Summer: 43–60.

Dunning, J.H. (1980) 'Toward an Eclectic Theory of International Production', *Journal of International Business Studies*, Spring–Summer: 9–31.

Greenway, D. et al. (1994) *Survey in International Trade*, Oxford: Blackwell Publishers.

Grosse, R. (1981) 'The Theory of Foreign Direct Investment', *Essays in International Business*, 3, December: 1–51.

Hine, R. (1992) *Regionalism and the Integration of the World Economy*, Oxford: Blackwell Publishers.

Lee, H. (1991) 'EC 1992 and Korea's Direct Investment in the EC, The Single European Market and its Implications for Korea and as an NIE', paper from a Joint Korean Development Institute Conference, Seoul.

Rahman, M.Z. (1983) 'Maximisation of Global Interests: Ultimate Motivation for Foreign Investments by Transnational Corporations', *Management International Review*, 23(4): 4–13.

Root, F.R (1990) *International Trade and Investment*, Ohio: South Western Publishing Company.

APPENDIX 3.1

Characteristics of firms in the survey

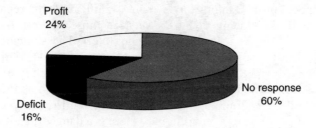

Figure 3.4 Profitability of subsidiary
Note: Profit (23); Deficit (15); No response (58).

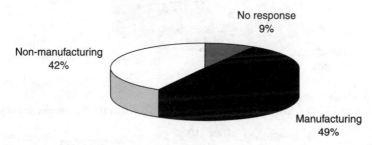

Figure 3.5 Survey response rate by sector
Note: Manufacturing (21); Non-manufacturing (18); No response (4).

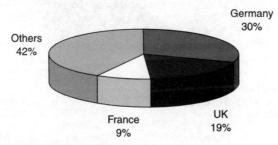

Figure 3.6 Investment by country
Note: Germany (13); UK (8); France (4); Others (18).

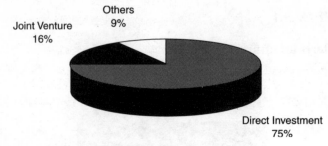

Figure 3.7 Investment by entry mode
Note: Direct Investment (32); Joint Venture (7); Others (4).

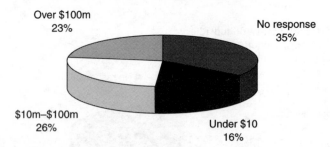

Figure 3.8 Capital of parent company
Note: Under $10 m. (7); $10 m.–$100 m. (11); Over $100 m. (10); No response (15).

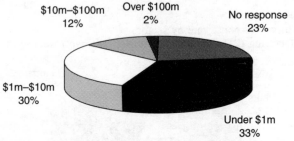

Figure 3.9 Size of investment amount to establish subsidiary
Note: Under $1 m. (14); $1 m.–$10 m. (13); $10 m.–$100 m. (5); Over $100 m. (1); No response (10).

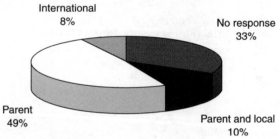

Figure 3.10 Source of financing
Note: Parent (20); Parent and local (4); International (3); No response (13).

4 The application of international strategic alliances to enhance competitive advantage: the experience of leading Taiwanese firms[1]

Jocelyn Chen

INTRODUCTION

This study illustrates through case studies the four stages by which Taiwanese firms conduct co-operative activities. The first stage involves absorbing inward basic technological know-how; the second stage the accumulation and assimilation of technology; the third stage, the enhancement of comparative advantages by outward transfer of mature technology to Less Developed Countries (LDCs), and/or establishment of overseas subsidiaries and/or joint ventures in LDCs; and at the fourth stage the acquisition of advanced technology by the purchase of foreign firms, and/or by formation of joint ventures with Multinational Corporations (MNCs) in Industrialized Countries (ICs) or in the domestic market. Success in each of the four stages is very much dependent on the attributes of, *inter alia*, technology, recipient firms and industry.

Many studies (Wortzel and Wortzel 1981; Wade 1990; Hobday 1994 and 1995; Levy and Kuo 1991) have indicated that Taiwan's industrial structure is moving away from labour-intensive industries to more technologically advanced manufacturing. For instance, the production of capital-intensive and technology-intensive industries accounted for 62.3% of total manufacturing production in 1993 (*Central Daily News* 1994a). Also, exports of capital-intensive and technology-intensive industries in 1991 accounted for 64.8% of total export production (Industrial Development & Investment Centre, Ministry of Economic Affairs (MOEA) 1992).

Taiwan ranks as the ninth largest Foreign Direct Investment (FDI) recipient in the world (*The Economist*, October 1994). Total FDI inflow into Taiwan from 1952 to 1993 was US$17,705 million involving some 6,895 individual cases (Investment Commission, MOEA 1993). Most FDI was from the USA ($4,716 million with 1,254 cases) and Japan ($5,056 million with 2,376 cases). Cases of foreign technical co-operation in the Taiwanese domestic market totalled 3,962 from 1952 to 1993. According to official records (Investment Commission, MOEA 1993) on Taiwanese firms' outward investment, total amounts and cases of outward investment were $7,281 million and 1,863 respectively. Outward investment concentrated on South East Asian and North American countries, particularly the USA. Approved Taiwanese outward investment in the People's Republic of China (PRC) totalled $3,590 million with 9,829 cases from 1991 to 1993 (Investment Commission, MOEA 1993).

The main purpose of this study, then, is to sketch a theoretical explanation for the pattern of Taiwanese firms' technological development in terms of their international strategic alliance behaviour.

First, the relevant academic literature will be reviewed, with particular attention given to the technological development of newly industrialized countries (NICs), especially technological development in Taiwan.

Second, a four-stage model of the form of strategic alliance employed by leading Taiwanese firms in their technological development will be discussed. Examples of these firms will be examined in relation to the Four Stage model, which is proposed for explaining their up-grading of technological capabilities. The observations are here limited to nine leading Taiwanese firms (see Appendix 4.1, p. 64) in different industries. The aim is to relate the experiences of Taiwanese firms in the context of the model.

Finally, there is a discussion on the effects of accumulated imported technology on firms' international competitiveness.

TECHNOLOGICAL DEVELOPMENT AND ACQUISITION CHOICES IN NICs (TAIWAN, SINGAPORE, HONG KONG, SOUTH KOREA)

Wortzel and Wortzel (1981) describe a simple marketing scheme to show how NICs' exporters graduate from supplying labour-intensive assembly services to exporting advanced goods into a foreign market. They systematically analyse the importance of export marketing to a firm's growth in East Asia, focusing on consumer electronics, athletics footwear and clothing.

The determinants of technological development and acquisition choices for companies in newly industrialized countries are examined by Contractor (1993). These choices for the acquisition of technology include independent development and imitation; licensing and contractual methods such as technical training and service agreements; import of capital equipment; partnerships and joint ventures with foreign firms; establishment of foreign investment affiliates; and the purchase of foreign firms.

Hobday (1994) finds that Asian firms have progressed from simple assembly tasks to more sophisticated product design and development capabilities. A simple market-technology model (see Table 4.1) examines how firms' domestic technology assimilation relates to export marketing in NICs such as South Korea, Taiwan, Hong Kong and Singapore. In addition, Hobday adds a technology dimension to provide a marketing-technology

Table 4.1 Stages of marketing and technology assimilation

	Marketing stages	Technology stages
1.	Passive importer-pull Cheap labour assembly Dependent on buyers for distribution	Assembly skills, basic production capabilities Mature products
2.	Active sales of capacity Quality and cost-based Dependent on foreign buyers	Incremental process changes for quality and speed Reverse engineering of products
3.	Advanced production sales Marketing dept. established Starts overseas marketing Markets own designs	Full production skills Process innovation Product design capability

4.	Product marketing push
	Sells direct to retailers and
	  distributors overseas
	Builds up product range
	Starts own-brand
		Begins R&D for products and
		  processes
		Product innovation capabilities

5.	Own-brand push Markets directly to customers Independent distribution channels, direct advertising Strong market research	Competitive R&D capabilities R&D linked to market needs Advanced product/process innovation

Source: Hobday, 'Export-led Technology Development in the Four Dragons: the Case of Electronics', 1994, p. 341.

model showing how successful NICs' firms gradually learn the techniques of manufacturing.

Hobday's (1994) marketing-technology model clearly has implications for the international product life cycle (Vernon 1966; 1975) and theories of the location of production (Dunning 1975). This simple export-led technology development model examines NICs' technology and marketing learning. The evidence also illustrates the importance of assimilative learning efforts on the part of NIC firms in electronics.

Hobday provides a useful approximation for understanding the dynamics of market and technological development in the NICs. NIC firms tend to start with simple assembly and manufacturing tasks and, once these are mastered, proceed to the more complex design and development work which is proposed in the marketing-technology model.

Hobday (1994) also presents a taxonomy of mechanisms by which NIC firms build bridges into international markets and acquire technology (see Table 4.2). Each mechanism provides both access to technology as well as a mechanism for exporting.

Under sales and exporting arrangements such as original equipment manufacture (OEM), joint ventures and licensing, NIC firms are presented

Table 4.2 Mechanisms of foreign technology acquisition and market entry by NIC firms

Licensing	A local firm pays for the right to manufacture a product under license from a foreign firm. This normally requires more technical capacity on the part of the local firm than does a joint venture.
OEM	Original equipment manufacturer (OEM) is a specific form of sub-contracting. Like a joint venture, it requires a close connection with the foreign partner. Under OEM deals, the local firm produces a good to the exact specification of the foreign company. The foreign firm then markets the product through its own distribution channels, under its own brand name. OEM often involves the foreign partner in the selection of equipment, training of managers, engineers and workers. It is to be contrasted with own design and manufacture, (ODM), where the local firm designs the product to be sold by the transnational corporation (TNC).
Sub-contracting	A local firm manufactures a component or sub-assembly for a foreign manufacturer located either within the NIC or overseas.
Strategic partnerships	These are joint technological developments under which the NIC firm develops a technology in equal (or near equal) partnership with a foreign company.
Joint ventures	Under jointly-owned companies the NIC partner gains direct access to training and technology. The foreign firm secures low-cost production. The NIC firm is a junior partner and a recipient of technology.
Company acquisitions	Recently NIC firms have purchased overseas companies to acquire skilled workers, managers, equipment and distribution outlets (e.g. the purchase of small US Silicon Valley companies).

Source: Hobday, 'Export-led Technology Development in the Four Dragons: the Case of Electronics', 1994, p. 337.

with a mechanism for technology transfer. Under OEM arrangements, the foreign corporation not only buys finished goods for export, but will often supply technical specifications, training, and advice on production and management. However, within the firms, sub-contracting and original equipment manufacture (OEM) mechanisms act as a training school for NIC firms, enabling them to overcome entry barriers and to assimilate manufacturing and design technology (Hobday 1995). In Taiwan, foreign involvements such as joint ventures, technical agreements, OEM contracts, venture capital investments, joint research projects, etc., have been preferred to direct investment (Lim and Fong 1991).

MNCs are often willing to assist in local assimilative efforts under OEM because they depend on the quality, delivery and price of the final output. Hobday's study confirms the view that technological learning is a cumulative, incremental process, and in his words 'NIC firms' strategies seem to begin with mature, standardised technologies and gradually work their way "backward" along the product life cycle towards new designs, process development and research'.

Generally speaking, Taiwanese firms' competitive advantage (Porter 1985; 1986) has been based on low-cost production. Therefore, in order to gain competitive advantage firms have focused on the control of costs, efficiency in manufacturing production, learning and absorbing technological and technical knowledge.

In addition, foreign direct investment has played an active and important role in Taiwan's development (Schive 1990; Lim and Fong 1991). Technological change has contributed greatly to Taiwanese firms' growth. However, for Taiwanese firms, technology is more easily acquired from abroad by imitation, licensing, foreign direct investment, or free goods, than internally by self-development. Many firms were the recipients of quite advanced technology from industrialized countries, then a modified form of this technology was channelled through both direct investment and technical co-operation agreements to firms in South-east Asia (SEA).

MODE OF APPLICATION OF STRATEGIC ALLIANCES IN TECHNOLOGICAL DEVELOPMENT

Interviews were undertaken over the period from December 1993 to March 1994, with senior managers of nine leading firms (see Appendix 4.1 for company details, p. 64). These case studies offer tentative support for the four stages model. The model (see Table 4.3) provides a useful framework for assessing the use of strategic alliances in each phase of technological development.

Stage I: Infancy

This involves **basic technology transfer**. In order to get basic manufacturing technology know-how, Taiwanese firms pay fees (royalty fees) for transferring technology from MNCs. At this stage, co-operation with MNCs raises the reputation of Taiwanese firms, and enhances their marketing capability.

The technological development of Taiwanese firms then concentrates on assembly skills, and basic production capabilities for mature products. This often involves cheap labour assembly. In this stage, Taiwanese firms are very dependent on buyers for distribution.

Methods for absorbing basic technology are typically via market-like arrangement, e.g. OEM, technology licensing agreements, sub-contracting, turnkey projects, and joint ventures (JVs). OEM was probably the most important channel for technology acquisition in Taiwan (Hobday 1994). Licensing is often cited as a quick means of acquiring technology

Table 4.3 The application of strategic alliances in technological development

Phase of technological development	Terminology	Attribute	Technological-marketing stage*	Type of strategic alliance
Stage I	Infancy	Basic Technology Transfer	Assembly skills, basic production capabilities, reverse engineering of product, Mature products	OEM, Licensing, Sub-contracting, joint ventures (JVs), Turnkey Project
Stage II	Adolescence	Growth in Technology Knowledge	Incremental process changes for quality and speed, Begin R&D for product & processes, Product innovation capabilities	ODM, Licensing, Sub-contracting, JVs in core business
Stage III	Maturity	Mature Technology	Full production skills, process innovation, Product design capability	FDI & JVs in LDCs, Licensing in LDCs
Stage IV	Rebirth	Learning Advanced Technology	Competitive R&D capability, R&D linked to market needs, Advanced product/process innovation	FDI & JVs in ICs, JVs with MNCs in domestic market, Technology co-operation

* Technological-marketing stages are developed from Hobday's marketing-technology model.

(Contractor 1985). Turnkey packages, where the seller supplies all engineering expertise, are sometimes the cheapest means to acquire production capability. Under sub-contracting, only production is delegated to recipient firms (sub-contractors). Therefore, production know-how can be transferred by sub-contracting. One example of a joint venture by a Taiwanese firm is TECO in the 1970s, which formed joint ventures with Japanese MNCs in bearings and electrical apparatus.

Harvey (1984) has given reasons for MNCs' willingness to transfer technology to LDCs. Large buyers from Japan, USA, etc. were very important for the growth of NICs' local firms. US and Japanese manufacturers and buyers came to Taiwan for access to cheap labour. In this trade, leading MNCs opened up export market opportunities and trained local technicians and engineers.

Technology was also acquired by imitation, reverse engineering and foreign training and education (Lim and Fong 1991; Hobday 1994, 1995). In Taiwan, the return of US-trained engineers is an important source of know-how. For instance, ACER employed a number of returned US trained engineers and overseas Chinese at its R&D centre during the early establishment stage and this policy has continued. 'Lite-on' was established by US-trained engineers who took over the divested firm from the US MNC.

Hobday interviewed a sample of leading Taiwanese start-ups at the Hsinchu Science-based Industrial Park in 1992. He found that senior staff from each firm had been trained in US companies, many in Silicon Valley. Some continued with training and licensing agreements with former US employers.

Taiwanese traditional industry mainly depended on OEM, with most of the equipment supplied by the licenser. Through OEM, firms absorbing basic technology, particularly in light industry, increased their capability to produce.

Hobday (1994) provided illustrative examples to show that joint ventures and foreign buyers' assistance played a very important role in the success of the start-up of the Taiwanese Electronics industry during the 1960s and 1970s.

Many firms started by learning from their MNC partners. For example, FEDS sent its employees to Japan for management and marketing training. Firms such as Shihlin, TECO and President, had licensing agreements with their MNC partners for technology transfer. The President Corporation, at its initial stage, purchased equipment from Switzerland and Japan. However, its technological know-how mainly came from its Japanese partners.

With regard to Taiwan Security Company, because the government has only recently relaxed restrictions on the development of the security industry, it is still at a basic technical level. Other industries such as electronics, machinery, and computer, however, have developed from the stage of infant technology into adolescence or mature technology.

Stage II: Adolescence

This involves the growth of core technological knowledge. In order to enlarge their market share, firms improve the quality of their products by developing their own R&D. Some firms form joint ventures or co-operate with MNCs to access product development technology and to improve quality. For instance, Tatung formed a joint venture with the Japanese Fujitsu Company in 1973.

In order to escape the necessity of continuing dependence on imported technology, Taiwanese firms are also beginning to develop their own innovative capability (Contractor 1993). In the 1970s and early 1980s, many firms established overseas offices for purchasing, for collecting valuable market information, and for offering after-sales services. For instance, both Tatung and FEDS had representative offices in USA.

In particular, a firm must overcome its technological dependency in terms of product design, quality control and process engineering. Hobday (1994) has illustrated the importance of assimilative learning efforts on the part of NIC firms. As firms' capacity expands and the number of customers increases they need to learn to control the quality and speed of production. The methods of technology development at this stage are own design and manufacture (ODM), licensing, sub-contracting, and purchasing foreign firms, in order to integrate technological competence.

In stage II, some firms have product design capacity and are able to conduct ODM for their foreign buyers. The ODM supplier has internalized the capability to design a product (or sub-assembly) for the international market. Under ODM a firm designs and manufactures a range of products with little or no assistance from the overseas purchaser. The foreign buyer then purchases the goods it requires and sells them under its own brand name. With the improvement of local firms' design capabilities, overseas manufacturers often purchase under ODM arrangements. Thus, ODM signifies a more advanced technological stage than OEM.

Stage III: Maturity

In this stage, local labour costs have risen, firms no longer receive benefits from their comparative advantage in cheap labour manufacturing procedures and they seek to license their mature technology to other manufacturers based in LDCs as an alternative to direct competition. In addition, Lim and Fong (1991) have indicated that Taiwanese firms have undertaken investments in LDCs either to source raw materials, or to exploit a firm's comparative advantage in industries where it can make cheaper products better suited to the host countries' markets, and operate on a small scale and with a lower level of technology than foreign firms from industrial countries. Some Taiwanese firms have moved or are planning to move abroad to exploit lower wage costs in countries like India, Indonesia, Thailand, Malaysia, and Vietnam. However, the pattern of foreign investment by firms is more nearly explainable by factor endowment (Dunning 1986). Technological co-operation/joint ventures are two types of Strategic Alliance normally undertaken by firms in this third stage.

At this stage, the firm has full production skills, and is capable of designing products. In order to extend comparative advantage and make use of cheap labour and raw material, firms undertake investment strategies such as establishing subsidiaries and joint ventures (JVs) in LDCs, and licensing their mature technology to LDCs. LDCs may then go through stages of technological development similar to those experienced by the NICs. Transferring mature technology to LDCs becomes essential for profit. In the assessment of technology transfer to LDCs, the ability of local collaborators and the opportunity to export goods have become the predominant concerns of Taiwanese firms.

Examples of firms in this stage are: Lite-On, which has invested in a joint venture in Thailand and also has established off-shore manufacturing sites in Malaysia, where ACER and TECO have similar establishments; and

Tatung, which has established a subsidiary in Thailand. Other examples of technological co-operation are highlighted in Lim and Fong (1991: 69): there were fifty-seven outward technical co-operation agreements in different industries between 1964 and 1986 where Taiwanese firms have sold technology to local firms in LDCs.

At the initial stage of foreign investment, firms are not familiar with the foreign environment and investment conditions. Most firms then choose export-only manufacturing in order to reduce risk, product cost and to maintain market share.

When firms are more familiar with the environmental conditions of investment, they co-operate with their business partners to form joint ventures to exploit the domestic market within the host country (LDC). For instance, ACER has invested in Mexico, Brazil, and Indonesia via the formation of joint ventures with its distributors. ACER is able to strengthen its strategic business alliance network and add a 'local touch' to its brand name. President Corporation's major investments in South-east Asia (SEA) and PRC were mainly joint ventures, and it also transferred know-how to its Indian partner (NAVA). According to its managers the motives of President are the pursuit of profits in host markets and the strengthening of internationalization. Table 4.4 shows the outward investments made by the firms interviewed.

Stage IV: Re-birth

This is **the stage of learning advanced technology**. In order to enhance international competitive capability, to improve product design capability, to market directly to customers, to access advanced product technology and innovation technologies, and to share the high risks in new product

Table 4.4 Outward investment in LDCs

Date	Company	Location and activity
1989	FETL	Take over Filsyn (polyester plant) in Philippines
1989	Lite-on	Manufacture of electronics in Thailand
1989	Lite-on	Joint venture for PC board in Thailand
1991	Lite-on	Manufacture of electronics in Malaysia
1991	President	Joint ventures in food and electronics industries over Thailand, Indonesia, Vietnam, Philippines, and PRC
1989	Tatung	Manufacture of colour-tube in Malaysia
1989	Tatung	Manufacture of CTVs in Thailand
1991	Tatung	Joint venture of Electronics in Malaysia
1991	Tatung	Joint venture of soft-ferrite core in Thailand
1991	ACER	Joint ventures in Mexico, Brazil and Indonesia
1991	ACER	Manufacture of PC board, monitors in Malaysia
1991	TECO	Manufacture of electric motors in Malaysia

ventures, leading Taiwanese manufacturers such as ACER, Tatung, etc. have conducted advanced technology transfer and joint ventures with MNCs or their local competitors at this stage.

But why would the leading MNCs want to share their expertise with Taiwanese firms that do not have access to a large market, nor have expertise of their own? Contractor (1993) suggests that Taiwanese firms might target mid- to small-size foreign high-tech firms that are in need of capital for further operation. Also, peripheral technology may be selected for transfer so that the supplier will not be put at a competitive disadvantage and will be able to earn income from the technology transferred.

Moreover, as Taiwanese firms' capabilities have increased, mutually beneficial technology partnerships with leading US and Japanese companies also provide an alternative for acquiring highly advanced technologies. By means of this international strategic co-operation, firms may have the opportunity to upgrade their technological capabilities. Simultaneously, they may have an opportunity to integrate a firm's upstream or downstream technology, to increase its innovative and R&D ability, and to enhance its competitive capabilities when collaborating with MNC partners. In order to meet increasingly sophisticated customer needs, firms will have to capture the higher value-added stages of production. At this stage, firms should embody sufficient skills to collaborate with MNCs to develop new products and processes.

Large firms from Taiwan have begun to acquire overseas firms to gain technologies (Contractor 1993; Hobday 1994). The mode of investment undertaken by firms in pursuit of technological development is to set up foreign subsidiary establishments in industrialized countries or to purchase existing firms in order to get related information on advanced-technological know-how and acquire well-established market distribution channels. Liu (1994) indicates that Taiwanese FDI in the EU is for information gathering, and for marketing in host countries. The purchase of total or partial stakes in a foreign company is often a speedy method of acquiring a ready-made technical capability (Contractor 1993). Several Taiwanese firms have gone abroad to access technology through acquisition. Table 4.5 gives some major examples.

The strategy of firms such as ACER, Tatung, and FETL for investments undertaken in USA, Japan, and EU was almost always merger and acquisition (M&A). M&A was also used for acquiring technological information, management techniques and marketing distribution. Greenfield investments remain few.

More recently, Taiwanese officials have promoted the island as a natural business hub for the fast-growing Pacific Rim (*Business Week* 1995). Having built competitive export industries, Taiwan is now able to attract foreign companies to invest and to supply Taiwanese firms, and to link increasingly with markets and suppliers in the East Asian Region. More multinationals are viewing the island's diversified economic structure as a

Table 4.5 Examples of overseas investments and acquisitions

Date	Company	Location and activity
1978	*Tatung	Los Angeles, manufacture of TV sets
1980	*Tatung	Atlanta, manufacture of TV sets
1980	*Tatung	Take over of Decca (UK) for TV set manufacture
1980	*ACER	Purchased Altos (US) to distribute computers in the US
1987	*ACER	Take over of Counterpoint (US) for minicomputer technology
1992	ACER	Subsidiaries of modular PC assembly in The Netherlands and Denmark
1991	FETL	Take over the PET Division of the Goodyear Rubber Co.
1992	FETL	Joint venture of manufacturing ethylene glycol in Canada
1991	President	Take over American biscuit manufacture factory
1991	Lite-on	Take over NPE company for product of power supply in UK

Sources: *Hobday (1994: 354), and author's research.

regional operations centre. The formation of joint ventures in Taiwan with MNCs is an increasing trend. For instance, China Electronics Ltd. has a joint venture with Japanese Elevam Company in producing CCFL (Cold Cathode Fluorescent Light; a main component of LCD) (*Central Daily News* 1995a); TIT Company and the American AMD Company (*Central Daily News* 1994c) co-operate in the production of CDUs; hard-disk drives are the object of co-operation between Asia Investment Co. and American HP Co. (*Central Daily News* 1994b). Other technological collaboration in Taiwan includes Taiwan's Solomon and the French Bull IC manufacturing (*Central Daily News* 1993). These joint ventures are no longer concerned with cheap labour, but are for accessing upstream components and R&D, for supplying the domestic market (this depends more on the attributes of product and industry), for penetrating the international market, and for accessing the development of new product or process technologies. Examples of the interviewed firms' co-operation with MNCs in the formation of joint ventures in Taiwan are in Table 4.6.

ACER has one main joint venture with Texas Instruments to make advanced memory chips (DRAMs), and another joint venture with MBB (a German aerospace company) to develop a special Hybrid IC (Integrated Circuit). ACER also has formed alliances with Daimler Benz and Smith Corona in micro-electronics technology and with Microsoft, Silicon Graphics and NEC in new product and chip designs (Lim and Fong 1991; Hobday 1994).

Tatung has joint ventures with MNC partners such as the Fujitsu Company, Japanese Precise Meter Company and American Otis Elevator Company. Technological co-operation and joint ventures with MNCs in the domestic market have a positive effect on Tatung's FDI activities. The

Table 4.6 Examples of inward co-operation investment in joint ventures with MNCs

Parent company	Main joint venture company	Area of main product	Taiwanese equity holding
ACER	1. Texas Instruments-ACER Inc.	1. DRAMs and ASICs	58%
	2. Ambit Microsystems Corp.	2. Hybrid micro-electronics	50%
FETL	1. LAFE	1. Industrial gas	35%
	2. Freudenberg-FE Co.	2. Polyester membrane	34.5%
Tatung	1. Tatung Precise Meter Co.	1. Speedometers, tachometers, fuelmeters, temperature-meters and tank indicators	All majority equity holding by Tatung
	2. Tatung Otis Elevator Co.	2. Elevator	
	3. Tatung Coatings Co.	3. Automobile finishes, electrodeposit, home appliance and industrial coatings	
TECO	1. Toshiba Compressor Co. (1990)	1. Magnetic contactors & switches	20%
	2. Royal Taiwan Co. (1993)	2. Family-style restaurant	49.99%
	3. Westinghouse Motor Co. (1988)	3. Marketing & sales of electric motors	25%
	4. YATEC Engineering Corporating (1992)	4. Electric systems engineering	39.99%

inward joint ventures of FETL with MNCs have served the company's diversification programme.

The main strategies of TECO in joint ventures, technological co-operation and FDI activities are aimed towards strengthening its position in its core business and expanding its business horizons into well-considered diversification programmes which are consistent with core strengths.

IMPLICATIONS

Special attention can be drawn to the different nature of joint ventures at each stage in Table 4.3. For example:

Stage I: Primary joint ventures involve basic technological knowledge transfer from MNCs to Taiwanese firms in which R&D intensity is low;

Stage II: Secondary joint ventures involve more progress in technological knowledge for improving product quality and R&D intensity is high;

Stage III: Tertiary joint ventures entail domestic expansion and high R&D intensity which is especially transferred to LDCs;

Stage IV: Quaternary joint ventures include international acquisitions in both ICs and/or in Taiwan, and R&D intensity is high.

DISCUSSION AND CONCLUSIONS

The success of strategic alliances in promoting technological development is for the most part dependent on industry characteristics, product features, firm-level capability, attributes of technology, environmental factors and opportunities.

Many firms simultaneously are at different technological stages and face different stages of technological competition. Firms may have different strategies to develop their technological capacity and to break through their technological obstacles by means of the application of strategic alliances. In this study, although based on a few cases, it has been shown that a life-cycle model of the use of strategic alliances may be a reasonable explanation of a firm's technological development.

Many Taiwanese firms carried out low-risk, small-scale investment and had a high probability of success in inter-firm co-operation. Thanks to international procurement, Taiwan has entered international markets, has supplied key markets and obtained technical information. Many local firms, including Tatung and ACER, acted as OEM suppliers and subcontractors, learning to imitate MNCs. Tatung exports around half of its colour TVs and personal computers under OEM agreements. TECO sells colour display terminals, video graphic adapters and TV monitors under OEM agreements with IBM, Wang and Hitachi. Lacking distribution outlets, most of Taiwan's larger electronics firms are dependent on OEM for export growth.

The study confirms Hobday's (1994) observation that local firms in NICs successfully coupled export and technological development under co-operative arrangements, such as JVs, licensing, OEM and sub-contracting.

Today, Taiwan's brand leaders still continue with OEM, for example, ACER manufactures approximately 50% OEM products for its customers and distributes around 50% of its own brands directly to customers. OEM enables ACER to increase output, to achieve economies of scale and to maintain the pace of technological and quality improvement.

Contractor (1993) suggests that, if Taiwan is to be known as one of the research centres of Asia, it should upgrade its industry and technology and attract more FDI. Attracting foreign company R&D activities to Taiwan would be a useful boost to this upgrading.

In recent years, decreasing tariffs and commodity taxes, the appreciation of the New Taiwan Dollar, liberalization of trade, the narrowing gap of prices between foreign and local goods, rising labour wages, and environmental protection campaigns, are all threats to Taiwan's competitive advantage and are the main reasons for Taiwanese firms becoming involved in outward investment activities. Most Taiwanese firms are small multinational enterprises (SMEs), which particularly focus on LDCs like South-east Asia (SEA) and PRC. Most entry modes in the PRC and SEA are joint ventures. It remains to be seen how these SMEs will upgrade their technologies on foreign soil.

Nevertheless, if Taiwanese firms wish to become fully internationalized, they must progress from OEM to building up their own brand names.

The examples from this study also confirm that firms' inward co-operation with MNCs helped firms to improve their technological knowledge and strengthen their competitive capability. But to extend their competitive capability in global business, Taiwanese firms must invest in skilled professional labour, R&D, and continue to upgrade their technology.

Finally, there is evidence of a circular phenomenon as all low value-added products are transferred from Taiwan to LDCs and high value-added products from industrialized countries are introduced into Taiwan's home market.

NOTE

1 The author wishes to express thanks to Trevor Buck and Dr Alistair Bruce of the University of Nottingham, and James Liu of Manchester Business School, and two anonymous referees for their valuable comments.

BIBLIOGRAPHY

Business Week (1995) 'The New Hong Kong? Don't Hold Your Breath: Taiwan Wants to Be a Major Asian Hub but has a Long Way to Go', No. 3402-732, 3 April.
Central Daily News (1993) 'Solomon and French Bull's Collaboration in IC Manufacturing: the largest Asian IC firm in Taiwan', 5 June, p. 8.
—— (1994a) 'Economic Strategy: Improving Investment Environment', 27 September, p. 8.
—— (1994b) 'Developing High Density Hard Disk Driver and Holding High Technology: Asia Investment Co. and HP's Co-operation', 20 October, p. 8.
—— (1994c) 'TIT and America AMD's Co-operation in Manufacturing 486 CPU', 29 October, p. 8.
—— (1995a) 'Taiwanese-Japanese Joint Venture: Taiwan Elevam for Producing Key Component CCFL', 30 March, p. 6.
—— (1995b) 'Japanese Firms Accelerate their Investment Pace to Match Taiwan', 13 April, p. 6.
Contractor, F.J. (1985) 'A Generalized Theorem for Joint Venture and Licensing Negotiations', *Journal of International Business Studies*, vol. 16, Summer: 23–50.
—— (1993) 'Technology Acquisition Choices for Newly Industrializing Countries: The Case of Taiwan', *The International Executive* 35(5), September/October: 385–412.
Dunning, J.H. (1975) 'Explaining Changing Patterns of International Production:

In Defence of the Eclectic Theory', *Oxford Bulletin of Economics and Statistics*, vol. 41: 269–95.
—— (1986) 'The Investment Development Cycle Revisited', *Weltwirtschaftliches Archiv*, 122(4): 667–75.
Harvey, M.G. (1984) 'Application of Technology Life Cycle to Technology Transfers', *Journal of Business Strategy*: 51–8.
Hobday, M. (1994) 'Export-led Technology Development in the Four Dragons: The Case of Electronics', *Development and Change*, vol. 25: 333–61.
—— (1995) 'East Asian Latecomer Firms: Learning the Technology of Electronics', *World Development*, 23(7), July.
Industrial Development and Investment Centre (1992) Ministry of Economic Affairs (MOEA), Taiwan, R.O.C., *Industrial Investment Information*, no. 129, 3 October.
Investment Commission, MOEA, Taiwan, R.O.C. (1993) *Statistics on Overseas Chinese & Foreign Investment, Technical Co-operation, Outward Investment, Outward Technical Co-operation*, December.
Levy, B. and W-J. Kuo (1991) 'The Strategic Orientations of Firms and the Performance of Korea and Taiwan in Frontier Industries: Lessons from Comparative Case Studies of Keyboard and Personnel Computer Assembly', *World Development*, vol. 19(4): 363–74.
Lim, L.Y.C. and P.E. Fong (1991) *Foreign Direct Investment and Industrialisation: in Malaysia, Singapore, Taiwan and Thailand*, Paris: OECD.
Liu, J.Y.S. (1994) 'Internationalisation Strategy and Transfer of Management Practices to the EC: the Experience of Taiwan', paper presented at the 21st Annual Conference of the UK Academy of International Business, UMIST (University of Manchester Institute of Science & Technology), 25–6 March.
Porter, M. (1985) *Competitive Advantage: Creating & Sustaining Superior Performance*, New York: The Free Press.
—— (1986) *Competition in Global Industries*, Boston: Harvard Business School.
Schive, Chi (1990) *The Foreign Factor: The Multinational Corporation's Contribution to the Economic Modernization of the Republic of China*, Stanford, Calif.: Hoover Institution Press.
The Economist (1994) 'A Survey of the Global Economy', vol. 333, no. 7883, 1–7 October.
Vernon, R. (1966) 'International Investment and International Trade in the Product Life Cycle', *Quarterly Journal of Economics*, 80(2).
—— (1975) 'The Product Life Cycle Hypothesis in a New International Environment', *Oxford Bulletin of Economics and Statistics*, vol. 41: 255–67.
Wade, R. (1990) *Governing the Market: Economic Theory and the Role of Government in East Asian Industrialisation*, Princeton, New Jersey: Princeton University Press.
Wortzel, L.H. and H. Vernon Wortzel (1981) 'Export Marketing Strategies for NIC and LDC-Based Firms', *Columbia Journal of World Business*, Spring: 51–60.

Appendix 4.1 Summary of interviewed companies, March 1994

Co. Name & Initial (Year of Establishment)	Sales NT$ m.	Assets NT$ m.	Net Income NT$ m.	Capital NT$ m.	Employees
1. Shih-lin Electric & Engineering (1955) Shih-lin	6,692	6,337	597.44	2,024	2,018
2. Far Eastern Dept. Store (1967) FEDS	12,962	10,485	700.86	3,692	2,265
3. Far Eastern Textile (1942) FETL	21,309	52,351	2,001.97	12,364	7,582
4. Teco Electric & Machinery (1956) TECO	11,911	14,796	1,630.52	4,368	2,963
5. Tatung (Electric & Machinery) (1949) TATUNG	33,103	51,849	1,215.88	8,836	10,500
6. Acer (Computer) (1976) ACER	12,242	16,336	55.95	4,598	8,319
7. Taiwan Lite-on Electronic (1975) LITE-ON	3,673	3,000	143.79	1,553	1,031
8. President (Food) (1967)	22,446	23,776	2,485.18	8,218	6,421
9. Taiwan Securities Co. (1988)	722	7,857	14.09	2,000	210

Note: Approximately US$1 = NT$26 (in 1994).

5 Italian firms in ASEAN countries: direct investment and non-equity linkages between Asian and Italian firms

Corrado Molteni

INTRODUCTION

Foreign direct investment (FDI) in Southeast Asia and in ASEAN countries, in particular, has increased conspicuously in the last decade. However, unlike the United States and Japan, the EU countries seem to be rather reluctant investors in the region. As pointed out by many European and Asian observers and scholars, the EU countries have collectively not established a significant corporate base in Asia and Europe remains, or seems to remain, a laggard in the region (for example, see Lim, Chow and Tsui 1994).

Economic statistics at least to a certain extent tend to confirm this view (see below). Lack of consistent and comparable data does, however, make it almost impossible to obtain accurate information on the dimension and the relative weight of European investment. Moreover, official statistics do not consider the so-called 'new forms of investments', which have emerged since the late 1960s, side by side with the more traditional forms of foreign direct investment, namely wholly or majority-owned subsidiaries (Oman 1984).

Examples of these new forms of investment include various types of non-equity linkages taking different contractual forms, such as sub-contracting, technical assistance and licensing agreements. These non-equity linkages do not require a direct capital participation from the European side but, like other investment, involve the transfer of managerial and technological resources and know-how from European to Asian firms, and thus contribute to the upgrading of Asian industries as well as to the development of industrial co-operation between Asia and Europe.

In particular, a small but increasing number of Italian firms operating in traditional sectors (textiles, footwear, furniture, etc.) and also in the machinery sector are particularly active in establishing and developing non-equity linkages with firms in ASEAN countries. This rather distinctive approach is the result of both the scarcity of financial and managerial resources affecting especially medium-sized Italian firms and their long experience of outsourcing and network-building.

This paper examines the reality of Italian involvement in ASEAN countries through equity and non-equity forms of investment, and focuses on a number of cases in Indonesia, Malaysia and Singapore. The advantages, disadvantages and risks of the two types of international investment are discussed.

EUROPEAN DIRECT INVESTMENT IN ASEAN COUNTRIES

As already mentioned, the available statistics on foreign investment in ASEAN countries do not provide a wholly accurate picture of European involvement in the region. Not only does the aggregate data, made available by the government agencies (Indonesia BKPM, Malaysia MIDA, BOI Philippines, BOI Thailand and EDB Singapore), vary in content and coverage, but there are also relevant discrepancies between investment which is approved and that which is actually undertaken. The picture is also not clear with regard to 'government-promoted' and 'non-promoted' industries, and also between authorized and paid-up capital. Thus, what we can infer from the available sources is just the trend rather than the real dimension of the phenomenon.

As far as the trend is concerned, all the available sources seem to register a strong increase of European investment since the second half of the 1980s. The value of 'approved applications' regarding European investment in four ASEAN countries (Indonesia, Malaysia, Singapore and Thailand) has in fact increased from approximately 500 million US dollars in 1986 to more than 2 billion in 1993.[1]

The relative position of Europe, however, has declined as Japanese investment has registered a real boom. Measured in dollars, Japanese investment grew more than threefold from 1987 to 1990, when it reached a record level of almost 7,000 million US dollars. Japanese firms, which in the past mainly invested in Asian newly industrializing economies (NIEs) have, since the second half of the 1980s, shifted their investment in manufacturing activities to ASEAN countries especially to Thailand and Malaysia and, more recently, to Indonesia. This shift has been spurred by the strong yen and attracted to Asia by lower labour costs and also by rapidly expanding local markets.

But Japan is no longer the only Asian investor. Capital-endowed Taiwan, Hong Kong and Singapore have also begun to invest in ASEAN. Indeed, according to a recent survey by the Asia Development Bank, in 1993 Asian NIEs account for more than 30% of foreign direct investment in Thailand, followed by Japan (23.8%) and the USA (19.9%). In Indonesia too the NIEs have won the race with 32.3% of all FDI, while in Malaysia the United States has provided 27.9% of FDI, followed by Japan and the NIEs with 26.4 and 17.5% respectively.[2]

From the above, it is evident that, notwithstanding the positive trend, Europe is falling behind Japan and other Asian nations as an investor. This is despite the fact that the European Commission has repeatedly advocated a strengthening of economic ties between the EU and the ASEAN countries, and despite all the locational advantages offered by the region.

These developments reflect first of all European companies' prevailing concern and interest for the overall important domestic market and for the areas geographically close to it, namely Eastern Europe and the Mediterranean countries: a concern clearly related to the reality of trade relations. In fact, although the incidence of the EU trade with ASEAN as a proportion of total EU trade has grown considerably since the second half of the 1980s, the region still plays a marginal role in the external economic relations of the EU and, as a consequence, European companies are not only less attracted by this market but they also have had fewer opportunities to train a high number of experienced managers with a good understanding of the economic, legal, social and political framework of ASEAN nations. Yet, Japanese firms have gradually developed relevant human capital thanks to the diffused practice of personnel rotation: a practice which has made it possible to have area specialists not only in the area but also at headquarters.[3]

THE ITALIAN EXPERIENCE IN ASEAN COUNTRIES: DIRECT INVESTMENT

For countries like Italy, which do not have a tradition of strong cultural, economic and political links with Asia, direct investment in ASEAN countries is an extremely risky option, available only to a limited number of companies. And if the Italian company does invest, it is often through affiliated companies established in other European countries. In cases such as these, the investment is not registered as an Italian one, but according to the country of the affiliated company. For this reason, therefore, the official number of subsidiaries of Italian companies or joint ventures with local partners in ASEAN is less than the actual number of participating Italian companies. To give an example, in a country like Indonesia, only a few Italian companies have so far officially invested and the amount of their investment registered in BKPM statistics (less than 50 million US$) accounts for a negligible percentage of all their investment.

Companies like FIAT (car assembly), Piaggio (motorcycles) and recently Pirelli (cables) have established joint ventures or production bases in the region, but the scope of their activities is still limited. The most significant, fully operating 'Italian' undertaking in the area is SGS-Thomson Microelectronics (ST), actually a French–Italian joint venture, legally based in The Netherlands (!), producing integrated circuits, discrete devices and sub-systems for computers, consumer products and telecommunications.[4]

In Asia ST has three production units: one in Malaysia (Muar in Johor) and two in Singapore (Toa Payoh and Ang Mo Kio), with more than 7,500 employees (4,000 in Malaysia and 3,000 in Singapore). These investments are part of an integrated, long-term Asian strategy which goes back to the end of the 1960s. Then, SGS – at the time a company of the Olivetti group – decided to open the first factory specializing in 'back-end' operations (i.e. assembly and testing) at Toa Payoh in Singapore for the assembly of epoxy and metal can transistors. This was a typical cost-reducing investment, since at that time labour costs in Singapore were about one twelfth of those in Italy and even less than those in Germany and Sweden, where the companies had two plants. It was also a 'follow the leader' type of investment since it was undertaken in the wake of the move by American competitors, which had already started to transfer their labour-intensive manufacturing activities to South-east Asia.

In 1974, following the rise of labour costs in Singapore, ST relocated the most labour-intensive operations in Muar (Malaysia) and in 1982 decided to open the second plant in Singapore. This time, however, it was a 'front-end' plant, that is a plant for the production of parts and components (wafers), and the first of this kind set up by a manufacturer of semiconductors in South-east Asia with the purpose of serving the local market. Thus, the company which started as a follower, cost-oriented investor, was fifteen years later a leading, market-seeker investor, a development brought about by the growth of the region's economy and the upgrading of its industrial and technological capabilities. The expansion of the local market is clearly confirmed by the growing importance of ST Asian sales: 18% of total sales in 1987 and 28% in 1993 (23% in Asia Pacific and 5% in Japan). This market is served by the Asian manufacturing units supported by a network of twenty-two suppliers, most of them located in Korea, Taiwan, Hong Kong and Malaysia.

According to the managers of ST in Singapore the advantages of localization in the city-state are as follows:

1. Lower labour cost and higher labour productivity.
2. Higher capacity usage ratio and, therefore, accelerated depreciation of fixed investments. Since 1984 Singapore's plants have been operating 24 hours a day for 365 days a year with two 12 hour shifts (workers work for four days and then rest for three days, then work for three days and rest the following four days).
3. Co-operative industrial relations.
4. Attractive fiscal and financial incentives for investments and for the training of personnel.
5. Public support and assistance provided by the Economic Development Board (EDB).
6. High level of infrastructures and advanced financial services available.
   (Interview with Italian manager of SGS-Thomson Singapore, 1994)

On the other hand, the company encountered serious problems of high levels of personnel turnover (job-hopping): from 12 to 18% yearly for non-production workers and even 20–30% in the case of blue collars. This is a problem that the company is trying to solve with the employment of foreign workers, mostly female workers from the Republic of China, hired with a two-year contract: a programme which has been developed in close co-operation with the Singaporean authorities.

However, the major task facing the managers of ST today is the building and the upgrading of research and development capabilities so as to make the Singaporean subsidiaries two integrated, autonomous production units. This process has just started with the co-operation, once more of the local authorities (in this case the National Science Technology Board, NSTB). In fact ST is presently involved in three research projects regarding 'back-end' and 'front-end' production technologies. The three projects were approved in August 1994, and will be partly financed by NSTB. The company is also participating in the government programme of upgrading the local supporting industry, co-operating with suppliers in the training of technicians and in developing ties with foreign (European) firms. These developments are in line with Singapore's policy aimed at transforming the island into a financial, manufacturing and research centre.When the building of autonomous research capabilities has been completed the process of re-localization, started in 1969 with the transfer of some labour intensive manufacturing activities, will have reached the stage at which even parts of the critical, strategic activities of the company can be successfully performed in Asia.

INDIRECT INVOLVEMENT: NON-EQUITY LINKAGES

The case of ST, however, is an exception. As has already been said, few other Italian companies have invested in wholly-owned subsidiaries or joint-ventures. There are, however, a good number of medium-sized firms established in Asia through non-equity linkages (sub-contracting and management agreements, technical licensing, etc.) with local companies. These non-equity linkages or alliances imply a continuous involvement in the form of managerial, technical and, in some instances, financial support, and a return from these investments in the form of fees and royalties or, more simply, the purchase at agreed conditions of the semi-processed or finished products.

However, since this form of investment is not subject to notification 'or recorded officially or systematically' it is not easy to obtain a clear, comprehensive picture of the phenomenon. Nevertheless, the information gathered so far confirms the fact that this type of involvement in Asia by Italian companies is rather significant and is assuming an increasing importance particularly in two ASEAN countries: Indonesia and Malaysia, where it has been possible to identify about a dozen cases of industrial co-operation between Italian and local entities.[5]

These agreements concern in particular companies operating in the so-called traditional, labour-intensive sectors: textiles and clothing, footwear, leather-goods, rubber products, building material and furniture, and also the machinery sector. In these sectors many Italian companies have already acquired experience in outsourcing and network-building and, since the end of the 1980s, with the liberalization of capital movements, have started to transfer this experience abroad: first in Eastern Europe and in the Mediterranean countries, and now in Asia.

There are three main purposes of this form of investment or industrial co-operation between Asian and Italian firms: (1) the development of natural resources and the acquisition of raw materials and intermediate goods (vertical integration); (2) the reduction of production costs (labour cost) and (3) entry into the local market, an investment sometimes required to bypass import restrictions.

As for the development of natural resources, Italian furniture producers have developed ties particularly with Indonesian companies for the production and the processing of various types of rattan and wooden furniture, according to the specifications of the Italian partner, who also provides the technical assistance and the training necessary to obtain the quality standards required by European consumers. However, in most cases the direct involvement of Italian firms has been more the result of an assertive, forward-looking policy of outsourcing, than Indonesian policy which severely restricts the export of the raw material (rattan and other high-quality woods). This is a policy which is aimed at keeping in the country the processing activities and the creation of value added. Italian firms have preferred to avoid direct investment through a joint-venture and have instead chosen industrial co-operation with a local partner. This is for two reasons: to keep their options open and maintain a high degree of flexibility in their operations and also to avoid the complex bureaucratic procedures and controls which come with the establishment of joint-ventures.

More numerous are the cases of industrial co-operation aimed at the containment of production costs. A good example is the operation in Indonesia of Miroglio Tessile, the fourth largest Italian group in the textile-clothing sector. This company has in the past developed an integrated network of suppliers, both in Italy and abroad, and has recently started an industrial co-operation scheme with an Indonesian partner to supply Miroglio with shirts and polyester clothes. The two partners have signed a carefully drafted agreement which includes an understanding on technical assistance. On the basis of this agreement a manager of Miroglio is taking care of all the quality control procedures, from the selection of the materials to the various stages of production. The final product is then exported for sale in foreign- European or third-markets using the brand name of the Italian firm. A licence agreement has also been signed in Indonesia by Benetton, although in this case all the production is distributed in the local market.

CONCLUSION

It is important to note that the decision to sub-contract part of the production is related to the fact that, in all of these cases, the manufacturing process is labour intensive and does not require particularly high technical competence and skill, and as these products are manufactured in large quantities they are also highly standardized.

If, however, the degree of technological and organizational complexity is rather high, direct investment still tends to be the only option available. This is also the case for some branches of the so-called traditional sectors in which advanced skills in product planning, design and manufacturing represent the main source of the firm's competitive advantage.

Whenever possible Italian firms, especially in the traditional sectors, seem to prefer a non-equity linkage with a local partner. This choice, instead of the establishment of a joint-venture or even a wholly-owned subsidiary provides relevant advantages for the Italian 'investor', advantages that can be crucial for a medium-sized company.

First, the amount of fixed investments is very limited and often no investment at all is required. Only in some instances, for example in the production of footwear, have Italian companies had to supply the local partner with production equipment and intervene in the reorganization of the factory lay-out. In all other cases the actual amount invested in plants and machinery has been quite limited.

Second, non-equity linkages assure the highest degree of flexibility and mobility, which has always been one of the sources of the competitive position of Italian firms operating, for example, in the fashion business.

Third, management costs are rather limited. Beside the training of the workforce, the Italian partner is normally in charge of the supervision and the control of quality, but this is normally achieved with a rather limited investment.

On the other hand, Italian firms face a serious risk when resorting to these forms of industrial co-operation in geographically and culturally distant countries. The risk is that of training potential competitors that might enter the market with similar, less costly products; a risk which can be avoided through the control of critical functions such as research, design and marketing and the control of the distribution channels, but a risk that smaller companies might not be able to avoid and prevent.

NOTES

1 Values calculated from BKPM, MIDA, BOI and EDB. More conservative estimates based on balance of payments data show, however, a less vigorous growth (see MITI 1994: 94).
2 See *Nihon Keizai Shinbun*, 8 November 1994.
3 Japanese companies investing in ASEAN countries can also rely on two important elements which are less available to European firms. The first is the strong

presence in the region of Japanese trading companies with their impressive capabilities of information gathering and diffusion. The second is the strong governmental support especially in the form of aid loans.

4 With a turnover of about 2.5 billion US dollars and 20,000 employees worldwide, ST is the leading producer of integrated circuits in Europe and the 11th in the world. A truly global company having plants in Europe, the United States and Asia, where, beside the manufacturing plants, it has five design centres and six applied research laboratories. Since 1993 it has established a large R&D centre in New Delhi, employing about 150 engineers and technicians. Information on ST activities in Singapore and Malaysia has been collected with the help of Giovanni Capannelli.

5 The research of data and information has been carried out by Ralph R. Klemp for Indonesia and G. Capannelli for Malaysia.

BIBLIOGRAPHY

Lim, Kian Guam, Chow Kit Boey, Tsui Kai Chong (1993) 'European Community Market Integration and Singapore', paper presented at Institute of Developing Economies Symposium on *Impact of EC Integration on Asian Industrializing Region*, Tokyo, June.

MITI, International Business Affairs Division (1993) *Dai 22 Kai Wagakuni Kigyoo no Kaigai-Jigyoo-Katsudoo (22nd Survey of Overseas Activities of Japanese Enterprises)*, Tokyo.

—— (1994a) *Charts and Tables Related to Japanese Direct Investment Abroad*, Tokyo, October.

—— (1994b) *Tsuushoo Hakusho (White Book on Trade)*, Tokyo.

Oman, C. (1984) *New Forms of International Investment in Developing Countries*, Paris.

6 Is Europe missing the Asia boat? An overview of EU–Asia Pacific[1] relations

Gordon Robinson

The prediction made at the turn of this century by the US Secretary of State that the Pacific would be the ocean of the future has turned out to have been remarkably far-sighted and the configuration of the world political and economic order has been fundamentally re-shaped by the movement of this region to centre-stage.

Asia Pacific's consistently high rate of economic growth has been sufficiently well documented not to require extensive description here. Suffice it to say that in the twenty-five years 1965–90, the eight most dynamic Asian economies attained a growth rate which was virtually double that achieved by the OECD countries as a whole. Of those twenty countries experiencing the fastest per capita GDP growth in the period 1960–85, nine came from this region. By comparison European countries, like Italy and Germany, could only manage 22nd and 28th ranking respectively (World Bank 1993).

This extremely rapid growth has continued into this decade. In 1993 the average growth in Asia Pacific was over six times faster than in the OECD. Whereas in 1960 Asia achieved 4% of global GNP by 1993 it had risen to 25% and the IMF predicts that the period 1990–5 will have seen a further 44% growth in GNP (European Commission 1994).

The region's emergence into world trade has been no less remarkable. It is predicted that by the year 2000 its present 25% share will have risen to 40% (World Bank 1993). Collectively, Japan, Hong Kong, The Republic of Korea, Singapore, Taiwan, China, Indonesia, Malaysia and Thailand increased their share of world exports from 8% to 18% between 1965 and 1990. Korea's exports grew particularly rapidly during this period.

This robust growth has been reflected in rising and equitably distributed living standards. In Korea, Taiwan and Singapore real wages have risen fivefold in the last twenty years. *The Economist* has estimated that by the end of this decade some 400 million consumers will have disposable incomes at least as great as the rich world average, making it a major and growing market in its own right (*The Economist*, 'Survey of Asia' 1993).

EUROPE AND TRILATERALISM IN THE PACIFIC

Asia Pacific occupies an increasingly central role in terms of trade, of production, particularly manufacturing, as a market and as a focus for powerful flows of FDI from both within and outside the region. Understandably it has become the major strategic target of the Triad Powers which recognize that it is upon this axis that the future balance of world power will turn. The struggle for global pre-eminence, particularly between the US and Japan, is now well and truly joined in this region.

In the last decade, particularly since the end of the Cold War, there has been a perceptible shift in US priorities from Europe towards this region. In order not to be denied the benefits of the region's growth and to head off any further major consolidation of Japan's position the US has moderated the Atlanticism which was the sheet anchor of its post-war diplomacy. As the US Assistant of State put it recently, Europe is still very important, but in relative terms, Asia has become more important, and not just for economic reasons. In the US foreign policy establishment many senior officials 'can scarcely conceal their feelings that all Europe has to offer is mature markets with few opportunities for expanded exports, foreign policy nightmares such as Bosnia and an unimaginative and backward looking pessimism' (*Financial Times* 22 November 1993). Underlining this is the shift which has taken place in the thrust of US trade from Europe to the Pacific. In 1993, for example, the US did half again as much trade with Asia as it did with Europe.

America's turn to the Pacific has partly been brought about by a recognition of Japan's growing integration into the region. This increased meshing of Japan and the Pacific economy will, according to a senior economist at Deutsche Bank, give Japan a 'force, coherence and structure that will change, and very profoundly, not only the global balance of economic, industrial and financial power, but also the international balance of political power' (*Straits Times*, Singapore 20 July 1994).

Like the US, Japan has re-oriented its trade towards the region. In 1991 Japan for the first time did more trade with the Pacific than with its former premier market, the United States, and in 1994 its trade surplus with the region was greater than its surplus with the US. A decade ago, Japan exported a third more to the US than it did to Asia. Now that position is reversed (*Financial Times* 6 December 1994).

Japan, of course, enjoys many advantages denied to its competitors, not least of which is geographic proximity. The growing integration of Japan into the region is marked not only by the expansion of its exports but also by the growing tendency for its imports to originate here as well. In 1993, for example, three quarters of the growth in its imports came from China and East Asia (Fornasari 1994). It has also prioritized the region for overseas investment which has been a prime target of the de-localization strategy of many of its corporations trying to reduce the impact of the ever hardening Yen.

So where do these shifts in the strategies of its major competitors leave Europe? Of the Triad, Europe is clearly the most disadvantaged and exposed and this is notwithstanding the strong historic and cultural ties which it still retains with the region. Indeed, there is probably no other major region in the world where Europe's loss of competitiveness is reflected and aggravated so clearly. It does not possess the same diplomatic and military clout of the US nor does it have Japan's economic dynamism nor its natural geographic advantages. On too many occasions Europe has viewed the region as a threat and reacted in a defensive and protectionist manner to the challenge which it poses. It was the Europeans, it should be remembered, who led the opposition to Japan's re-insertion into the world economic order after 1945, while Japan, Korea and a number of other Asian countries have been on the receiving end of determined efforts to block their exports to Europe.

Unlike either Japan or the United States, which do about a third of their trade intra-regionally, Europe's trade is much more parochial in character with something like two-thirds of its trade done within Europe itself. Western Europe's imports from France alone are equivalent to its imports from the eleven major economies of Asia Pacific and in 1991 Austria and Switzerland held a larger share of EU trade than Japan. The liberalization going on in Eastern and Central Europe is also tending to draw the EU's attention away from Asia. As the Chairman of the Hong Kong Development Council has recently pointed out, it is far too often the case that European executives are pre-occupied with forging links with the emerging economies of the old Soviet bloc. The danger is that these priorities will 'keep investment and management attention out of Asia – or at least on the margins – at a time of unparallelled opportunity' (*Financial Times* 10 November 1993).

Finally, it would seem that Europe has an image problem in Asia. According to a survey carried out for the European Commission, Europe is far too often perceived in the region as an exhausted backwater, protectionist, old world snobs, colonialists and even racist. Too often for comfort, Europeans are seen as 'economic losers and swaggering imperialists with outsize egos and shrinking wallets' (*Financial Times* 19 September 1994). Something of the same sentiment was expressed by Lee Kuan Yew in his address to the students of the National University of Singapore in the summer of 1994 in which he advised aspiring MBAs to go to American rather than European Business Schools (*Straits Times*, Singapore 23 July 1994).

THE EU AND ASIA PACIFIC: THE CASE OF TRADE

The role of Asia Pacific in world trade is characterized by the rapidly growing volume which it is generating, a shift toward high-value-added manufacturing, an increasing tendency towards regional integration and self-sufficiency, and the growing attraction it has for the Triad powers.

The expansion of trading activity can be measured by the fact that in the last decade East Asian trade has doubled to $1 trillion of which Japan accounts for half. Trade within South-east Asia has grown too, if not quite so rapidly, to a total of $350 billion in 1991 (European Commission 1994).

A very significant aspect of this growth, however, is that a large and growing part of it is endogenous. At the beginning of the 1990s, intra-regional trade exceeded trade with the US by two-thirds and was more than double its trade with Western Europe (Kirchbach 1992). Indeed, the European Commission claims that, with the exception of South Asia, it has led to a decline in dependence upon developed country markets to a degree never seen before (European Commission 1994).

In terms of exports to outside of the region, the European Union is the second most important market after the US. The fact that the US already has the lion's share of its trade deficit with Asia Pacific and is not happy to see it grow much further, has meant that Europe has become a much more inviting market. This is fairly clear, for example, with South Korean motor vehicle and electronics exports and according to Han (1992) is evidence of a widespread desire to penetrate the European market by all means.

The growing importance of the European market can be gathered from the fact that in 1993 Europe was the destination of 27% of exports from the region. By the same token, Asia Pacific has also grown very rapidly as a market for European goods. Whereas in 1980 the exports of the nine member states of the EC totalled $15 billion, by 1993 the twelve member states were sending $93 billion worth of goods there, a sixfold increase in just over a decade. In 1980 Asia Pacific represented only 7% of EU exports; by 1993 it had grown to 20%, making it a more important market than the US.

This impressive growth in two-way trade has not, however, been to Europe's advantage. Asia Pacific's exports to Europe in 1993 were worth $128 billion while those of Europe amounted to just over $93 billion leaving a trade gap of some $34 billion, with Japan alone contributing $25 billion to the deficit (European Commission 1994).

A sectoral analysis of this trade makes uncomfortable reading for the EU. Asia Pacific has improved its performance in cars, non-electrical machinery, consumer electronics, footwear, leather articles and toys. South Korea, for example, boosted the share of electrical and electronic appliances as a percentage of its total exports to Europe from 10% to 35% in the period 1982–90 (Han 1992).

By comparison Europe only achieved an improvement in aircraft, silk products, animal feed and the food industry (Kirchbach 1992).

Although there have been disagreements between trade liberals and protectionists about the most appropriate response to adopt to this growing volume of imports from the Pacific, the EU's response has been largely defensive. Increasingly quotas, non-tariff barriers, and anti-dumping actions have been the means chosen to stem the tide of imports. In addition, the shift within EU trade policy towards giving Member States more freedom in determining trade policy has created greater space for countries like France to exercise more national discrimination.

EU protectionist measures have become more stringent in terms of products and rules of origin. Asian newly industrializing economies (ANIEs) have been particularly targetted as have products such as VCRs and computers. The most recent case of trade restriction is the proposal for a duty of 20% on certain types of television sets from Malaysia and an impost of 30% on TV imports from Thailand and China (*Financial Times* 16 September 1994).

Imports from Korea have been subject to particular opposition. In the three years 1985–8 alone, its share of exports affected by non-tariff barriers grew from 29.5% to 43.5%. In the period 1985–90 there were nineteen anti-dumping investigations which were directed especially at hi-tech and capital intensive goods (Han 1992). Both in these cases and the most recent ones against TV imports, SGS Thomson and Phillips have been markedly effective in bending the Commission's ear. This pressure has been ruthlessly effective in impeding the import of Korean electronics products.

The trade position is not all bad news for Europe, however. Kirchbach maintains that despite the somewhat downbeat conventional wisdom Europe did manage to strengthen its position in Asia in the 1980s. Evidence that European companies can do well is not hard to find and Italian exports are a case in point.

The devaluation of the lira and its exit from the Exchange Rate Mechanism put its real exchange rate back to where it had been in the 1970s. This, plus the fact that key sectors of its industry are to be found in the small- and medium-sized sector, has meant that Italy has been able to switch relatively easily from stagnating European markets to those in Asia. It is generally agreed that the size and flexibility of Italian engineering firms has allowed them to adapt well to the specific needs of the modernizing economies of Asia where less complex technology allows operatives to be trained more easily and on the spot.

China is a good example of this. In 1993 Italian exports doubled over the previous year and a particularly strong performance has been made by machine tools and engineering equipment. Equipment for the textile industry, of which Italy has considerable experience, has figured centrally in this export drive. The country has also been able to trade on the high reputation which it has in consumer goods. Clothes, shoes, luxury goods and furniture compete on price as well as quality. Italy is also an interesting case of an EU country whose trade is becoming less, and not more, oriented towards its European partners.

THE EU AND ASIA PACIFIC: THE CASE OF INVESTMENT

The very rapid growth experienced by Asia-Pacific has been driven forward and accompanied by a very sharp increase in FDI. The growth in foreign investment is even more significant if it is borne in mind that Asia Pacific is the only region in the world not to have been affected by the overall decline of FDI flows from the developed to the less developed world which has occurred in the last few years. In fact, in 1990, 90% of this investment went into eighteen developing countries, of which eight were in Asia Pacific (Fry 1994).

Between 1980 and 1988 FDI in Thailand, for example, more than tripled while in Indonesia foreign investment projects approved by the Government grew tenfold in the five years 1986–91. In both cases a very high proportion of investment went into export-oriented industries, a phenomenon which was also true of other emerging economies in the region. In rank order, the most important recipients were Singapore, China, Malaysia and Thailand. During the period 1985–90, for instance, foreign investors, principally from the US and Japan, accounted for 84% of all investment in Singapore's manufacturing sector (European Commission 1993).

The key investor in the region has been Japan which excepted the region from the downward trend of its FDI which took place after the peak of the late 1980s. The most recent pattern of investment, in fact, shows that the country is shifting its focus from the US and Europe towards China, Asean and the rest of Asia. It has been calculated that by the end of the century Japan will hold some 37% of all FDI in the region when it will be more significant to Japan than the United States (*Straits Times*, Singapore 20 July 1994). This investment, from which countries like Thailand have considerably benefited, generates a degree of profitability which is five times the global average achieved by Japanese firms (Fung 1994).

As well as Japan and the US, which saw its FDI flow into the region twice as fast as to anywhere else in the world (*The Economist* 1993), the other leading investors are to be found within the region itself. The self-sufficiency which is becoming evident in trade is also making itself felt in the sphere of savings and investment. Examples of this are Taiwanese investment in Malaysia, Korean investment in China, and Singaporean FDI in Malaysia, Indonesia and other parts of ASEAN.

There is also growing interest in investing in Europe, partly as a result of problems being experienced in the US and also as a means of overcoming the ever growing hurdle of trade restriction which the EU has erected. Korean investment has been growing very strongly since the mid-1980s and in 1989 it was twenty times greater than in 1985 (Han 1992).

Given the clear opportunity which the region presents to outside investors, what is the EU doing? According to the European Commission, Europe is trailing behind Japan and the US (European Commission 1994). Perhaps because of the attention which has been given to pan-European mergers in preparation for the Single Market, and also to Eastern Europe, there has even been a sharp decline of EU FDI into Asia Pacific over the last few years. It has been calculated that in the first part of this decade only about 10% of the region's FDI was coming from Europe, a picture which is hardly reassuring (European Commission 1994).

The relatively poor position held by Europe is clear from the picture of investment in China which, with its annual growth rates of 12–13%, is the most rapidly expanding economy in the region and also, according to some forecasts, likely to be the fulcrum of the world economy in the next century. Since 1979, when China inaugurated its open-door policy towards foreign investment, some $275 billion has been pledged, of which $85 billion has actually been used. In comparison with Taiwan, Hong Kong, Japan and the US, Europe's contribution has been derisory. Only the UK and Germany figured in the top ten foreign investors (sixth and ninth respectively) while their joint contribution of $4.7 billion was a third of the US figure of $14.6 billion and way below the $150 billion which originated in Hong Kong. However, given the special circumstances attending investment from Hong Kong, a more realistic comparison might be with of Japanese FDI which amounted to $18.4 billion (*Financial Times*, 'China Survey' 7 November 1994).

Much the same picture emerges from Vietnam. In a league table of the top ten investors since 1988, France, The Netherlands and the UK occupy the last three places and the total of their investment is barely half that provided by Taiwan, the most important source of FDI (*Financial Times* 8 December 1994). With the help of Taiwanese investors the government of Vietnam is currently planning a new city of more than 500,000 population to the south of Saigon with the aim of establishing a business and financial centre which will rival Shenzen and Shanghai (*Financial Times* 3 January 1995).

Within what is an unimpressive performance in terms of FDI, relative to the EU's main competitors, the UK maintains its strong global position as the key European investor while it also occupies the position as the biggest exporter of invisibles as well (*Financial Times* 22 September 1993).

On the surface, then, it would seem that the EU still has a lot of ground to make up not just on Japan and the US but also on countries like Taiwan and Hong Kong. There are, however, some arguments which are advanced in mitigation. The Commission argues that a considerable part of EU investment is not picked up in the statistics since it is generated locally by the subsidiaries of the many long-established European firms which operate in the region. Others make the point that Europe, particularly countries like Germany, has traditionally had a high export-to-investment ratio (Kirchbach 1992). It is further maintained that the present preoccupation of corporate investors with intra-European mergers and acquisitions, which has clearly distracted attention from Asia, will produce longer-term competitive benefits.

ASIA PACIFIC: THE OPPORTUNITIES FOR EUROPE

It is tempting to be too downbeat about the position of the EU in the region and overlook the genuine opportunities which exist for many sectors of business. Aerospace, infrastructural development, and assistance with the sound management of the physical and natural environment are all cases in point.

Aerospace, it may be recalled, is one of those areas where Europe's competitive advantage has recently improved. Given this, it is therefore fortuitous that Asia Pacific is experiencing the most rapid air traffic growth in the whole of the world. In China alone, air traffic grew by 30% in 1993 while at Kuala Lumpur it is expected that passenger throughput will grow from 9 million in 1991 to 55–60 million by the year 2020.

Singapore International Airlines and Cathay Pacific, which are the first and third most profitable airlines in the world, are working hard to service a regional demand which is growing at 7% a year, well ahead of the global average of 5%. Indeed, SIA is in the market for over fifty new large jets, a possibility which conjures up the spectre of a bitter battle between Airbus and Boeing of the kind which Airbus recently lost in Saudi Arabia.

The large aircraft manufacturers expect the region to outperfom every other part of the world in the next twenty years. After the year 2000 the region will overtake the US as the world's largest commercial jet market with new deliveries averaging about $16 billion for the years 2001–10. Even now China is Boeing's largest customer and in the future it is expected that the region will take up 40% of the global demand for wide-bodied jets. Airbus has calculated that Asia Pacific will be the major force in 'determining requirements for the future development of even larger aircraft to match growth demands' (*Financial Times* 18 February 1994).

Competition, however, is likely to be extremely fierce. Needless to say, Boeing will be at the forefront but a considerable effort is also being made by the Japanese. Mitsubishi, Kawasaki and Fuji Heavy Industries are making great efforts to get themselves established and already 15% of the Boeing 767 airframe and 20% of the 777 is provided by the Japanese. Samsung and Daewoo are also trying to gain market share, while Hyundai have teamed up with Yakovlev who are less sensitive about technology transfer than their Western rivals.

Because full-scale independent production of big jets is not yet possible, regional manufacturers have chosen the path of collaboration with Western airframe, aero-engine, components and systems manufacturers. As well as selling direct to Asian airlines, who, with their plans to considerably enlarge their fleets, show that they have very deep pockets, established European manufacturers have sought collaboration or joint venture agreements with Asian partners to strengthen their presence. Some of these have worked out, such as BAE's plan to produce a regional jet with Indonesia, while others like BAE's project with Taiwan have fallen foul of companies' reluctance to transfer technology.

The rapid growth of air traffic has created its own opportunies for European companies in the related field of infrastructure. The traffic at Kai Tak airport in Hong Kong, which is the third largest in the world, is growing at 10% a year and its facilities are at or very close to their handling possibilities. Presently, two-thirds of flights are delayed and the congestion is predicted to worsen, especially if the second airport is not completed on time. Very few airports in the region are free from the constraints imposed by a demand which is outstripping infrastructural capacity. Delays and congestion, it is suggested, will soon grow to European proportions (IATA, *Financial Times* 31 August 1993).

The opportunity for European companies in terms of construction and provision of infrastructure is very clear and it is to be hoped that the kind of political difficulties which hampered British firms in the building of the new Kuala Lumpur airport can be avoided. The prize to be won is very considerable; trillions of dollars will have to be spent on other parts of the infrastructure. In the next five years Indonesia plans to spend $12.5 billion to develop its surface communications, Malaysia will likewise have to invest $4 billion in power generation over the next ten years otherwise the lack of capacity which blacked out the whole of the peninsula in 1992 could easily stymie its development plans. China's need for telecommunications, rural electrification and transport infrastructure holds out enormous possibilities for European companies as does Taiwan's need for environmental expertise to head off what could be an environmental disaster if the present model of economic development is not modified.

The business opportunities for European companies are therefore very clear, but other possibilities exist for the EU to make its influence felt. Even though Europe is clearly not punching its weight, it should not allow the current wave of pessimism about its global competitive position to blind it to the value of the long-standing economic, diplomatic and sentimental ties which it still has with the region. It is worth recalling that after Japan the EU is the second largest disburser of aid to Asia and presently gives three times as much as the US (European Commission 1994).

The EU should also be sensitive to the need – which is expressed in the region – for it to play a balancing role, particularly to that of Japan. The growing anxiety that the region is slowly being turned into Japan's backyard (Pelkmans 1990) offers Europe a clear and present opportunity. Proton Malaysia's recent decision to loosen its links with Mitsubishi and explore an arrangement with Peugeot-Citroen is evidence that some operations are turning to Europe because of their concern with the Japan's managerial style and its reluctance to expedite technology transfer. Asia also needs the stimulus which European companies can bring and it is accepted that it 'will also pay a price if European companies are not fully engaged in the region [as] leaders in high technology production' (Fung 1994).

That the stakes for Europe in Asia Pacific are considerable is too evident to need much reiteration. As the Singapore Ambassador to the European Commission put it recently, 'Europe's presence in Asia is integrally tied up with its wish to remain a key player in the world economy . . . if Europe allows itself to lose out in Asia it will be losing out world-wide' (Seet-Cheng 1994). It is quite clear that if European companies are not able to take a full part in the growth of Asia Pacific it will affect their profits and competitiveness, not only in Asian markets, but also globally.

The danger is that Europe will find itself on the sidelines and be condemned to play a marginal role. The Commission's 1994 Green Paper on Asia makes it quite plain what a failure to fully engage in the region would result in. If the EU loses out it will have 'political costs, and at the very least will exacerbate the calls for more defensive policies from those who view Asia as a threat rather than as a valuable partner . . . [this] . . . in turn will further reduce the benefits to be gained from Asia and so on in a spiral of decline'.

CONCLUSIONS

From what has been implied in this chapter the question of whether Europe is missing the Asia boat seems to invite an unambiguously affirmative answer. What might be useful in conclusion is to examine why the situation has arisen and whether or not the conditions exist for Europe to recover the position.

The first and most obvious cause is geographic. It is not a Pacific Power and therefore does not enjoy the economic, diplomatic and, in the case of the US, security intimacy which physical contiguity confers.

Some of the reasons derive from the political and historical conjuncture. It has been extremely unfortunate for Europe that the acceleration of the whole integration project has occurred precisely at that moment when the mounting challenge from Asia Pacific demanded a clear, vigorous and outward looking response. Instead, the EU, perhaps unavoidably, has had its political energies consumed by the Single Market Programme, monetary union, enlargement and the whole debate over subsidiarity and states' rights. This historical conjuncture has also been marked by the collapse of the Cold War which has not only removed one of the main driving forces of European integration but has also introduced very serious elements of instability. These developments have skewed Europe's policy agenda and given it a very introverted momentum, a characteristic which, it must be said, is most unhelpful to any policy of constructive engagement in Asia Pacific.

Some of Europe's difficulties can be explained by the problems which derive from the inherent nature of the European integration project itself, particularly those created by the conflict between national and Community competence. The tension which this has produced is very clear in the area of trade policy where there is a constant tug of war between protectionists and liberals over the issue of the defence of EU industry in the face of Asian imports. The frequent recourse to the protection of national rights over trade policy has made the development of a consistent, convincing and open trade strategy towards Asia difficult to bring about with the consequence that countries in Asia Pacific have understandable reservations about Europe's reliability as a trade partner.

There is also the problem of how best to pursue and co-ordinate trade policy and strike the correct balance between bilateral relations and those which are developed and mediated through the EU's institutions themselves. There is also damaging rivalry between European companies on the ground as was the case in the recent competition between European defence contractors to supply the Korean military. This was so cut-throat that the challenge from US suppliers was almost completely ignored.

There is, finally, the issue of attitude. Far too often the business and policy-making community has buried its head in the sand and not given the Asian challenge the importance which it demands. The response has often been slow, complacent or reactive. Instead of the offensive participation which the situation demands European business has far too often been prepared to skulk in the trenches (Doehler 1994).

The question which has not been directly posed in this chapter is whether, and to what extent, the situation is retrievable. Even though this issue cannot be addressed outside of the debate about the speed and direction of European integration and the issue of competitiveness to which it is clearly related, one thing is fairly clear. The precondition of any recovery is the political will and determination to pursue a co-ordinated policy toward the region. It is to be hoped that there is still time left and that the momentum of Japanese and US policies has not already foreclosed its options.

NOTE

1 For the purpose of this discussion, Asia Pacific refers to Japan, China, Taiwan, Hong Kong, South Korea, Indonesia, Malaysia, Singapore, Thailand, Cambodia, Laos, Vietnam, and Burma (Myanmar).

BIBLIOGRAPHY

Doehler, A. (1994) 'Why is Asia of Importance to the EU?', *Interactive Forum*, Brussels.
The Economist (1993) 'A Survey of Asia', 329 (30 October).
European Commission (1993) 'The European Community as a World Trade Partner', *European Economy* 52: 79–86.

—— (1994) 'Towards a New Asia Strategy', *Communication from the Commission to the Council*, Brussels: COM (94)314 Final, p. 14.

Fornasari, F. (1994) 'What are the Obstacles to a Better EU Economic Presence in Asia?' Paper presented to the *Inter-Active Forum: Towards a New European Economic Strategy for Asia, European Commission, Financial Times, Speakers' Papers*, Brussels. (Hereafter, *Interactive-Forum*, Brussels.)

Fry, M.J. (1993) *Foreign Direct Investment in Southeast Asia. Differential Impacts*, Singapore: Institute of Southeast Asian Studies.

Fung, V. (1994) 'Why is Asia of Importance to the EU?', *Interactive Forum*, Brussels.

Han, S. (1992) *European Integration: The Impact on Asian Newly Industrialising Economies*, Paris: OECD.

Kirchbach, F. von (1992) 'Euro-Asian Trade: The Stepchild in Triadic Relations Takes Over', *Intereconomics* 27(5): 245–50.

Pelkmans, J. (1990) 'ASEAN and EC-1992', *National Institute Economic Review*, November: 99–109.

Seet-Cheng, M. (1994) 'How Can the Obstacles to an Improved EU Presence be Overcome?', *Interactive Forum*, Brussels.

World Bank (1993) *The East Asian Miracle. Economic Growth and Public Policy*, New York: Oxford University Press.

7 Globalization of European enterprises: the case of East Asia

Wolfgang Klenner

Globalization is an undisputed issue for companies developing strategies for sustaining or creating their competitive advantage. In this context, quite a few European companies have already extended their export market and manufacturing base into Asia to take part in Asia's booming markets.

However, the concrete steps towards globalization are debated extensively. One point of controversy is the question of standardization.

STANDARDIZATION VERSUS ADAPTATION TO LOCAL CONDITIONS

On the one hand it is argued that economies, societies, cultures and, therefore, national markets, are becoming increasingly similar. Hence, companies would be well advised to promote worldwide standards and pursue a standardized approach towards sourcing, production, marketing and other functions. In this connection the success of American companies such as IBM, Coca Cola, and McDonald's are frequently cited as examples of corporations which operate globally by serving clusters of customers with the same characteristics.

On the other hand, however, it is argued that internationalization of business should proceed through adaptation to individual markets. Globalization, therefore, is promoted by companies gaining competitiveness by exporting an ever-increasing portion of their products or services outside their own country and by importing globally an ever-increasing portion of the required raw materials and intermediate commodities. This can be promoted, as well, by standardization with respect to selected competitive variables such as product mix, branding, advertising, sales promotion, etc. However, respective decisions should be made on a case-by-case basis, taking account of the business, product, size and other features of the companies and of the specific features of the region into which the company's market should be extended.

ARGUMENTS FOR INDIVIDUAL APPROACHES

What would be the most appropriate concept of globalization for European countries aiming at penetrating Asia's booming markets? Even if doing business in Asia is not much different from doing business elsewhere, it seems that there are at least three arguments for a strategy of adaptation to local conditions:

- In spite of the progress made towards 'open regions', East Asia and South-east Asia are not at all homogeneous regions. They are splintered into many areas of economic activity with quite different economic structures, cultures, languages and history. This diversity cannot properly be dealt with by unified strategies. Culture, for instance, is extremely important, as has been shown by cross-cultural studies. Culture and the understanding of culture play an important role in problem identification and internal communications. Taking the cultural aspect into account is extremely important when managing staff and correcting wrong decisions. Market entry, product decisions, investment decisions and business transactions can all be influenced by cultural factors.

- It seems that hardly any Asian competitors, when penetrating European markets, base their strategy on the concept of total standardization. Most Japanese firms, for instance, entered European markets on a trial-and-error basis, carefully adjusting products, qualities, services, marketing methods and other variables to European 'atmospherics' by first selling via the sogo shosha. Investment on a larger scale was only initiated after Japanese firms had become sufficiently accustomed to their export country. If Asian firms had to conform to Western conditions, European firms therefore, ought, to adjust to 'Asian' conditions. It might be argued that Japanese companies succeeded in transplanting their concepts of 'lean production' and 'just-in-time' delivery, not common in Western practice, to Europe. However, lean production and just-in-time delivery in themselves require a meticulous and thorough adaptation to individual conditions. (Lean production combines the advantages of craft and mass production, whilst avoiding the high cost of the former and the rigidity of the latter. Just-in-time delivery means co-ordinating the flow of parts within the supply system on a day-to-day basis (Womack, Jones, and Roos 1990: 13, 62).)

- European enterprises are under-represented in East Asia in comparison to their important position within the world economy. Why is that? The main reason seems to be their lack of ability and willingness to adjust to Asian complex local conditions. Even in the past, European enterprises were not very successful in penetrating Asian markets, as can be seen from the fact that in the last few centuries most European enterprises were located in port cities such as Shanghai, Hong Kong, Canton, Nagasaki, Yokohama – internal Asian markets were left to their Asian competitors. It is revealing that Coca Cola's concept of marketing in Asia was not simply the strategy of 'standardization': they developed a different recipe for Sprite in order to be successful on the Japanese market!

LOCATION AS STRATEGIC VARIABLE

The expansion of a firm's business into Asian markets requires adjustments of variables such as organizational form and location policies. This chapter will focus on location policies.

It will be argued that European enterprises, when deciding on locations for operations in East Asia, would be well advised to learn from their successful Asian competitors. A few general trends of investment strategies of Asian firms within the region will be elaborated by way of illustration.

COSTS AND BENEFITS OF CENTRAL LOCATIONS

In order to examine a number of crucial issues of investment strategies of Asian firms, a distinction will be made between peripheral and central locations. Industrial hubs with worldwide communications and transportation networks, will be defined as central, while less developed regions will be termed peripheral. The costs and benefits of both locations will be assessed.

Investing and operating in Asia's central locations can be very costly, even more so than in Europe. Property prices are extremely high, not only in Tokyo and Seoul, but also in Hanoi or Saigon. Wages in Asia's industrialized countries are equally high. Moreover, in countries such as Japan, it can be extremely difficult for foreign companies to hire qualified local personnel and to build up loyalty among local employees.

Central locations, however, also have considerable benefits. They provide the best communication and transportation networks and allow insights into the present state and future trends of the most dynamic markets with discriminating customers. They are also usually the centre of operations for the most important Asian competitors and subsidiaries of European competitors. Thus, a central location provides access to the latest intelligence when planning future decisions on products, research, production technology, organization, marketing, world market strategies, etc.

The proximity of influential government bodies, industrial organizations and research institutions is also invaluable. In Japan, they often have an important role in determining future trends of technological research, norms and standards, sectoral and regional development priorities.

The availability of top-quality local personnel from first-rate schools and universities is another asset, enabling firms to utilize the most modern technologies and advanced organizational schemes; similarly, central locations are usually more attractive for expatriate personnel wishing to relocate with their families.

However, two important points should be made. The realization of many of the advantages of a central location, presupposes an excellent local and expatriate staff, willing and able to analyse the market, collect information on competitors and establish connections with ministries and other organizations. Not all central locations in East and South-east Asia, however, provide similar advantages. Operations at two or more complementary centres might therefore be advisable.

COSTS AND BENEFITS OF PERIPHERAL LOCATIONS

Setting up operations in a peripheral location entails a completely different set of considerations, including what might be called 'opportunity costs'.

Peripheral locations do not usually provide the company with sophisticated inputs in the widest sense. Everything, apart from labour, property and natural resources, has to be provided by the company itself. Technical and organizational know-how, market knowledge, and sometimes even electricity generators, have to be brought in by the foreign investor. There is no easy access to, or dialogue with, influential state organizations, competitors or research institutes, and simply being present in Asia does not, therefore, necessarily guarantee first-hand insights into Asian market developments.

There are two striking advantages of peripheral locations: one is low costs of property and labour – provided, however, that this is not offset by a low quality-factor – and the other is easy access to natural resources. Another important consideration is that by virtue of their isolation, companies setting up in peripheral locations often enjoy preferential relations with local administrations and closer interpersonal relations among their staff. Similarly, the presence of an expatriate population is often much appreciated in such locations, bringing with it spending power and international connections.

THE DUAL APPROACH OF ASIAN COMPETITORS

How, then, is it possible to combine the advantages of central and peripheral locations, while at the same time minimizing their disadvantages? It might be instructive to study how Asian competitors approach this issue.

When looking at Japanese, South Korean, Taiwanese and other companies it is clear that many of them have quite complex networks of production facilities and operation centres spread all over East and South-east Asia. Even small Asian companies with only a few hundred employees will often have a dozen or more subsidiaries. There is usually one or more head office and/or factory in a central location, applying capital-intensive technologies, plus a wide range of operation bases in Asian peripheries, taking advantage of the low costs factor and, in some cases, natural resources.

The individual operational bases are interconnected through sophisticated networks which provide information on products, inputs, prices, etc. Moreover, they are able to liaise in the selection of additional operational bases which offer cheaper labour than that which is available at existing production locations.

The strategies of Asian firms become clearer when we study the way in which various networks of companies' subsidiaries in central and peripheral locations have developed over the last two or three decades. A few general trends can be observed:

- There seems to be a preference for a larger number of smaller projects within different areas of the region, rather than one or two large-scale projects.
- Many of the larger projects seem to be the result of consolidation and expansion of smaller investments.
- Companies do not hesitate to set up a new base, as soon as a new market, or an (even) cheaper source of labour has been identified. The result of this strategy is often a 'downward' shift of operations from one location to another.

Asian firms have adopted this kind of investment pattern with considerable success. Moreover, Japanese companies became extremely flexible and competitive. Let us look at one example: a Japanese company with subsidiaries in low-cost countries, and a European company producing in Europe, are competing on the Chinese market. Both, during the first round of negotiations, offer best quality for a high price. The Chinese partner, however, requests a reduction of 40% in the price. On top of this, since imports have to be brought in line with China's tight planning process, an early decision and delivery of commodities is required.

The European company is not usually able to lower its prices substantially, even if it were prepared to sell without profits in order to gain a foothold in the Chinese market. Moreover, due to European holiday-terms and other social regulations, it is difficult or even impossible to agree on early delivery as stipulated by China's planning schedules.

The Japanese company with its network of Asian subsidiaries, is in a completely different position as far as costs and time schedules are concerned. If the requested price for top-notch quality is not accepted, a comparable but cheaper product, with the same brand name but with components made by low-cost subsidiaries, could be offered. Moreover, with subsidiaries in Thailand or Indonesia, the Japanese firm is not subjected to the same 'social regulations' as its EU competitors, and can easily comply with short-term delivery requirements.

Asian firms thus demonstrate how they cope efficiently with differences and changes in the economic, cultural and political sphere of East and South-east Asian countries. The key-word in this context is flexibility.

PROBLEMS OF EMULATING 'ASIAN' STRATEGIES

European companies would do well to emulate 'Asian' strategies in order to exploit low costs, quickly penetrate new markets and gain in flexibility. However, they should not expect, simply by following these investment patterns, to automatically become as successful as their Asian competitors. Even if expected gross margins are good, net margins often turn out to be much lower. An awareness of the most important reasons why this is so might help to overcome comparative shortcomings:

- Asian companies are usually already well-established in a central location within the region, and are thus able to build up their network of subsidiaries abroad. European companies (alone or pooling their efforts) often have to 'buy in' to a central location, a process which, by now, is extremely costly.

- European companies usually appear 'later' on peripheral Asian markets than their Asian rivals. Asian competitors might be yielding profits already, and may even, because of rising factor costs, be considering shifting operations to cheaper locations. They are inevitably one step ahead of European corporations in the region. Consequently, the latter have to pay higher prices for property and labour. A recent example is Vietnam, where property prices in Hanoi and Saigon are now as expensive as those in Singapore or Sydney. Many European corporations that are looking to break into this market, therefore, face less favourable cost-structures than their Asian competitors in the initial phase of operations.

- European companies are often not as practical as, for instance, those run by Japanese or overseas Chinese, when it comes to adapting to the difficult political, legal and personal environment in which any investment in Asia has to operate. They find it difficult to extend personal networks in order to gather information, to stabilize sources of supply and markets and to cement certain key-relationships in their organization in order to fend off uncertainty. They are generally unable to build relationships based on regional or family ties. Moreover, they have difficulties in adjusting to Asian practices, such as the preference for taking a small share in a variety of projects, thus fostering a network of local business partnerships.

- To European enterprises the cost of doing business in East and South-east Asia is usually high because their organization tends to be more complex and more heavily staffed with highly-paid expatriates than that of their Asian rivals. And even if European subsidiaries are not headed by European expatriates, many Europeans find it difficult to compete with the 'workaholism' of their more driven Asian counterparts.

The specific comparative disadvantages for European corporations investing and competing in Asia are clear, but these should not discourage European investment, since any corporation failing to invest here will find itself in a weaker position globally. Moreover, these disadvantages are not insurmountable. Much can be done to improve the situation by carefully selecting local personnel, improving flexibility and taking other measures, listed above, aimed at better adjusting to local conditions. European firms aiming at Asian markets must be prepared to take these specific strategic considerations on board, while at the same time retaining those features and elements which are an essential part of the firm's global identity.

BIBLIOGRAPHY

Buckley, P.J. and Pervez, N.G. (eds) (1993) *The Internationalisation of the Firm: A Reader*, London: Academic Press.

Coulson-Thomas, C. (1992) *Creating the Global Company: Successful Internationalization*, London: McGraw-Hill.

DeAnne, J. (1990) *Global Companies and Public Policy: the Growing Challenge of Foreign Direct Investment*, London: Chatham House Papers, Royal Institute of International Affairs.

Dunning, J.H. (1993a) *The Globalization of Business: the Challenge of the 1990s*, London and New York: Routledge.

—— (1993b) *Multinational Enterprises and the Global Economy*, Wokingham, Reading, Menlo Park: Addison-Wesley Publishing Company.

Guex, P. de (1988) 'L'autonomie des filiales des entreprises multinationales suisses: une analyse contextuelle', *Schweizerische Zeitschrift für Volkswirtschaft und Statistik* 3: 317–32.

Jeannet, J-P. (1988) 'Global Integration of Business Strategies', *Die Unternehmung. Hrsg. von der Vereinigung der schweizerischen Betriebswirtschaftler* 42: 318–28.

Levitt, T. (1983) 'The Globalization of Markets', *Harvard Business Review* 61 (May/June): 92–102.

Porter, M.E. (1990) *The Competitive Advantage of Nations*, London and Basingstoke: Macmillan.

Redding, S.G. (1990) *The Spirit of Chinese Capitalism*, New York: de Gruyter.

Rodrik, D. (1988) 'The Economics of export-performance requirements', *The Quarterly Journal of Economics* 102: 633–50.

Samiee, S. and Roth, K. (1992) 'The Influence of Global Marketing Standardisation on Performance', *Journal of Marketing* 56 (April): 1–17.

Szymanski, D.M., Sundar, G.B. and Varadarajan, P.R. (1993) 'Standardisation versus Adaptation of International Marketing Strategy: An Empirical Investigation', *Journal of Marketing* 57 (October): 1–17.

Tanaka Hiro (1994) 'Chokusetsu tooshi no kooka in: Nihon yushutsuniuu ginkoo kaigai tooshi kenkyuujo' (ed.) *Kaigai tooshi kenkyuujo hoo*, Tokyo, September: 4–35.

Tse, D.K. *et al.* (1993) 'Does Culture Matter? A Cross-cultural Study of Executives' Choice, Decisiveness and Risk Adjustment in International Marketing', *Journal of Marketing* 52 (October): 81–95.

Wehrli, H.P. (1988) 'Globale Strategien im Kontext von Führung und Organisation', *Die Unternehmung. Hrsg. von der Vereinigung der schweizerischen Betriebswirtschaftler* 42: 178–89.

Womack, J.P., Jones, D.T., and Roos, D. (1990) *The Machine that Changed the World*, New York: Rawson Associates Macmillan Publishing Company.

8 Opportunities for trade and investment in South Korea

Sang-Kun Nam

INTRODUCTION

Thirty years ago, South Korea was one of Asia's poorest agrarian societies with a small and stagnant economy. It has since achieved impressive economic development with an average 8% annual GNP growth rate. The key to this growth was the adoption of an outward looking development strategy which made exports the engine of growth – a strategy that reflected an insufficient endowment of natural resources, a limited domestic market and an abundant labour force.

The World Bank listed South Korea as one of the fastest growing countries in the world, and its emergence as a major trading nation in the world is by now a familiar economic success story. Less well known, however, are the details of business opportunities in Korea in terms of foreign trade and investment.

South Korea has its own advantages. It has a well-educated and trained labour force as well as a substantial market of 45 million people. Its industries have already reached international standards. The infrastructure is also continuously expanding, having high priority. Furthermore, South Korea's location is ideal for foreign businessmen seeking market opportunities in the Asia Pacific region.

South Korea has become more attractive for European business firms and their products as its dynamic market has continued to grow. Likewise, the European Union has steadily increased in importance as a market for Korean products. From this point of view, it was timely and opportune that in June 1993 the EC Council of Ministers approved a communication by the EC Commission on 'Relations between the EC and South Korea: Towards a growing partnership'.

This article is designed to enable European businessmen to have a better understanding of the South Korean economy, government policies on external trade and investment, economic relations between South Korea and the EU, the favourable investment climate, etc. in order to reveal business opportunities that South Korea offers.

GENERAL INFORMATION ON SOUTH KOREA

South Korea in brief

Located in North-east Asia, the Korean peninsula borders in the north on China and Russia and extends southwards to Japan. The land area, 221,487 km^2 making up the entire peninsula, has since 1945 been divided into two: north and south. The Republic of Korea in the south covers 99,221 km^2, and is a little more than twice the size of Switzerland.

South Korea has a population of almost 43.6 million. Since 1962, population growth has slowed from 2.9% a year to 0.5%. Only about 30% of the total area is available for agricultural, industrial and other purposes. Some 70% of the population is urbanized, and over 12 million of the population live in Seoul alone, making it one of the ten largest cities in the world.

South Korea has 5,000 years of history, and its society is homogeneous with the same language and the same ethnic group. Education has been at the heart of South Korea's growth, training and supplying the manpower needed for rapid industrial and economic expansion. The national literacy rate is in excess of 95% and the unemployment rate is around 2.4%.

The South Korean economy

In the last three decades, South Korea's economic growth has been among the fastest in the world. The country has transformed itself from a subsistence-level economy into one of the world's leading newly industrialising countries.

South Korea's strong growth performance has been based on an outward-oriented and high-investment strategy supported by prudent macroeconomic policies, and sustained by high domestic savings and continuous access to foreign borrowing and overseas markets. An outward-looking growth strategy has facilitated rapid trade expansion, diversification of the export base and increasing integration of South Korea into the international economy.

In 1962 at a time when the first Five Year Economic Development Plan was launched, South Korea began to induce the foreign investment which has made a great contribution to the development of the national economy by way of expansion of production, employment and improvement of the balance of payments. Since then, South Korea's industrial structure has been rapidly modernized through the concerted efforts of government and private enterprise to produce technology-intensive, high value added items, through investment in research and development.

In the 1970s, increasing defence burdens and on-going trade deficits led South Korea to shift its industrial policy towards particular industries, targeting import substitution and strategic export industries. Trade liberalization was an important feature at the initial development stage and has proceeded forthwith since the late 1970s.

In the early 1980s, decentralization of micro-economic policy was introduced and more reliance was placed on market signals for resource allocation. Korea's trade showed a surplus in 1986, for the first time in its history, and this surplus continued until 1989. During this period, Korea began overseas investment in order to shift its declining industries to the developing countries, as well as to avoid trade frictions with the advanced countries.

In the late 1980s, however, the favourable external economic environment – mainly, low oil prices, low international interest rates, and the depreciation of the US dollar – greatly contributed to a good performance of exports, a high rate of capital formation, high GNP growth (over 10% per annum), and a large and growing trade surplus.

The high growth rates strained capacity utilization and generated inflationary pressures. The trade surplus caused international trade conflicts while democratization of the nation released bottled-up labour demands. Consequently, exports declined in 1989, for the first time in a decade.

Thanks to relatively stable inflation, the surge in the Japanese Yen value, and continued wage restraint, the Korean economy has steadily recovered since 1993 during which the economy grew by 5.6% in real terms and this recovery continued into 1994. Exports are picking up, triggering capacity expansion, and fuelling domestic demand. In the first quarter of 1994, GNP grew at an annual rate of 7.3%, almost double the year-earlier 3.8%, and exports amounted to 19.9 billion dollars in the same period, up 9% from a year earlier. By the third quarter of 1995 growth was 9.8%. Expectations are now of a slowdown to around 7% with inflation running at 4%.

The Korean Development Institute has estimated and forecast growth of 9.3% in 1995 and 7.5–7.8% in 1996, respectively. According to the new Five Year Economic Plan launched in 1993, Korea is expected to export $136.3 billion by 1998 and import $128.1 billion, and GNP per capita will reach $14,076.

South Korea's economy is heavily dependent on international trade, and in this respect, has been confronted with many challenges. Most serious is that South Korea has been losing international competitiveness across industries mainly due to rising levels of wages, the growth of the labour union movement, increases in production costs, lack of investment in R&D, and the rise of regionalism.

In an attempt to overcome these drawbacks, South Korea has been actively pursuing strategies towards globalization of its industries, while liberalizing its growing domestic market. To this end, South Korea needs a firm grasp of the changes in the new world economic order and to implement more flexible policies and more articulate strategies in terms of foreign trade, investment, and technology.

Table 8.1 Trends in major South Korean economic indicators

Indicators	1988	1989	1990	1991	1992	1993
GNP per capita ($)	4,127	5,210	5,659	6,518	7,007	7,966
Real GNP Growth (%)	12.4	6.8	9.3	8.4	5.0	5.6
Exports ($ bn)	60.7	62.4	65.0	71.9	76.6	82.2
Imports ($ bn)	51.8	61.5	69.8	81.5	81.8	83.8
Consumer Price Inflation (%)	7.2	5.0	9.4	9.3	4.5	4.8

Source: The Bank of Korea.

OPPORTUNITIES IN FOREIGN TRADE

External trade has played an important role in the process of economic development for Korea. Exports have contributed 20%–50% of South Korea's economic growth from the 1960s to the present.

Although South Korea suffered chronic balance of payment deficits, a surplus was registered from 1986 to 1989 and in 1993. From 1990 to 1992, however, the balance reverted to deficit, due to difficulties in the transition to a democratic industrialized nation and increased protectionism abroad. In 1993, total trade volume reached $166.0 billion and accounted for 2.15% of world trade, a performance that ranked South Korea as the twelfth largest trading nation in the world.

Exports

With an export-oriented policy during the Five Year Economic Development Plans, annual export growth averaged 41.4% and 35.6% in the 1960s and 1970s respectively. In the 1980s, this growth rate dropped to 13.0% because of worldwide recession. Korea's exports were $71.9 billion in 1991, up 10.5% from 1990 and $82.3 billion in 1993, up 7.3% from 1992. This 1993 figure accounted for 2.3% of world exports, ranking South Korea as the thirteenth largest exporter internationally.

The development of Korean exports began in primary sectors such as agricultural and mineral products, moving to light industry products such as textiles and footwear, then to heavy and chemical industry products such as iron and steel, petro-chemicals and automobiles. However, in 1993, South Korea became the largest exporter of shipbuilding and memory chips in the world, the leading producer of pianos, electronic household appliances, cars, footwear, and the third largest textile manufacturer.

Imports

South Korea is one of the fastest growing markets in the world. Annual import growth averaged 20% during the 1960s and 1970s, and 12% in the 1980s. Imports increased to $81.5 billion in 1991, up 16.7% on the previous year. These increases in import figures were mostly due to import

Table 8.2 Exports by major countries in 1993

Ranking	Country	Export ($ bn)
1	USA	465
2	Germany	362
3	Japan	361
4	France	209
5	UK	183
6	Italy	168
7	Canada	145
8	Hong Kong	135
9	The Netherlands	134
10	Belgium/Luxembourg	116
11	China	92
12	Taiwan	85
13	South Korea	82

Source: The Korea Foreign Trade Association.

Table 8.3 South Korea's export structure by industry (Unit: %)

Industries	1975	1980	1985	1990	1992
Primary	16.4	7.7	5.2	5.1	4.3
Manufacturing products	83.6	92.3	94.8	94.9	95.7
Light industry products	72.9	48.4	37.7	38.5	33.0
Heavy-chemical products	10.7	43.9	57.0	56.4	62.8
Total	100.0	100.0	100.0	100.0	100.0

Source: The Korea Foreign Trade Association.

liberalization, tariff reduction, growing demand for overseas consumer goods and continued general domestic market expansion. Major import items are crude oil, grains, capital goods and consumer products.

Trade with Europe

Trade with Europe has been somewhat neglected not only for reasons of geographical distance but also because of cultural differences. However, the integration of the EU has many implications for South Korea, with its heavy dependence on export markets. South Korea has emphasized diversification of its export markets in order to reduce its dependence on the US and Japanese markets, and thus, trade between South Korea and the EU has increased rapidly since the mid-1980s.

South Korea recorded a trade surplus with the EU during 1985–90, but showed deficits of $151 million in 1991 and $351 million in 1992. Meanwhile, the volume of bilateral trade increased from $4.3 billion in 1980 to $18.8 billion in 1992 as shown in Table 8.4.

Table 8.4 Trends in South Korea's trade with the EU (Unit: million dollars)

Export/import	1975	1980	1990	1991	1992
Export	798	2,710	8,876	9,728	9,233
Import	544	1,614	8,421	9,879	9,585
Balance	254	1,096	455	−151	−351

Source: The Korea Foreign Trade Association.

In 1992, the EU's share of Korea's imports was more than 11%, while more than 12% of Korea's exports went to the EU. The EU accounted for almost 11.2% of South Korea's external trade, and the volume of trade between the EU and South Korea amounted to 6.3% of South Korea's GNP. From the EU's point of view, however, South Korea is the thirteenth largest import partner and the twentieth largest export partner, accounting for only 1.8% of the EU's imports and 0.8% of the EU's exports.

The trade structures of South Korea and the EU are rather complementary in the sense that South Korea imports capital equipment and high-tech

Table 8.5 South Korea's exports to the EU by commodity
(Unit: million dollars, %)

Commodities	1986	Share	1992	Share
Primary goods	135	3.1	198	2.2
Chemicals	62	1.4	383	4.2
Plastic, rubber & leather	240	5.6	475	5.2
Non-metallic mineral products	37	0.9	27	0.3
Textiles	1,360	31.6	1,697	18.4
(Textile products)	*1,091*	*25.3*	*1,228*	*13.3*
Household goods	456	10.6	1,054	11.4
(Footwear)	*232*	*5.4*	*645*	*7.0*
Iron/steel and metals	230	5.3	580	6.3
Electrical and electronics	1,259	29.2	3,130	33.9
(Industrial electronics)	*313*	*7.3*	*1,301*	*14.1*
(Electronic parts)	*312*	*7.2*	*883*	*9.6*
(Home appliances)	*517*	*12.0*	*894*	*9.7*
Machinery & transport equipment	489	11.4	1,595	17.3
(General machinery)	*11*	*0.3*	*274*	*3.0*
(Transport equipment)	*394*	*9.2*	*781*	*8.5*
(Passenger cars)	*42*	*1.0*	*679*	*7.4*
(Ships and boats)	*323*	*7.5*	*230*	*2.5*
Miscellaneous goods	37	0.9	93	1.0
Total	4,305	100.0	9,234	100.0

Source: Ministry of Trade, Industry & Energy.

products which the EU exports, while exporting industrial supplies and consumer goods which the EU imports. Table 8.5 shows the commodity composition of Korean exports to the EU, characterized by a change from light industry goods towards heavy industry goods, while Table 8.6 exhibits the commodity composition of EU's exports to Korea gradually changing in favour of machinery and transport equipment.

OPPORTUNITIES FOR INVESTMENT

Overseas investment

Before the 1980s, Korea's overseas investment was meagre. It rose during 1982–3 after the second oil crisis, followed by a brief downturn in 1984 due to the decrease in investment for development of natural resources.

The upsurge of overseas investment began in 1986 when South Korea established its first current account surplus. Overseas investment continued to rise through the 1990s, given the necessities of securing raw materials, circumventing trade barriers, establishing and expanding overseas markets, and getting access to advanced technology and new materials.

Table 8.6 The EU's exports to South Korea by commodity

Commodities	1986	Share	1992	Share
Agricultural & fishery	497	8.2	497	5.2
Mineral products	83	1.4	98	1.0
Chemical products	1,755	29.1	2,353	24.6
Organic chemicals	934	15.5	831	8.7
Medicinal materials	362	6.0	624	6.5
Leather, fur	148	2.5	315	3.3
Non-metallic minerals	84	1.4	153	1.6
Textiles	172	2.8	408	4.3
Textile fabrics	91	1.5	215	2.3
Iron/steel and metals	527	8.7	715	7.5
Iron and steel	356	5.9	380	4.0
Machinery and transport	2,202	36.5	4,264	44.5
General machinery	1,319	21.8	2,767	28.9
Scientific measurement	215	3.6	435	4.5
Aircraft and parts	311	5.1	387	4.0
Electrical and electronics	660	10.9	1,026	10.7
Industrial electronics	190	3.2	286	3.0
Electronic parts	189	3.1	357	3.7
Heavy electric equipment	241	4.0	285	3.0
Miscellaneous goods	140	2.3	210	2.2
Total	6,050	100.0	9,585	100.0

Source: Ministry of Trade, Industry & Energy.

Table 8.7 Cumulative overseas investment in South Korea (end 1992)
(Unit: thousand dollars)

Region	No. of projects	Share (%)	Amount
North America	523	42.56	1,918,124
South-east Asia	1,133	37.26	1,679,054
Europe	171	8.57	368,188
(EU countries)	131	6.53	294,704
Other regions	311	11.61	541,266
Total	2,138	100.00	4,506,632

Source: The Bank of Korea.

Foreign investment into Korea

Trends

Since 1962, inward foreign investment in Korea increased rapidly until 1973. The trend was halted in 1973 when the government imposed restrictions. The flow of foreign investment thereafter stagnated until the end of the 1970s.

In the early 1980s due to the loosening of regulatory control and an improvement in the investment environment, an increase in investment was noted. However, in the period between 1987 and 1990, the figures for approval of foreign investment projects released by the Ministry of Finance showed a decline both in number of projects and volume. At the same time, some foreign companies pulled out of Korea and this trend continued up to 1990.

In the 1990s, foreign investment in Korea steadily increased to $802.6 million in 1990, $894.4 million in 1992 and $1,044 million in 1993, while the number of foreign investment projects fell to 278 in 1993 from 306 in

Table 8.8 Foreign investment by region (Unit: thousand dollars)

Regions	62–71	90	92	93	Total*
America	139,501	335,369	433,691	343,835	3,466,269
(USA)	*120,324*	*317,465*	*379,182*	*340,669*	*3,259,165*
Asia	104,415	257,321	170,272	391,583	4,922,653
(Japan)	*98,017*	*235,895*	*155,161*	*285,943*	*4,465,611*
Europe	20,732	206,943	282,218	307,424	2,643,810
(EU)	*20,420*	*177,932*	*231,802*	*295,250*	*2,266,651*
Middle East	405	42	4,279	87	44,979
Others	978	2,940	4,016	1,345	130,867
Total	266,031	802,635	884,476	1,044,274	11,208,578

* Cumulative total.

Source: Ministry of Finance.

Table 8.9 Foreign investment trend by industries (Unit: thousand dollars)

Industry	62–76	90	92	93	Total
Agriculture/Fishery	10,082	–	809	127	24,301
Mining	4,590	–	1,388	–	17,563
Manufacturing	907,609	583,416	648,012	526,817	7,394,176
Service	223,175	218,693	244,267	517,330	3,772,538
Total	1,145,456	802,635	894,476	1,044,274	11,208,578

Source: Ministry of Finance.

1990. In the meantime, cumulative foreign direct investment in Korea from 1962–93 was $11,208 million. Japan invested $4,465 million, followed by the USA with $3,259 million, and then Europe with $2,643 million, including the EU countries with $2,266 million.

Cumulative foreign investment from 1962 to 1993 was in the following industrial sectors: manufacturing, such as chemical, electronics, transport equipment, etc., $7,394 million; services in the fields of hotels, finance, insurance, foreign trade, etc., $3,772 million; and agriculture and fisheries $24,301 million.

Investment with the EU

(1)   South Korean investment in the EU

Korean direct investment in the EU has increased since the mid-1980s. It is considered essential for South Korea to increase further its direct investment in Europe in order to diversify export markets and circumvent trade frictions.

South Korea's direct investment in the EU has drastically increased in the last five years from $41 million in 1988 to $126 million in 1992. But its share in the EU remained at 5% of total investment, still modest, compared to that in North America (46.4%), and in South-east Asia (33.8%). However, South Korea's investment in Europe is expected to increase in the years to come in order to take advantage of the expanding markets associated with extended European integration.

South Korea's investment in the UK increased to $4.9 million in 1992, an increase of 45.4% compared with 1991. Of Korea's cumulative investment in the EU 41.8% ($294 million) had been invested in the UK. So far, there are ten Korean manufacturers in the UK, and some fifteen Korean financial institutions maintain their European headquarters there.

Table 8.10 South Korea's investment in the EU countries (Unit: thousand dollars)

Host country	1991	1992	Cumulative amount
Germany	14,458	32,372	63,629 (49 projects)
France	8,455	29,763	45,757 (16 projects)
UK	33,918	49,347	123,235 (32 projects)
Italy	4,535	583	5,884 (11 projects)
Netherlands	738	7,589	9,048 (10 projects)
Belgium	0	0	6,797 (3 projects)
Denmark	0	0	0
Spain	3,238	1,611	8,649 (5 projects)
Ireland	2,000	361	24,861 (3 projects)
Greece	0	0	0
Portugal	0	4,769	6,844 (2 projects)
Luxembourg	0	0	0
Total	67,342	126,935	294,704 (131 projects)

Source: Ministry of Finance.

(2) European investment in South Korea

Investment from the EU amounted to $177.9 million in 1990 and increased to $295.8 million in 1993, an increase of 21.5% compared with 1992. Total accumulated EU investment in Korea, from 1962 to 1993, was $2,266 million, accounting for 19.8% of the total foreign investment in the country.

The investment climate in South Korea

South Korea's fast growing economy and its open-door policies offer very favourable investment opportunities to foreign investors. Protection of intellectual property rights, a well-educated labour force, and an efficient

Table 8.11 European investment by countries in Korea (Unit: thousand dollars)

Country	1990	1992	1993	Total
Netherlands	36,315	43,785	131,223	978,199
Germany	62,330	120,485	35,929	520,897
UK	44,841	23,694	70,823	339,775
France	22,439	29,202	39,674	265,024
Denmark	2,940	10,306	14,186	56,834
Italy	1,367	1,572	2,860	27,627
Belgium	5,230	2,405	180	24,104
Spain	1,470	130	375	2,392
Greece	200	–	–	100
Total	177,932	231,802	295,250	2,266,651

Source: Ministry of Finance.

and reliable infrastructure, including electricity, transportation, communication, industrial water and industrial estates are in place.

Protection of intellectual property rights

Trade in intellectual property has increased rapidly in recent years, both through its embodiment in goods and through flows of foreign direct investment and licences for the use of technologies and trade names.

This growth reflects, in part, the increasing globalization of indigenous business as firms employ sophisticated forms of international activity to exploit the value deriving from their innovation and creativity. Government measures to protect intellectual property rights such as patents, trade marks, copyrights, and related devices have taken on greater importance in influencing the rules governing international trade and investments.

- Patents
  The patent system grants the right to exclude others from making, using or selling an invention for a certain period of time with the condition that the holders are obligated to make their invention publicly available. Protection for practical devices is governed by the Korean Utility Model law. Most provisions of the Patent Law apply *mutatis mutandis* with respect to utility models. A recent development of the Patent Law is a provision that protection shall not exceed 20 years from the date of the patent application.

- Trademarks
  Any person who uses or intends to use a trademark in Korea shall be entitled to register it with the Korean Industrial Property Office and is required to file the trademark application in order to protect the trademark under the Trademark Law. The duration of trademark protection is 10 years from the date of registration and may be renewed for periods of 10 years.

- Industrial designs
  The duration of protection is 8 years from the date of registration but it cannot be renewed. To bring standing laws in line with international practice, recent improvements have been made to protect well-known industrial designs not yet registered in Korea.

- Trade secrets
  Trade secrets protection is governed by the Unfair Competition Prevention law. The purpose of this law is to protect trade secrets and to maintain good order in commercial trade by preventing competition by means of unfair business methods such as illegal use of another trademark or tradename which may be well-known in Korea. Also, violation of trade secrets protection constitutes unfair competition under the law.

- Copyright
  The principal body of law governing copyright protection in Korea is the Copyright Law. But there are several other laws protecting copyright in works of authorship other than printed materials.

  Works protected by such copyright laws include literary, artistic, musical, photographic and cinematographic works, as well as computer programs. The copyright protects the expression itself as embodied in copyrighted work, while patent rights protect the new idea stipulated in the claim.

Tax system

The tax system comprises both national and local taxes. National taxes are divided into internal taxes and customs duties. Internal taxes include both direct and indirect taxes. Direct taxes consist of corporate tax, income tax, etc., while indirect taxes include value-added tax (VAT).

Wages and fringe benefits

Wages must be paid regularly and in full, once or more per month on a fixed day or days. The minimum wage in Korea was set at about 250,000 won per month in 1995 (1 US$ = 791 Korean won as of 19 January 1996).

Large Korean companies usually provide many non-taxable benefits for employees such as transportation, meals, housing loans, as well as cash gifts for weddings and funerals. All employees are entitled to a physical examination when they commence employment, and companies with five or more employees must pay for an annual physical as well.

Work hours

The standard working week is 44 hours, 8 hours a day on weekdays and 4 hours on Saturday in the manufacturing industries. Extension on overtime requires prior approval by the Ministry of Labour.

Eight hours of work a day should be accompanied by at least 1 hour of rest. Anything above the standard working week is considered overtime and is subject to compensation at 150% of the standard hourly rate.

Paid holidays

An employee is entitled to one paid holiday per month which can be accumulated or taken separately. In addition, the employer is required to grant eight paid holidays for those employees who maintain perfect attendance over one year.

Laws concerning labour unions

The Labour Dispute Adjustment Law and the Labour Union Act apply to foreign-invested enterprises as well as to domestic enterprises. Should labour disputes arise, according to the procedure stipulated in these laws, official institutions will conciliate, mediate and arbitrate such labour disputes.

POLICIES TOWARDS FOREIGN TRADE AND INVESTMENT

Foreign trade policy

Goals of foreign trade policy

Until the 1980s, South Korea's trade policy emphasized export growth and import control, as the economy suffered from chronic trade deficits and a shortage of foreign exchange. However, following dramatic economic growth in the latter part of the 1980s, and as the nation came to assume new responsibilities commensurate with its enhanced global role, the major trade policies that the South Korean government has recently been pursuing are:

– active participation in the formation of a new global trade order, and a greater role in the international economy
– sustaining the momentum of the import liberalization programme and other market-oriented measures
– removing some of the institutional barriers blocking access to the South Korean market.

Import liberalization

Korea graduated from GATT-sanctioned balance of payments protection in October 1989, and has agreed to progressively liberalize items that had been import-restricted under the GATT provision by July 1997. Korea has submitted to the GATT its import liberalization schedule for the 1992 to 1997-period, and the import liberalization ratio stood at 99.2% as of the beginning of 1996. Those changes represent the positive approach of Korean economy to the World Trade Organization system, and at the same time, are construed as preparatory groundwork for membership entry to the OECD which is expected during 1996.

Table 8.12 Import liberalization ratio

1981	1985	1991	1994
74.7%	87.7%	97.2%	98.5%

Other major policies in brief

- Tariff reduction

   In accordance with the goals of the Uruguay Round, South Korea is implementing tariff reductions in tandem with import liberalization. South Korea's tariffs, which averaged 23.7% in 1983, were reduced to 18.1% in 1988, when the first five-year-tariff reduction plan ended. The second tariff reduction plan was effective through 1994 and further reduced tariffs to 7.9%, the average level of OECD nations.

- Opening of the service industry

   The government has partially opened the services in such sectors as banking, insurance, advertising and telecommunications. Further liberalization of services will be carried out in accordance with the UR agreement.

- Export and import procedures

   Most of South Korea's export transactions are made under irrevocable letters of credit, either on a sight basis or usance basis (the time-limited allowance on the payment of foreign bills of exchange). Export on D/P and D/A terms – Documents against Payment and Documents against Acceptance Bill respectively – are also permissible. In addition, certain strategic items such as vessels are exported on a deferred payment basis.

   On the other hand, import procedures differ according to the items to be imported and the terms of payment. In the case of importing goods by commercial letters of credit, the importer should obtain an import licence from an authorized foreign exchange bank and open an irrevocable letter of credit to the foreign supplier through the bank.

- Foreign exchange

   To ease inflationary pressure from the overseas trading sector, the currency limit of $10,000 on individual possession was removed during the second quarter of 1994.

Foreign investment policy

Trend of foreign investment policy

In the past, South Korea concentrated its efforts on inducing foreign loans, direct investment and technology. Many incentives were introduced to encourage foreign businesses to invest in South Korea.

Now the government emphazises the need for local businesses to become internationally competitive through open competition with technologically advanced foreign firms. Accordingly, the government has gradually lifted restrictions imposed on foreign investors and treats them as domestic investors.

Foreign investment policy

The basic policy direction of the government on foreign investment is to facilitate market access and provide domestic status to foreign firms after their establishment. To this end, the government is trying to liberalize and simplify the investment procedures in accordance with overall economic policy. This policy seeks to grant national treatment to foreign investors so that freer and fairer competition can exist between domestic and foreign companies, thereby promoting an efficient free market economy.

South Korea has been pursuing liberalization policies for foreign direct investment and implementing them by reducing tariffs, and liberalizing imports and service markets. Further efforts have recently been made to improve the economic climate for foreign investment by deregulating and simplifying investment procedures, protecting overseas intellectual property, allowing foreign investors to buy land, and so on.

- Laws governing foreign investment

  The Foreign Capital Inducement Act (FCIA) is the basic law governing foreign investment, along with sub-legislation such as the Presidential Decree, Working Rules (Ministerial Decree) and the Regulations on Foreign Investment (Notification of the Minister of Finance).

- Establishment of corporations

  Anyone who wishes to establish a corporation in South Korea must register with the Court after completing the subscription of paid-in capital, and this procedure is equally applicable to the foreign investor wishing to establish a business corporation.

  Also, the FCIA requests foreign investors to register with the Ministry of Finance after completing the subscription of approved/notified investment capital.

- Financial liberalization

  Foreign banks have received national treatment since 1984, and capital and securities markets have been liberalized step by step. Foreign investment in South Korean stock was permitted on a limited basis. Since the Korean stock market opened to foreign investment in 1992 on this limited basis, the UK has been far ahead of other countries.

  The government has made various efforts to further develop the financial markets through deregulation and market opening. In this regard, the government's Financial Liberalisation Plan announced in July 1993 entailed measures which seek to decontrol the interest rate, revise monetary policy tools, develop the short-term money market, improve the credit control system, and liberalize foreign exchange and capital accounts.

- Financing

  There are no discriminatory measures in the legal system imposed on foreign invested firms in connection with financing, but in practice there are some difficulties which a newly established firm might face because of credit deficiency and lender's preference for a mortgage.

- Taxation

  A foreign corporation is liable for corporation tax only on the income derived from sources within South Korea. Corporation tax on income is assessed and collected in the same manner as applied to a domestic corporation and corporation taxes are assessed at graduated rates ranging from 20% to 34%. In addition, corporations are liable for inhabitant tax which is generally 7.5% of the corporation income tax amount. However, if foreign invested firms are granted tax incentives (reduction or exemption) by the government, special treatment, other than the above mentioned, may be applied under the FCIA.

- Tax incentives

  The government is still providing tax incentives for foreign investments which bring high technology into South Korea. In this connection, income tax or corporate tax is exempted after acceptance of notification of a technology licence agreement.

- Guarantees on foreign investment

  The FCIA guarantees full repatriation of principal and profits by foreign invested firms. And the properties of foreign-invested firms are guaranteed and protected by relevant laws and decrees from requisition or expropriation.

- Negative list

  A negative list system is applied to inward foreign investment. In this respect, South Korea is planning to open up for foreign investment 132 out of 224 business sectors which are currently restricted (19 of the 132 sectors will be partially opened).

  The remaining 92 sectors that will remain closed are related to mass media, real estate, financial services and energy sectors or areas which pertain to public morals. These sectors are generally considered inappropriate to be opened to foreign direct investment due to their sensitive nature.

- Intellectual property right (IPR)

  Protection of IPR is being pursued by cracking down on violators, by upgrading the legal framework and institutions for protection, and by raising public awareness of IPR. These are based on the recognition that effective protection of IPR is critical in order to foster technical development in South Korea and attract high-technology from abroad.

South Korea's efforts to improve the foreign investment climate

- The new foreign investment guidelines

  The Ministry of Finance announced in December 1993 new foreign investment guidelines offering a set of incentives to foreign investors to boost foreign investment in Korea and promote capital co-operation with foreign countries.

From 1 January 1994, South Korean enterprises were allowed to introduce freely any foreign technology, except defence related technology, without prior approval from the government. Foreign business concerns operating here will be allowed to purchase land in South Korea without any limitations for the purpose of business operations or to house their staff.

As a means of improving the investment environment, the government has lowered corporation tax for foreign companies operating in South Korea to 15% from the previous 25% by revising the Corporate Tax Law.

Also, approval processes for foreign investment about which foreign investors have recently complained have been simplified from 20–30 days to 3 hours.

- Opening of the bond market to foreign investors
  South Korea's bond market will be opened to foreign investors, but stock market liberalization will progress slowly. This is because expectations of massive foreign currency inflows may raise the spectre of renewed inflationary pressure. Foreign financial institutions are guaranteed the opportunity to do business in South Korea on an equal footing with their local counterparts.

CONCLUSION

The basic goal of the economic development strategy of South Korea is to increase its growth potential by strengthening the international competitiveness of its economy. Globalization and liberalization are essential parts of this strategy.

The importance of globalization has heightened further since the UR Agreement and the establishment of regional economic integration such as

Table 8.13 New incentives for foreign investment

Problem	Remedies	Date
Land costs	Scrap approval required for land purchases for manufacturing	March 1994
Finance costs	Permit offshore borrowing equal to 50% of foreign equity (75% for high-tech firms)	January 1994
Taxes	Cut retained earnings tax to 15% from 25%. Negotiate with OECD countries on transfer-pricing tax	January 1994
Labour unrest	Set up labour relations centres to help foreign-invested firms	July 1994
Protectionism	Cut number of closed sectors from 224 to 92	1994–1997

the European Union and the North America Free Trade Agreement. To further liberalize the growing domestic market, however, the foreign investment climate has largely been improved by removal of excess regulations and obstacles such as land acquisition and tax burdens.

As mentioned earlier, South Korea has advantages including well-trained manpower, an ever-expanding domestic market, a well-established infrastructure, and industries that meet international standards. In a nutshell, opportunities for doing business with South Korea are very promising.

Europe has begun to perceive the necessity of broadening its economic relations with Asia Pacific. In that sense, Europe can use South Korea, which offers vast opportunities to European businessmen in terms of foreign trade and investment, as a stepping stone for advancing deeper into the most dynamic region in the world. Accordingly, more trade with Europe is expected, and European investments in South Korea are most welcome.

9 Levels of culture and Hong Kong organizations

Sid Lowe

INTRODUCTION

The concept of organizational culture is based upon the assumption that organizations exist largely as independent entities promoting the independent organization as the central unit of analysis.

In the context of Hong Kong this can be seen as a somewhat ethnocentric perspective as the principal industries are characterized by interlocked networks of small enterprises whose cultural strength lies in the trust-based relationships and linkages between rather than within firms. The basic proposition of this chapter is to submit that the industrial 'recipes' of Hong Kong networks are a reflection of broader Confucian, Buddhist and Taoist influences and a consonance between the macro and meso levels of culture is a contributory influence to the apparent economic success of Hong Kong. A supplementary proposition is that 'mental programming' at the cultural level in a 'collective' *Gemeinschaft* and 'high power distance' society like Hong Kong is relatively more important in influencing economic activity than mental programmes at the individual level.

The chapter concludes with a discussion of the consequences of national, industrial and organizational cultural differences influencing the structure and strategy of Hong Kong enterprises and a critique of the appropriacy of Western management theories for Hong Kong businesses.

First we shall examine the influence of culture on organizations in Hong Kong. Hong Kong has been investigated as a particular case rather than as a representation of a general Overseas Chinese business culture since it is becoming clear that within 'East Asia' there is considerable diversity of Asian management systems (Min Chen 1995) which enables us to characterize an Overseas Chinese 'style'. This is not homogeneous in the societies where Chinese businesses operate and an examination of Hong Kong must include 'etic' (Hofstede 1984: 33) idiosyncratic aspects which cannot be generalized.

The literature reviewed is based heavily upon the work of Hofstede (1980, 1984, 1991) which is broadly recognized as seminal in the field and which has enabled a benchmark perspective on the study of culture as a basis upon which to develop a co-operative approach amongst social scientists interested in culture. In this respect the literature examined is not exhaustive or faultlesss but provides important perspectives of 'blind' social scientists seeking to identify and improve understanding of the enigmatic cultural'elephant' (Hofstede 1984: 15).

In other words, the study of culture reveals different perspectives which are at times concurrent and at others competitive. No single perspective is absolutely 'right' and a search for such absolute truth is probably impractical and possibly itself culture-based. The author has found the perspectives offered by the cited authors to be informative in the somewhat tortuous task of studying 'culture' and invites the reader to share in the realizations they offer.

DEFINING CULTURE

Definitions of culture range from the very broad to the very narrow reflecting the extent to which culture permeates human experiences at different levels. Hofstede (1991: 5) recognizes the levels of culture by providing a narrow and a broad definition. The former concerns 'civilization' or 'refinement of the mind' and the concomitants of education, art and literature. The broader definition which is derived from social anthropology and deals with more fundamental human processes (including those within the narrow definition), is the main concern for Hofstede and also for this chapter. This broad definition is given as 'the collective programming of the mind which distinguishes the members of one group or category of people from another' (Hofstede 1984: 21).

LEVELS OF MENTAL PROGRAMMES

Values are defined by Hofstede as 'a broad tendency to prefer certain states of affair over others' (Hofstede 1984: 18). Values are attributes of individuals and collectivities (Hofstede refers to *norms* in the latter case), they are non-rational but influence our 'subjective definition of rationality' (ibid.) Values have both intensity and direction, the *desired* (phenomenological) and the *desirable* (deontological) must be treated seperately. Hofstede warns against the 'positivistic fallacy' (Hofstede 1984: 19) of equating the *desired* and the *desirable* which 'leads to a confusion between reality and social desirability' (ibid.). Values are central to Hofstede's study who assumes them to be, along with many social psychologists (e.g. Schwartz 1992: 1), as criteria affecting how actions are selected and justified, how people and events are evaluated and how reality is socially constructed. This reflects a broader underlying assumption that culture is something a collective entity *has* and which has constituent variables which are measurable.

It seems clear that, using this assumption, values and culture are inter-related and interdependent as *'values are among the building blocks of culture'* (Hofstede 1984: 21).

Culture confers identity on a human group at a macro (societal/national) level. Hofstede uses the term 'sub-culture' to describe micro-level systems like organizations or ethnic groups. Culture for Hofstede therefore concerns societies as social systems in homeostatic, quasi-equilibrium with societal norms or value systems at the centre interacting with 'ecological' origins and institutional 'consequences' (ibid.).

Hofstede contends that analyses of values at the individual level cannot be equated simultaneously with analyses at the ecological (collective, societal, cultural) level and to do so is an 'ecological fallacy' (Hofstede 1984: 24) which confuses two separate and incompatible levels of analysis. This proposition is challenged most frequently by other psychologists concerned that 'the ecological or culture level approach (of Hofstede) does not yield individual level dimensions of values' (Bond 1988: 1,009) and challenged by another study finding 'in contrast to Hofstede's (1980) findings, the dimensions derived at the two levels in our research appear to be closely related' (Schwartz 1992: 2).

It is also suggested by Hofstede that mental programmes are intangible and exist as 'constructs' which are terms we use to define them into existence. This is fraught with problems when we come to research as constructs are vulnerable to subjectivity and to the values of their creator and his/her own cultural background. Consequently we have the situation in cross-cultural studies of researchers, with their own subjective perspective, trying to measure the subjective reality of individuals and organizations in another culture. To avoid research results which are meaningless, except to the researcher at the time of writing, it is essential to be eclectic in research methods.

Organizational culture is, in Hofstede's terms, one of 'Culture's Consequences' in that it is both an institutional consequence of, and a reinforcement to, societal norms and their environmental origins. In this context 'organizations are structured in order to meet the subjective cultural needs of their members' (Hofstede 1991: 142). Organizational Culture is, in this perspective, not the same as National Culture in that it operates at a different level but both have some common characteristics. In support of this Hofstede quotes Guilford to define Culture alternatively as 'the interactive aggregate of common characteristics that influence a human group's response to it's environment' (Hofstede 1984: 21).

The Cultural Environment of Hong Kong at a macro level has been delineated by Hofstede (1980) within a set of cultural maps of the world and categorized initially on four dimensions including 'Power Distance' (PDI), 'Uncertainty Avoidance' (UAI), 'Individualism-Collectivism' (IDV) and 'Masculinity-Femininity' (MAS). Hong Kong is classified as high power distant, low uncertainty avoidance, collective and masculine.

Hofstede has more recently (Hofstede 1991) added a fifth dimension to his model. This new dimension, derived from the construction of a 'Chinese Values Survey' by The Chinese Culture Connection group (Bond 1987), is directly relevant to this study since it concerns 'Confucian Dynamism' which principally relates to the degree of long-termism inherent within a society. This dimension was named in this way since the research indicates that societies influenced by Confucianism (such as China, Hong Kong, Taiwan, Japan and Korea) all share markedly high degrees of long-termism relative to all other countries. Hofstede points out that the Chinese Values Survey (CVS) resulted in identification of three out of four dimensions identified in his own 4-D study. *None of the CVS factors, however, were correlated with uncertainty avoidance.* This is explained as a fundamental difference between Western and Eastern (particularly Chinese) cultures which means that Western cultures have a fourth dimension related to the search for 'Truth' whereas Chinese societies are more concerned with 'Virtue'. The implication is that the identification of this Chinese 'emic' cultural dimension is one of the fundamental reasons for the relative success of countries in the Pacific Rim influenced by Chinese culture as:

> By showing the link between Confucian Dynamism and recent economic growth, the CVS research project has demonstrated the strategic advantage of cultures that can practise Virtue without a concern for Truth.
>
> (Hofstede 1991: 172)

Hong Kong culture in Hofstede's terms

Hofstede characterized Hong Kong culture in his 4-D study as similar to Anglo-American culture in that it has weak Uncertainty Avoidance (or a willingness to accept ambiguity and low propensity to mitigate uncertainty through a formal, unitary and consensual structure) and strong Masculinity (assertive, competitive and materialistic). On the other dimensions Hong Kong differs sharply from Anglo-American culture by being Collectivist (loyalty to other people in family, clan or organization is the moral basis of culture) and having a large Power Distance (hierarchical inequality between dependent subordinates and powerful leading members of society) plus a Long-Term Orientation, and see themselves more as a part or product of the environment than their Western counterparts.

Confucian/Taoist/Buddhist societies have a self-concept which is traditionally oriented, reflecting collective interdependence and social control based upon 'face' which is a 'social ego' more akin to feminine value systems despite the prevailing higher MAS scores in these countries. Logically therefore masculine values differ between the East and the West since their interaction (in the East) with Collective values and high PDI would seem to modify masculine values to a more benign form than the more interpersonally aggressive, competitive Western equivalent. This is reflected in the CVS findings suggesting that values in Hong Kong 'suggest "feminine" valuing more than "masculine"' when measured on a scale constructed by Chinese minds (Bond 1987: 152).

Hofstede considers that a combination of Uncertainty Avoidance (rather than IDV) and PDI is the critical influence. Hofstede theorizes that four main implicit models of organizations result from differences in UAI and PDI. In low UAI/low PDI countries like Britain the implicit model is a 'village market' wheras in low UAI/high PDI countries like Hong Kong the implicit model is the 'extended family'. These correspond, according to Hofstede, to Williamson's concept of 'market' organizations and Ouchi's concept of 'clans' (Hofstede 1990: 149).

Schwartz's Universals in the content and structure of values

Schwartz (1992) provides the most recent research of note in this area. The model being constructed by Schwartz, if validated, promises to provide a refinement of the Hofstede model.

For Schwartz, the concept of values is derived by reasoning that values represent, as conscious goals, three universals of human existence concerning individual, social interaction and group needs. This is a substantive challenge to Hofstede's model in that, if further validated, it is likely to become regarded as a refinement of Hofstede and a seminal work in the field. Schwartz proposes that in addition to formal features the primary content aspect of a value is the motivational concern it expresses. A universal typology of the different contents contains eleven distinct universal motivational types of values (at the individual level) of which ten are derived from the empirical data using Smallest Space Analysis. A set of dynamic relations amongst motivational types of values in terms of compatible or conflicting consequent actions is proposed and supported by the results.

The individual level analysis shows some interesting findings. The value types are shown to form a circular motivational continuum rather than discrete entities. Thus partitioning into discrete value types is recognized as an expediency to facilitate research. The theorized dynamic relations amongst value types propose two higher level dimensions which are contiguous regions of compatible value types. These two dimensions 'organize value systems into an integrated motivational structure' (Schwartz 1992: 60).

The first is labelled 'openness to change versus conservation' as they oppose the Self-direction plus Security value types (motivating people to follow their inner-directed interests in uncertain directions) to the combined Security, Conformity and Tradition value types (motivating people towards outer-directed avoidance of uncertainty to preserve the status quo in close relationships with other people, institutions and traditions). This dimension appears to resemble Hofstede's Uncertainty Avoidance but, as we shall see in the examination of the second of Schwartz's higher level dimensions, there is sufficient reason to believe that it is substantially different or that UAI is perhaps the work-related context to Schwartz's trans-situational and abstract dimension.

The second, labelled 'self-enhancement versus self-transcendence', opposes Hedonism, Achievement and Power value types (motivating people to enhance their individualistic interests) against the combination of Universalism and Benevolence value types (motivating people to enhance the welfare of others and transcendence of selfish interests). At a broader level an individual interest region (Self-direction, Stimulation, Hedonism, Achievement, Power) and a collective interest region (Benevolence, Tradition, Conformity) are linked to complete the continuum by boundary regions that serve mixed interests (Universalism, Security). Schwartz emphasizes that the above 'interests facet' is not the same as Hofstede's Individualism–Collectivism since at the collective level of analysis, 'For example, the values wealth, social power, and authority, which primarily serve the interests of the individual person in our current analysis, tend to receive greater cultural priority in collectivist cultures in a culture-level analysis' (Schwartz 1992: 13).

The motivational continuum at individual level proposed by Schwartz can be shown diagrammatically in Figure 9.1 (below).

Accordingly, the implication is that clustering of values, as in Hofstede's study, is considered arbitrary by Schwartz since values exist relatively

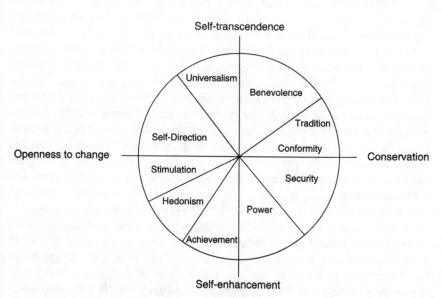

Figure 9.1 Schwartz's Continuum of Value systems at individual level.

within a continuum defined by adjacent compatibles and opposite conflicts. Further, Schwartz suggests that Hofstede's method of standardizing scores to construct an index is flawed since 'standardizing changes the patterns of intercorrelations among values within groups' (Schwartz 1992: 53) and proposes an alternative procedure which he claims does not distort the structure of value relations in the same way.

Schwartz proposes *pace* Hofstede that the individual and the collective level dimensions of value systems are closely related structurally. The configuration of values and value types between the individual and cultural level shows some variation but the main differences between cultures are in terms of value priorities or in the hierarchical ordering of the relative importance afforded to values and value types. Schwartz also finds, at the individual level of analysis, important differences in how PRC Chinese respondents construe the relations among collective and mixed interest values. The Chinese samples deviated from the universal or 'ideal' structure in that the values that constitute Universalism, Benevolence, Tradition, Conformity and Security could not be partitioned into regions representing each type. Instead they were partitioned into three uniquely Chinese value types consonant to the major 'religious' influences in Chinese culture: Taoism, Confucianism and Buddhism. Schwartz reports that Hong Kong was 'closer to the ideal structure and did not show this alternative pattern' (Schwartz 1992: 48) although Hong Kong was amongst those samples that deviated most from the ideal structure. This finding would seem to support the proposition that value structures in Hong Kong are influenced by both Western and Chinese value system in a process of 'crossvergence' (Ralston *et al.* 1993). Because Schwartz sees universality in the structure of values anchored in two higher-level dimensions, he proposes hypotheses based upon this structure about the relations of value priorities with other variables. 'Two statements summarize the implications of the interrelatedness of value priorities for generating hypotheses: (1) Any outside variable tends to be similarly associated with value types that are adjacent in the value structure. (2) Associations with any outside variable decrease monotonically as one goes around the circular structure' (Schwartz 1992: 54). As a result the whole pattern of associations regardless of statistical significance rather than the significance of single correlations or mean differences is considered to reflect the validity of the theory. Predicted associations between outside variables and value priorities are represented graphically with a sinusoid curve.

For the purpose of this chapter the most interesting prediction using this method is the hypothesis regarding differences in value priorities between persons from communal societies versus contractual societies. Schwartz hypothesizes that Tradition, Conformity, and Benevolence are more important in communal societies (such as Hong Kong) in contrast to the higher importance of Self-direction, Stimulation, and Universalism in contractual societies (such as UK).

Schwartz compares his Taiwan (communal) sample with New Zealand (contractual) and finds the highest priority afforded to Security followed by Power and Conformity in Taiwan with the emergence of Benevolence as an unexpected priority in the New Zealand sample. Schwartz concludes that it may be preferable to compare the value priorities of cultures on value types derived from analysis at the cultural level as they are configured slightly differently from their individual equivalent (Schwartz 1992: 57).

In doing so Schwartz is effectively conceding that Hofstede's cultural-level approach, which avoids the 'ecological fallacy', is more appropriate in this case suggesting that, even if the individual and cultural levels are structurally similar, they should be regarded as separate for purposes of analysis.

Hofstede's model, which is largely vindicated in a recent replication study within IBM (Lowe 1994), still remains the seminal work in the field despite the promise of refinement afforded by Schwartz. The 'consequences' of cultural difference for countries and organizations is as valid now as proposed in the original study by Hofstede (1980).

Hofstede's pioneering study has resulted in a considerable amount of interest and research. The implications are wide and some of the more important 'consequences' for Hong Kong organizational culture can now be examined.

CHINESE CAPITALISM: A DIFFERENT SPIRIT

The first 'consequence' of a persistently very different cultural environment from most Western countries is a rather different type of economic activity. The linkages between societal values and economic performance within Overseas Chinese communities have been investigated in some depth by S.G. Redding at the University of Hong Kong (Redding 1990). In his work, Redding shows the central importance of values and particularly those associated with familism in partially explaining the source of recent economic success amongst the Overseas Chinese. Redding also emphasizes the importance of manager-owners who created cultures in the form of family businesses which are cultural artefacts peculiarly well suited to the socio-cultural environment and particularly well placed to exploit opportunities in the economic environment. He describes a distinctive and coherent Spirit of Chinese Capitalism largely through investigating the values of founder-leaders who 'together constitute a spirit of Chinese Capitalism' (Redding 1990: 15).

ECONOMIC CULTURE: THE 'SOFT' SIDE OF DEVELOPMENT

Redding's rationale of the success of the Overseas Chinese centres on the concept of an 'economic culture' (Redding 1990) which describes connections between socio-cultural values and economic behaviour conducive to development. Taoist, Buddhist and Confucian (or more appropriately neo-Confucian) ideals and especially familism are one essential source of socio-cultural values which, through the vehicle of the Chinese family business, enable successful economic behaviour. It is dangerous to regard the concept of economic culture as deterministic. According to Redding 'The Overseas Chinese have an apparent distinct economic culture, that is describable, and the outline of its determinants can be drawn. It is still necessary to place it in a larger framework of explanation if the question of macro-economic performance is to be considered' and 'it is necessary to reassert that (culture) is not seen as the dominant cause of economic success, obliterating or ignoring other factors like economic policy. Culture is one of several key features, deserving a respectable place in any account' (Redding 1990: 12).

NATIONAL CULTURAL INFLUENCES ON ORGANIZATIONS

The terms culture and organization have been described in different ways. Ideologies can penetrate an organization from at least six layers (large-scale, national, community, industry, occupational and other organization's cultures) according to one source (Trice and Beyer 1993: 46) and these cultural influences may be regarded as one noncoterniminous type as opposed to culture coterminous with the organization's boundaries (Gregory 1983: 374).

Hofstede's approach of comparative explanation of work-related values is categorized and labelled variously using different typologies (Ajiferuke and Boddewyn 1970; Adler 1983) re-emphasizing that this approach is not the only perspective and only one particular type of 'blindness' amongst social scientists.

Despite the lack of consensus amongst perspectives Smircich concludes that there is 'an apparent trend for the cultural metaphor to replace the open systems metaphor as an analytical framework in organization studies' (Smircich 1983: 354). Smircich identifies current research themes where the intersection of culture theory and organization theory is evident and traces how culture has been developed in organization studies as a critical variable as well as as a root metaphor. This typology would put Hofstede's work in the category of 'Culture as an Independent Variable' or comparative management.

Within the comparative management perspective linkages between national culture and organizational culture are vital to understanding the role of culture in comparative differences in economic behaviour and performance amongst nations as 'national culture influences corporate culture by providing the universal values and moral principles which condition the deepest and highest in abstraction levels of organizational culture' (Nicolaidis 1993: 386). This view synthesizes Scheins' framework of organizational culture with the economic theory of the entrepreneur and supports the idea of the critical role of the leader as a pivotal catalyst in harmonizing national and organizational culture in the context of contingency factors in the environment. Corporate culture influences the beliefs and values affecting the behaviour of individuals but the relationship between the variables is not straightforward as is dependent upon the broader (ethnic/national) cultural environment (Laurent 1983).

Structure and strategy

Differences in cultural norms result in differences in behaviour in group tasks with Asian and other collectivist cultural traditions displaying more co-operative behaviour than individualist traditions (Cox *et al.* 1991). National culture influences the expectations of individuals and stakeholders involved and the power relationships that result influence the purposes and strategies of the organization (Johnson and Scholes 1993, ch. 5). Cultural assumptions regarding relationships amongst people (involving Individualism–Collectivism) and the relationship with the environment (involving Uncertainty Avoidance) will affect the interpretation of strategic issues, strategy formulation and implementation which are, therefore, culturally contingent (Schneider 1989). Western typologies of strategic planning approaches are unlikely to be appropriate for Hong Kong where strategy is characterized by a variant of the 'Adaptive' approach (Chafee 1985) which one might label 'speculative incrementalism' dissimilar to planned, rationally sequential ideal types influential in Anglo-Saxon economies (Warrington 1982).

In this view 'excellence' is created in Hong Kong where there is consonance between the national/ethnic and organizational culture (Feldman 1988) when consequent innovative behaviour exploits strengths and opportunities whilst overcoming weaknesses and threats. The implication is the proposition that macro-level culture may be more influential on economic behaviour in collective societies like Hong Kong than in individualist societies since 'the process of enculturation is more successful in some cultures than others' (Claryse and Moenaert 1991: 1–20). This idea of the differential importance of levels of 'mental programming' between cultures is another area for potential research into a basic proposition that collective, internally co-operative 'culture' focused societies do not contain the same inherent limits to growth as individualistic, internally competitive 'personality' focused societies.

ORGANIZATIONAL CULTURES ARE DIFFERENT

Redding's concept of economic culture is consonant with the Strategic Choice School within Contingency Theory in that there are no panaceas or single variable determinants of organizational success and attempts to refute universal prescriptions of 'excellence'. Rather the design of organizations can be seen as taking place within an environment with culture as a macro-level influence upon both those who are influential in constructing organizations and those who participate in it.

Using this perspective it is not the environment that determines the nature of organizations and strategies but the *perception* of the environment through a 'cultural filter' of values and beliefs adopted and cultivated by management decision-makers and adopted in the practices of organizational members. By implication national/ethnic culture will influence the extent to which organizations are typically dynamic 'Prospectors' or conservative 'Defenders' or 'Analysers' (Miles and Snow 1978).

The organizational 'paradigm' (Johnson and Scholes 1989: 39) of core beliefs develops a support system or 'Cultural Web' of symbols, rituals and myths, routines, control systems, power and organizational structures. The successful organization will have adopted a paradigm which allows it to achieve 'strategic fit' with its environment and, in particular, with its market.

A main task for future research, therefore, is to examine why the family-based culture inherent in local Hong Kong organizations has, on the whole, enabled them to prosper particularly well in increasingly chaotic environments. One proposition for future investigation is that the success of Hong Kong firms is due in large part to their adoption of 'cultural filters' which enable them to 'develop an attitude of receptivity and high adaptability to changing conditions' (Schneider 1989: 153). They seem to have achieved this adaptability despite (or even because of) shortages of Western business skills and techniques in Marketing, Human Resources and other areas.

Hong Kong Chinese firms are in comparison to Western organizations more cohesive, family-based, collective and holistic. Relationships are founded on a belief in tradition and moral debt amongst people who 'instinctively avoid conflict of loyalties' (Bedi 1991: 2). Another result of this are distinctive 'industrial recipes' or wider cultural reference groups (Spender 1989). For instance, industries seem dominated by networks which enable formations of temporary 'organizations' in some industries which exploit specific contracts and disband to seek new opportunities on completion. Both networks and constituent organizations are dominated by family-based hierarchies similar to the patron-client hierarchies from the recent rural past. The essence of these structures is to attempt to integrate the interests of both patrons and clients in a system of mutually beneficial support in what may be described as a 'moral economy'. As a result successful cultivation of both networks inside the organization and within the industry is a pre-requisite of success requiring skills at fostering trust, mutual loyalty and balancing autocratic power with paternalistic responsibility. Hong Kong organizations are consequently relatively 'weak', as the strength, flexibility and durability of Hong Kong business is within the 'recipes' of networks rather than organizations (Redding 1990). This means, in research terms, according to Chen, that it is desirable to concentrate attention on the networks rather than on individual organizations (in Hamilton 1991).

Social and cultural values reflecting Confucian ideas and other influences are, consequently, at the core of understanding the Overseas Chinese model of capitalist development.

CONSEQUENCES FOR MANAGEMENT IDEAS IN HONG KONG

Hofstede's work adds considerable weight to casting doubt on the universal validity of Western (usually American) management theory since management 'is very much an American concept, just as earlier the entire discipline of economics was very much an Anglo-Saxon discipline' (Hofstede 1984: 253). Management theory has largely been developed within a Western cultural milieu which results in solutions for markets and hierarchies and ignores or marginalizes the role of networks as 'hybrids' rather than as a distinctive alternative structural form.

Consequently all management theories should be examined for culturally relative validity in this view. Hofstede widely examines and critiques, in terms of cultural relativism, Western theories relating to Motivation, Leadership, MBO, Planning and Control, Organization Design and Development, Humanisation of Work, Industrial Democracy and others (Hofstede 1984 ch. 9).

Hofstede suggests that Leadership and Industrial Democracy is largely influenced by Power Distance and IDV in a society. He suggests that 'neither McGregor nor Likert nor Blake and Mouton nor any other US leadership theorists I know has taken the collective values of subordinates into account' (Hofstede 1984: 259) and suggests that industrial democracy is basically a contradiction for Chinese organizations 'in which participative structures in work situations are combined with a strictly controlled hierarchy in ideological issues' (Hofstede 1984: 269).

In terms of organization design Hofstede considers PDI and UAI to be influential in the Aston Studies (Pugh and Hickson 1989) dimensions of concentration of authority and structuring of activities.

Organizations are likely to be 'structured in order to meet the subjective cultural needs of their members' (Hofstede 1991: 142). Hofstede reports empirical evidence provided in the work of Stevens supporting the proposition that this translates into organizational structures of Hong Kong and other Asian firms which are a distinct form of 'personnel bureaucracy' as the 'equivalent implicit model of an organization in these countries is the (extended) "family", in which the owner-manager is the omnipotent (grand)father. It corresponds to large Power Distance but weak Uncertainty Avoidance, a situation in which people would resolve the conflict described by permanent referral to the boss' (Hofstede 1991: 143). In contrast the implicit model of organizations in Britain (where PDI and UAI scores are both low), according to Stevens' evidence was 'a "village market" in which neither hierarchy nor rules, determine what will happen' (Hofstede 1991: 142). The consequences for studies when organizations from Hong Kong and the UK are compared are that it must be realized that we are probably not comparing like with like and every effort must be made to ensure that future research avoids ethnocentric bias.

The cultural characteristics of a country affect conceptions of human nature produced in a society which will influence the managerial theories produced therein. One influence is the degree of individualism which, according to Hofstede, provides an environment where theories of motivation such as those of Maslow are inappropriate for collective societies where higher motives are unlikely to be 'self-actualization' (as in Anglo-Saxon cultures) but rather the interests and honour of the ingroup and the harmony and consensus within the society collectively. Real motivators (as opposed to 'hygiene factors' in Herzberg's terms) are likely to be different in Hong Kong from the UK because of power distance.

In Hong Kong, large power distance leading to dependence should be seen as a real motivator as 'the motivator should rather be labelled the *master*. He differs from the "boss" in that his power is based on tradition and charisma more than on formal position' (Hofstede 1991: 154).

Similar motives might be expected in Hong Kong and the UK, in theory, in terms of McClelland's 'need for achievement' (and esteem) since both countries have weak UAI and strong MAS scores (Hofstede 1991: 124) although how achievement is interpreted may differ between societies because of differences in Long-Term Orientation, Individualism and differences in the nature of Masculinity.

Other needs such as 'respect, harmony, face and duty' (Hofstede 1991: 126) are somewhat neglected in the somewhat ethnocentric view of the world provided by Maslow, McClelland and other Western management theorists and as a result these theories in their original form do not qualify as adequate foundations for a cross-cultural study. This extends to more recent theory also as Hofstede explains the 'popularity in the United States of "expectancy" theories of motivation, which see people as pulled by the expectancy of outcomes, mostly consciously' (Hofstede 1984: 255) as explicable in terms of the assumed 'calculative invovement' of highly individualistic Americans in organizations. By implication expectancy theories are not considered to be appropriate in a collective society like Hong Kong.

Other more recent management theories must be examined to see if they pass the 'test' of cultural relativism implicit in Hofstede's work. In International Business and Management studies considerable potential exists for culturally based deconstruction of theories originating in the West and claiming universal validity.

This is largely a task for a subsequent study but it should be noted that Hofstede does not consider Peters and Waterman to have fully passed the 'test' of cultural relativity since his prescriptions for 'excellence' in organizational culture are universal and not environmentally or culturally contingent. Hofstede objects and disagrees with Peters and Waterman's book *In Search of Excellence* where 'eight conditions for excellence are presented as norms. The book suggests there is "one best way" towards excellence' (Hofstede 1990: 199). Hofstede maintains that (culturally derived) implicit models of organizations cannot explain why Hong Kong and Singapore 'have been doing very well in modernizing themselves' (Hofstede 1991: 140) but restates that structure of organizations has cultural antecedents. Combining Mintzberg's five typical configurations of organizations with his four cultural dimensions leads him to posit that the implicit model for Hong Kong organizations is the 'simple structure' whereas in the UK it is the 'adhocracy'. Characteristics of each implicit model are quite different particularly concerning preferred control/co-ordination and key parts of the organization. Essentially the focus, according to this model, within Hong Kong organizations is the 'owner' whereas in UK organizations it is the 'support staff' reflecting a fundamental difference in power distance. If one accepts this then it seems clear that Hofstede is providing a theoretical basis which is empirically supported by the work of Redding indicating that organizational structure is one vehicle through which the comparative cultural advantage inherent in Hong Kong (relative, for example, to the UK) manifests itself in economic activity. This is not to suggest that simple organizations working in networks are *per se* somehow more effective than 'adhocracies', rather it suggests that in Hong Kong 'this special form of organization is peculiarly well adapted to its sociocultural milieu (Redding 1990: 4), enhancing the possibilities for culturally contingent excellence.

BIBLIOGRAPHY

Adler, N. (1983) 'A Typology of Management Studies Involving Culture', *Journal of International Business Studies*, Fall: 29–47.
Ajiferuke, M. and Boddewyn, J. (1970) ' "Culture" and Other Explanatory Variables in Comparative Management Studies', *Academy of Management Journal* 13: 153–63.
Bedi, H. (1991) *Understanding The Asian Manager*, London: Allen & Unwin.
Bhagat, R.S. and McQuaid, S.J. (1982) 'The Role of Subjective Culture in organizations: A Review and Directions for Future Research', *Journal of Applied Psychology* 67(5): 653–85.

Bond, M.H. (1987) 'Chinese Values and the Search for Culture-Free Dimensions of Culture: The Chinese Culture Connection', *Journal of Cross-Cultural Psychology* 18(2), June: 143–64.

—— (1988) 'Finding Universal Dimensions of Individual Variation in Multicultural Studies of Values: The Rokeach and Chinese Value Surveys', *Journal of Personality and Social Psychology* (6): 1009–15.

Chafee, E.E. (1985) Three Models of Strategy', *Academy of Management Review*, 10(1): 89–98.

Chen, M. (1995) *Asian Management Systems; Chinese, Japanese and Korean Styles of Business*, London: Routledge.

Claryse, B.J. and Moenaert, R.K. (1991) 'Culture's Consequences on Innovation: A Study of Cultural Dimensions', (unpublished) paper presented in workshop on 'Innovation', August: University of Kiel, Germany.

Cox, T.H. *et al.* (1991) 'Effects of Ethnic Group Cultural Differences on Cooperative and Competitive Behaviour on a Group Task', *Academy of Management Journal* 34(4): 827–47.

Douglas, M. (1973) *Natural Symbols: Explorations in Cosmology*, New York: Vintage.

Douglas, M. *et al.* (1992) 'Institutions of the Third Kind', in M. Douglas (ed.) *Risk and Blame*, London: Routledge.

Feldman, S.P. (1988) 'How Organisational Culture Can Affect Innovation', *Organisational Dynamics* 17, Spring: 57–68.

Goodstein, L.D. (1981) 'American Business Values and Cultural Imperialism', *Organisational Dynamics*, Summer: 49–54.

Gregory, K.L. 'Native-view Paradigms: Multiple Cultures and Culture Conflicts in Organisations', *Administrative Science Quarterly* 28: 359–76.

Hamilton, G.G. and Chen, E. (eds) (1991) 'Business Networks and Economic Development', University of Hong Kong, Centre of Asian Studies Occasional papers and Monographs, no. 99.

Hofstede, G. (1980) *Culture's Consequences: International Differences in Work-Related Values* (unabridged edn), London: Sage. Abridged edn 1984.

—— (1981) 'Do American Theories Apply Abroad? A Reply to Goodstein and Hunt', *Organisational Dynamics*, Summer: 63–8.

—— (1982) *Scoring Guide for VSM*, IRIC, PO Box 143, 2600 AC Delft, The Netherlands.

—— (1991) *Culture and Organisations*, London: McGraw-Hill.

Hunt, J.W. (1981) 'Applying American Behavioural Science: Some Cross-Cultural Problems', *Organisational Dynamics*, Summer: 55–62.

Johnson, G. and Scholes, K. (1993) *Exploring Corporate Strategy*, 3rd edn, London: Prentice-Hall.

Kerr, C. *et al.* (1960) *Industrialism and Industrial Man*, Cambridge, Mass.: Harvard University Press.

Kluckhohn, F.R. and Strodtbeck, F.L. (1961) *Variations in Value Orientations*, Westport, CT: Greenwood Press.

Laurent, A. 'The Cultural Diversity of Western Concepts of Management', *International Studies of Management and Organisation*, XII(1–2): 75–96.

Lowe, S. (1994) 'Hermes Revisited', 1994 International Symposium on Pacific Asian Business, 7th. Annual Proceedings: The Dynamics of Global Co-operation and Competition, P.A.M.I. Honolulu, Hawaii, USA.

Miles, R.E. and Snow, C.C (1978) *Organisation Strategy, Structure and Process*, London: McGraw-Hill.

Nicolaidis, C.S. (1993) 'National Culture, Corporate Culture and Economic Performance: An Interdisciplinary Synthesis', Proceedings of the 20th Conference of the UK Academy of International Business, Pontypridd, April, vol. 2 'International Strategies': 377–98.

Parsons, T. and Shils, E.A. (eds) (1951) *Towards a General Theory of Action*, Cambridge, Mass.: Harvard University Press.

Pugh, D.S. and Hickson, D.J. (1989) *Writers on Organisations*, 4th edn, London: Penguin.

Pyatt, T.R. and Kwok, C.C.H. (1993) 'The Nature of South East Asian Business Networks and Buyer Behaviour', Proceedings of AIB Western and Southeast Asian Regional Meeting, June: 'Asian Success & International Business Theory'.

Ralston, D. *et al.* (1993) 'Differences in Managerial Values: A Study of U.S. and PRC Managers', *Journal of International Business Studies*, 2nd quarter: 249–73.

Redding, S.G. (1982) 'Cultural effects on the Marketing Process in Southeast Asia', *Journal of the Market Research Society* 24(2): 98–122.

—— (1986) 'Participative Management and its Varying Relevance in Hong Kong and Singapore', *Asia Pacific Journal of Management* 3(2), January: 76–98.

—— (1990) *The Spirit of Chinese Capitalism*, Berlin: W. de Gruyter.

—— (1994) 'Competitive Advantage in the Context of Hong Kong', *Journal of Far Eastern Business* 1(1), Autumn: 71–89.

Ronen, S. and Shenkar, O. (1985) 'Clustering Countries on Attitudinal Dimensions: A Review and Synthesis', *Academy of Management Review* 10(3): 435–54.

Schneider, S.C. (1989) 'Strategy Formulation: The Impact of National Culture', *Organisation Studies* 10(2): 149–68.

Schwartz, S.H. (1992) 'Universals in the Content and Structure of Values: Theoretical Advances and Empirical Tests in 20 Countries', in Zanna (ed.) *Advances in Experimental Social Psychology*, Orlando: Academic Press.

Smircich, L. (1983) 'Concepts of Culture and Organizational Analysis', *Administrative Science Quarterly* 28: 339–58.

Spender, J.-C. (1989) *Industry Recipe: The Nature and Sources of Management Judgement*, Oxford: Basil Blackwell.

Triandis, H.C. (1982) 'Review of Culture's Consequences: International Differences in Work-Related Values', *Human Organisation* 41(1), Spring: 86–90.

Trice, H. and Beyer, J. (1993) *The Cultures of Work Organizations*, Englewood Cliffs, NJ: Prentice-Hall.

Trompenaars, F. (1993) *Riding the Waves of Culture*, London: The Economist Books.

Tse, D. *et al.* (1988) 'Does Culture Matter? A Cross-Cultural Study of Executives' Choice, Decisiveness, and Risk Adjustment in International Marketing', *Journal of Marketing* 52 (October): 81–95.

Usunier, J.-C. (1993) *International Marketing: A Cultural Approach*, London: Prentice-Hall.

Warrington, M.B. (1982) 'Will Hong Kong's Entrepreneurs Move to Planning?', *Long Range Planning*, 15(3): 168–75.

Yeung, D. and Kenneth Chung, K.C. (1993) 'Marketing and Purchasing Strategies in the Life Insurance Industry of Hong Kong', Proceedings of AIB Western & Southeast Asian Regional Meeting, June: 'Asian Success & International Business Theory'.

10 Japanese product transplants in Asia and consumer choice

Yong Gu Suh

INTRODUCTION

In the globalizing world of the 1990s, firms are increasingly carrying out their sourcing, assembly and production of parts for their products in foreign countries. This has led to the issue of product 'transplants', a common example being that of Japanese automobile transplants in Europe and the United States. More recently, as the yen has strengthened continuously, Japanese manufacturers are moving into Asian developing countries to take advantage of the region's low wages. This chapter analyses the implications of product transplants from the viewpoint of consumers and welfare, using the Japanese case as an example.

There is considerable evidence that firms in the 1990s will carry out increasing parts of their assembly, sourcing and production of products in foreign countries through strategic alliances or foreign direct investment. This has led to the well-known issue of 'transplants'. Japanese firms have been especially successful in using the strategy of product transplants in world markets. Rehder (1989) predicted that by the early 1990s Japanese-owned or -managed factories transplanted to the United States would be producing over 25% of the total US automobile output.

A similar phenomenon is expected in Europe, which is why the issue of Japanese automobile transplants has become such a sensitive one in the European Community. This European debate has been analysed in more depth by Choi (1992). The Japanese approach to global assembly, sourcing and production is now being adopted by other foreign firms including Asian dragon countries such as Taiwan and South Korea. It is still too early to be sure whether these countries will achieve the same success as Japan.

The purpose of this chapter is to address the issue of product transplants from a 'consumer' perspective. It is likely that a Western consumer will not view a Sony product 'made in' Malaysia, as the equivalent of a Sony product made in Japan because country-of-origin information affects consumers' product evaluations (Bilkey and Nes 1982). Japanese product transplants are on the increase, however, including not only automobiles but also other industries such as electronics, appliances and semiconductors.

Owing to transplants, hybrid products in which country of brand and country of manufacture are different have become more common. The success of hybrid products being produced in transplant facilities ultimately depends on consumers' attitudes and intentions to buy such products. Thus, we try to analyse the implications of consumer perception on product value in relation to hybrid products (e.g. SONY Made in Malaysia).

REPUTATION AND CONSUMER CHOICE

Globalization has become an increasingly researched topic in economics and management. Most of the research, however, has been from the viewpoint of a firm's strategy, and how globalization affects the behaviour of firms. We believe globalization can have an impact on consumer choice, through a firm's or country's reputation.

International sourcing, production and assembly form a major part of the globalization process of firms. International sourcing, where a substantial proportion of a product is made in various countries can help to 'blur' the image of a firm's reputation, or corporate identity from the viewpoint of consumers. For example, depending on local content laws and other criteria, a product may carry the 'made in' label of the country where it is assembled, rather than where the parts are produced, or where the firm's headquarters are located. But from the viewpoint of consumer choice, it may matter that a Sony product carries the 'made in Malaysia' label versus the usual 'made in Japan' label. This is because a country's or a firm's image and reputation can play an important role in consumer choice (Bannister and Saunders 1978; Bilkey and Nes 1982; Johansson and Nebenzahl 1986; Han and Terpstra 1988). In a world of imperfect information, consumers often base their choice on signals such as country, firm or brand images, based on stereotyped views. Bannister and Saunders (1978: 564) noted:

> generalised images created by variables such as representative products, economic and political maturity, historical events and relationships, traditions, industrialisation and the degree of technological virtuosity will have effects upon consumer attitudes additional to those emanating from the significant elements of the products.

As firms continue to adopt greater globalized practices, the 'made in' label may be one that consumers use to discriminate against certain products. In choice behaviour, the 'made in' concept is closely related to the 'country image' perceived by consumers. Since the 'made in' label can be an important extrinsic informational cue for potential buyers, country-of-origin information may play a major role in consumer choice towards hybrid international products.

Japanese firms, those most widely using global production techniques and transplants, face the greatest possible such consumer bias or stereotyping. Japan, as a country faced negative images in the 1960s and even early 1970s. However, country or firm images can change over time (Nagashima 1970, 1977). Since the late 1970s, Japan has developed a formidable reputation for product quality. An example of this quality reputation is Toyota's joint venture with Holden in Australia. The joint venture requires that half of the output be branded Toyota and the other half Holden, although the products are identical. This has led to automobile dealers discovering that consumers purchase the car with the Holden brand name only if they are given certain additional credit incentives or discounts. Although the products are identical and even from the same factory, in a world of imperfect information and brand name reputation, i.e. Toyota versus Holden, consumer choice was affected.

Germany also presently enjoys a premium reputation for products carrying the 'made in Germany' label. The reputation of its workers and high technical skills have allowed German firms successfully to enter new markets where they had no prior experience relative to their competitors.

Country-of-origin bias or stereotyping exists because of imperfect information, and statistical discrimination by consumers. Statistical discrimination here can be defined as prior judgements about a product's quality based upon the overall image or perception of the country where the product is manufactured. This in turn prevents a consumer from making an objective judgement about the product's quality; the 'made in' label has a greater influence on the consumer's choice. Chiang and Masson (1988: 261) have analysed this issue in more depth with reference to Taiwanese products:

> information imperfection may cause consumers to practice statistical discrimination against imports from developing countries. Consumers often associate the quality of such goods with their country of origin.

Product transplants in the United States and Europe by Japanese firms did not face this origin bias in terms of either the ability to command a premium or the need to sell at a discount. This is because in the eyes of most consumers, the 'made in' Japan, United States or Europe label all carry a high quality premium. However, as in the example of Australia's Holden, brand names such as Toyota may indeed hold a premium over the brand names of other firms from developed countries, such as Australia.

JAPANESE TRANSPLANTS IN THE ASIAN DEVELOPING COUNTRIES

There is a hierarchy of countries in terms of consumers' product evaluations (Wall, Leiefeld and Heslop 1989). Transplants by developed country MNCs in other developed countries will have less impact on consumers'

SONY	Malaysia	audio, colour-TV, VCR, Camcorders
	Thailand	audio products, semiconductors
	Indonesia	tape recorder
	Taiwan	VCRs, telephones Audio

Figure 10.1 Sony's transplants in Asia
Source: Company Brochure 1992, March.

perception of hybrid products. However, the situation may be different if a premium brand name carries the made in label of a developing country. An increasingly common example concerns Japanese products assembled in South-east Asia. Sony transplants are shown in Figure 10.1. Most of these investments were intensified in the late 1980s. Consumers have to make a choice between the premium associated with the brand name, and the possibly negative stereotyped view of the developing country of origin: Malaysia, for example.

This is a choice that Asian consumers have been facing since the late 1980s and a choice that European consumers will face in the 1990s as Japanese transplants in automobiles, electronics and various other industries begin entering the European markets in substantial numbers.

In Asia, Japanese, along with Taiwanese and Korean firms, have been shifting production rapidly to low-wage countries in South-east Asia such as Thailand, Malaysia and Indonesia and, more recently, China. For example, in 1992, an average manufacturing worker in Malaysia earned US$120 a month. In Japan, the figure was over twenty times that amount. In other more developed Asian countries such as South Korea and Taiwan, the average was $800 a month (Hale, 1994). Thus, cost considerations have caused Japanese firms to shift sourcing, assembly and production rapidly to South-east Asia. Further, the continuing rise of the Japanese yen since 1990 has further deterred domestic production. Figure 10.2 shows movements in the exchange-rate of the yen to the US dollar since the mid-1980s.

As a result, Japan's investment in transplants in Asia is speeding up. Some examples are shown in Figure 10.3. The latest investment wave seems to be different from that of the early 1980s in terms of orientation and breadth.

To Japanese manufacturers, endaka, or a strong yen, has two main effects. In the short term, it worsens manufacturers financial accounts. In the longer term, major exporters are forced to increase production at off-shore plants, where the costs of labour, space and components have fallen sharply in yen terms, relative to domestic costs.

These developments have sparked a debate on whether the Japanese economy will hollow out, as American manufacturing industries did in

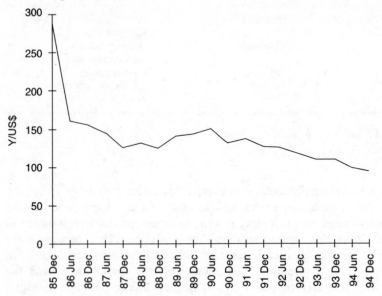

Figure 10.2 Japanese yen to 1 US dollar
Source: Extel Financial Research Service.

Company	Country	Product
ALPS	China	Magnetic heads
Epson	Singapore	Semiconductors
Fujitsu	Thailand	Floppy-disk drives
Hitachi	Malaysia	VCRs
Matsushita	China	Big-screen TVs, VCRs
Nintendo	China	Game Boy machines
Sanyo	Singapore	CD players
Sharp	Philippines	Washing machines
Sony	China	TVs, CD players, camcorders
Toshiba	Thailand	Cathode-ray tubes for PCs

Figure 10.3 Japanese companies' planned manufacturing investment into Asia
Source: Nomura Research Institute, *Business Week*, 23 May 1994.

the early 1980s. Concern over hollowing out was first raised in the mid-1980s when the yen began rising against the dollar after the 1985 Plaza Accord. The Japanese overcame that crisis by inducing asset inflation (the so-called bubble economy) of the late 1980s which compensated for loss of exports. In addition, the Japanese yen weakened for a while during the late 1980s (see Figure 10.2). However, the worst recession in Japan since the Second World War followed the bubble economy and the continuous strength of the yen since the early 1990s made it difficult for Japan to sustain its growth without structural change.

The result is that Japanese products, such as those of Sony, carrying a 'made in Malaysia' label have been competing with Korean and Taiwanese brand names such as Samsung or GS (former Goldstar) made in their home countries. Asian consumers, faced with the choice between a Sony made in Malaysia versus a Korean Samsung 'original' made in Korea and given similar price levels, would choose the Sony 'made in Malaysia' if brand name is the strongest influence. The success of Sony transplants in Asia suggests that Asian consumers, including Korean and Taiwanese, seem to prefer the Sony brand, even though the products were manufactured in a developing country such as Malaysia or Thailand.

Roth and Romeo (1992) examined country of origin effects in terms of the fit between countries and product categories: the importance of country of origin may differ among products. For example, Japanese automobiles have a favourable match between country image and the importance of country of origin as a product feature. Willingness to buy can therefore be enhanced by promoting country of origin. For other countries, country of origin information could be detrimental to automobile evaluation. Other products may not be so sensitive. The generality of this framework has not been examined in detail. More complex analysis is necessary to take into account price differences and retailer types as well as brand name and country of origin information.

INFORMATIONAL CUES AND QUALITY GUARANTEES

The product transplants discussed above raise the general question of branding, reputation and quality. Questioning the limitations of consumer information about quality, Nelson (1970) made the distinction between 'search' and 'experience' goods. The quality of search goods can be evaluated through search, the most obvious procedure available to consumers in obtaining information. The quality of experience goods, on the other hand, can be evaluated only after consumption. However, despite the importance of such categorizations, most consumers will use a variety of 'irrational' criteria sometimes for choosing among products.

From an information-theoretic perspective, consumers evaluate a product on the basis of informational cues. Such cues have been separated into two categories, namely intrinsic and extrinsic (Jacoby *et al.* 1977). While intrinsic cues are directly related to product quality (e.g. design and performance), extrinsic informational cues (e.g. brand name, store image and price) are used as surrogates to infer quality. Since consumers are often unable to detect a product's true quality, they utilize extrinsic cues in evaluating it. Given this perspective, brand or a firm's name and country of origin information are likely to be factors important in consumer choice. Consumer reports, advertising, friends or associates who have tried the product will also be influential sources of information.

Countries can *acquire* reputation, just as brand or firms' names do. Japan

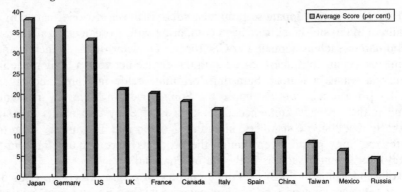

Figure 10.4 Quality league
Source: Bozell–Gallup poll, *Financial Times*, 11 February 1994.

now enjoys one of the world's highest reputations for quality (see Figure 10.4). It has had a dramatic change of image, summarized in the following remarks by Akio Morita (1986: 85), the founder of Sony, on its image three decades ago.

> After all, international rules require you to state the country of origin on your product – but we certainly did not want to emphasize it and run the risk of being rejected before we could demonstrate the quality of our products. But I must confess that in the early days we printed the line *Made in Japan* as small as possible, once too small for US Customs, which made us make it bigger on one product.

Nowadays, the rationale for consumers choosing Sony products manufactured in transplants in developing countries may be the belief that the company is willing to 'guarantee' the quality of a product that bears its name. Thus, a strong positive brand name may override a negative country image.

Three questions must be addressed: are there spill-over effects of brand name among product lines?; how important is a brand name compared with other informational cues such as country-of-origin information and price?; and do consumers from different cultures (e.g. Asia and Europe) perceive products from transplants differently?

First, is it possible that the superiority of the Sony design and the quality of its components dominate the inferior country images and less skilled labour of developing countries such as Malaysia and Thailand? Sony has incentives to maintain a certain level of quality in all products using its name, because of the potential negative repercussion to all Sony products. Scherer and Ross (1990: 578) explain the potential effects of such reputational linkages:

> The link between image and behaviour is perhaps strongest for firms selling a broad line of consumer durable goods. Companies like General

Electric or Sunbeam are acutely aware that the poor performance of any single appliance can, through its adverse effect on their reputation, impair the sales of other lines. Though this does not guarantee good performance, it at least increases the probability that the image-conscious producer will try hard to maintain adequate standards.

An extreme case of such negative repercussions has been shown in cases of product tampering. Mitchell (1989), in his empirical study of the Tylenol capsule poisoning case of the early 1980s, showed that the negative publicity caused by the product tampering affected all the other products of Tylenol's manufacturer, Johnson & Johnson:

> Johnson & Johnson ran an advertisement advising consumers how to exchange Tylenol capsules for a refund of tablets. The advertisement made no mention of Johnson & Johnson. This suggests that Johnson & Johnson was fearful that consumers might associate the company name with the poisonings, thereby damaging its reputation across its entire product line, from band aids to baby powder, in addition to the other products in the Tylenol line.
>
> (Mitchell 1989: 613)

Second, to what extent do consumers' perceptions of the quality of products from developing countries change when other informational cues are given? The relative importance of these informational cues may be different for different products. Furthermore, the question of the relative significance of brand name and country of origin is far from settled. Gaedeke (1973) tested American respondents using US branded products made in developing countries. He found that country of origin information did not significantly affect opinions about the quality of branded products in general. On the other hand, Han and Terpstra (1988) examined the effects of country of origin information and brand name on consumer evaluations of uni-national and bi-national products. In contrast to Gaedeke's findings, they found that sourcing country stimuli had more effects than brand name on consumer evaluation of bi-national products (e.g. US branded/foreign made). These contrasting findings show the function of brand name as a quality guarantee in relation to country of origin is still not well understood. To test the relative importance of the factors of country-of-origin, brand names, and prices, a more integrated framework of analysis is needed.

Third, do European and Asian consumers have different quality perceptions of Japanese products made in the Asian developing countries? In the remainder of the 1990s, European consumers will encounter more and more Japanese brands made in the Asian transplants, Japanese consumers have faced the same question: for example, in 1993, Japan became a net importer of colour TVs, mainly produced by Japanese transplants in Southeast Asia (Holyoke and Lindorff 1994).

CONCLUSION

In our rapidly globalizing world, the phenomenon of product transplants has become increasingly common. Japanese firms in general have placed great importance on product transplants and have used them successfully in world markets.

As has been shown in Bannister and Saunders (1978) and Bilkey and Nes (1982), consumers can be biased against a firm or country because it has a negative image. Japanese firms faced such a negative bias in the 1960s and early 1970s. But since then, Japanese firms and products have gained a reputation for high product quality. Consumers may make little distinction between products from Japanese transplants in the United States and Europe and those made in Japan. This may not be the case if firms from Japan manufacture their products in developing countries. The Sony example suggests that in Asian markets at least, consumers seem to have shown that they prefer Japanese products made in Malaysia to other, less prestigious, brands manufactured in their original countries. The Japanese firm has the dual advantage, therefore, of perceived high quality and low production costs leading also to competitive prices. Clearly the continuance of the quality image will depend upon the transferability of Japanese production skills.

In the 1990s, Japanese firms will enter European markets in greater numbers. Product quality, technology and reputation may allow them to repeat if not surpass their past successes in the US market. Whether the quality premium of Japanese products made in countries such as Malaysia will be able to shift European consumers from the more expensive ones made with US or European labels is a topic worthy of future research.

BIBLIOGRAPHY

Bannister, J. and Saunders, J.A. (1978) 'UK Consumers' Attitudes Towards Imports: The Measurement of National Stereotype Image', *European Journal of Marketing* 12: 562–70.

Bilkey, W.J. and Nes, E. (1982) 'Country-of-Origin Effects on Product Evaluations', *Journal of International Business Studies*, Spring/Summer: 89–99.

Chiang, S. and Masson, R. (1988) 'Domestic Industrial Structure and Export Quality', *International Economic Review* 28(2): 261–70.

Choi, Chong J. (1992) 'Rivalry in East Asia', *Journal of World Trade*, October: 99–103.

Gaedeke, R. (1973) 'Consumer Attitudes Toward Products 'Made-In' Developing Countries', *Journal of Retailing* 49(2), Summer: 14–24.

Hale, D.D. (1994) 'Stock Markets in the New World Order', *Columbia Journal of World Business* 24(2): 22–6.

Han, C.M. and Terpstra, V. (1988) 'Country-of-Origin Effects for Uni-National and Bi-National Products', *Journal of International Business Studies*, Summer: 235–55.

Holyoke L. and Lindorff, D. (1994) 'A Yen for Asia', *Business Week*, 23 May: 18–19.

Jacoby, J. *et al.* (1977) 'Information Acquisition Behaviour in Brand Choice Situations', *Journal of Consumer Research* 3 (March): 109–16.

Johansson, J.K. and Nebenzahl, I.D. (1986) 'Multinational Production: Effect on Brand Value', *Journal of International Business Studies*, Fall: 101–25.

Mitchell, J. (1989) 'The Impact of External Parties on Brand Name Capital', *Economic Inquiry* 27: 601–18.

Morita, A. (1986) *Made in Japan*, London: Penguin Books, pp. 85–6.

Nagashima, A. (1970) 'A Comparison of Japanese and US Attitudes toward Foreign Products, *Journal of Marketing*, January (34): 68–74.

—— (1977) 'A Comparative Made-in Product Image Survey among Japanese Businessmen', *Journal of Marketing*, July (41): 95–100.

Nelson, P. (1970) 'Information and Consumer Behaviour', *Journal of Political Economy*, July/August: 311–29.

Rehder, R. (1989) 'Japanese Transplants: In Search of a Balanced and Broader Perspective', *Columbia Journal of World Business*, Winter: 17–28.

Roth, M.S. and Romeo J.B. (1992) 'Matching Product Category and Country Image Perceptions', *Journal of International Business Studies* 23: 477–97.

Scherer, F. and Ross, D. (1990) *Industrial Market Structure and Economic Performance*, Chicago: Rand McNally.

Wall, M., Liefeld, J. and Heslop, L.A. (1991) 'Impact of Country-of-Origin Cues on Consumer Judgements in Multi-Cue Situations: A Covariance Analysis', *Journal of the Academy of Marketing Science* 19(2): 105–13.

11 The internationalization process and control style of MNCs: the case of Korean electronics companies

Yeon Hak Kim and Nigel Campbell

INTRODUCTION

As the multinational corporations (MNCs) emerged as the main actors in the international business field, the control mechanisms in the MNC context have attracted considerable academic interest in recent years. Numerous studies have been conducted on issues concerning the relationships between HQ and subunits of an MNC (see Martinez and Jarillo 1989, for a review). However, existing studies have yet to produce a comprehensive explanation of the control mechanisms in the MNC context because of certain limitations. We believe that the limitation of existing studies is that their frameworks are mostly based on a single and narrow perspective on control and thus the validity of their explanations is limited. Another limitation is that they are static in their analysis. Most of the existing studies analyse organizations in a given time without referring to the possibility of dynamic changes. Considering that MNCs are living organizations, a static analysis alone may not be enough to explain control phenomena in MNCs.

To address these issues, first we propose a framework of control processes and control style which can be useful to provide a better understanding of control in the MNC context. Second, we describe and explain the longitudinal change of the internationalization process and control style of an MNC and their relationship with the MNC's long-term performance.

To give an explanation by comparing the changing patterns of control styles in different organizations, we select two Korean electronics companies, GoldStar Corporation[1] and Samsung Electronics Corporation (SEC), for our case companies. These companies are two of the biggest consumer electronics companies in the world outside Japan. They have been developed from small domestic/export firms into MNCs in a relatively short period of time and thus provide us a good basis for explaining the changing patterns of control style and their fit with the environment as the internationalization process goes on.

To gain an understanding of how SEC and GoldStar have changed their control styles, intensive interviews were conducted during January 1992 and May 1993. Altogether forty interviews were conducted, each lasting from one to three hours. In addition, documents and archival records were collected and analysed.

Apart from the introduction, this chapter is composed of three parts. The first part deals with the theoretical framework; the concept of the control process, control styles and their ideal fit with the environment. In the second part, we describe and explain the longitudinal changes of the internationalization process, and the control styles in Korean electronics companies. Finally, in the third part, we summarize the discussion.

THEORETICAL FRAMEWORK

Sub-processes of control

Many different processes are involved in control, thus a single or narrow perspective does not give a complete understanding of these processes. Hence, this chapter separates them into three types – feedforward, feedback and socialization. Feedforward control is linked to the literature on cybernetics (Ashby 1963; Beer 1967). The cybernetic perspective of control is about the nature, location and use of models for control (Berry *et al.* 1991: 117), both those formally defined and those implicitly used by managers. Feedforward control includes such activities as environmental scanning, objective setting, strategy formulation, negotiating business targets and budget preparation. Feedback processes are found in the literature on management control (Anthony 1965). Management control is about the nature of the organizational structure in relation to the location of managerial and operational decisions. Thus, feedback control includes comparing actual performance with budget, reporting, monitoring, reward and punishment.

Some authors writing about control limit their analysis to easily documented feedforward and feedback processes (Simons 1990; Green and Welsh 1988; Lorange *et al.* 1986). Others, such as Maanen and Schein (1979), Doz and Prahalad (1984) and Martinez and Jarillo (1989) stress the importance of the informal and undocumented processes. The nature of these latter processes is influenced by the way managers in the firm are socialized (i.e. how they are recruited, what training they receive and what career paths they follow). Kim (1995) summarized the strategic control processes as in Table 11.1.

Four control styles

To give a better explanation of the changes of control processes, the typology of four control styles is proposed. Control style refers to the balance between the three sub-processes of control in real organizations. This typology is based on two dimensions, the complex-less complex control and the clan-bureaucratic control. Traditionally the dichotomy of

Table 11.1 Three sub-processes of strategic control

Sub-processes	Typical activities
Feedforward process	– environmental scanning – strategy formulation – negotiating business target – budget preparation
Feedback process	– comparing actual performance with budget – reporting – monitoring – reward and punishment
Socialization process	– recruitment – education and training – career paths – communication channels

Source: Modified from Kim 1995: 61.

clan control vs bureaucratic control was widely used (e.g. Jager 1982, 1983; Lebas and Weigenstein 1986; Binberg and Snodgrass 1988; Beechler 1990) to describe the control styles of organizations from different countries. However, it seems that this dichotomy was not comprehensive enough to describe the control styles of many organizations. For instance, there are different types of clans (e.g. family clan and professional clan) and there are different types of bureaucratic processes (e.g. feedforward process and feedback process) and these differences have been ignored in existing studies.

Thus, we suggest a two-by-two matrix of control styles which would give a better representation of control styles in real organizations (see Figure 11.1).

more complex control	*Professional clan control*	*Broad bureaucratic control*
less complex control	*Family clan control*	*Narrow bureaucratic control*

Figure 11.1 Typology of four control styles

A company where wide and common socialization processes among managers from different backgrounds are emphasized is classified as *a professional clan control company*. While a company where the socialization processes are narrow and where a single clan (mostly a family) monopolizes important positions in the company is classified as *a family clan control company*.

A company where both the feedback and feedforward processes are emphasized is classified as *a broad bureaucratic control company*. While a company where only feedback process is emphasized is classified as *a narrow control company*. A brief description of each control style can be drawn as follows:

Family clan control company: A company where socialization processes between different clans are limited and preferential treatment is given to the members of a privileged clan. The privileged clan in this type of company is normally a blood-kinship clan (Alvesson and Lindkvist 1993) and the ties among the clan members are stronger than any other social ties. Thus the co-operation and dedication among the clan members are very strong. This type of company is very common in East Asian countries (e.g. some Korean chaebol[2], Chinese family businesses).

Professional clan control company: A company where wide socialization processes among managers from different backgrounds are emphasized. The relationships between these managers are Economic-co-operative and Socio-integrative (Alvesson and Lindkvist 1993) and wider socialization processes are applied to most of them. The so-called 'Z type' companies identified by Ouchi (1981) are examples of this type. This control style, noted for the shared values and common objectives among managers in the organization, was hailed by many scholars (e.g. Ouchi 1981; Jager 1982, 1983; Lebas and Weigenstein 1986; Binberg and Snodgrass 1988) as the answer to improving the organizational efficiency of Western companies.

Narrow bureaucratic control company: A company where the feedback processes are emphasized as the main control mechanisms. A narrow bureaucratic control company normally focuses on quantifiable and rather short-term performance such as profitability and productivity. The financial control company described in Goold and Campbell (1987) is a typical example of this type.

Broad bureaucratic control company: A company where both the feedback control and feedforward control processes are emphasized as control mechanisms. Since HQ initiates most strategic decisions, a broad bureaucratic control company usually has a large HQ and a large environmental scanning and planning staff. Many MNCs with integrated worldwide operation can be classified as this type.

We proposed four generic types of control styles and described the characteristics of these four styles above. In practice though, the control styles of many companies may lie somewhere in between the four styles. Thus, we propose that these styles are to be used for relative comparison between various companies rather than measuring the absolute control style of a firm.

Environment and control styles: the concept of fit

Having characterized four different control styles, we now examine the fit between the environment and the control styles. Among the many dimensions of environment, the 'uncertainty' dimension has attracted by far the most research interest and is regarded as the most important one (Lawrence and Lorsch 1967). Recently, though, the dimension of 'the need for global integration' has attracted considerable academic interest especially among the so-called 'process school' (Prahalad and Doz 1987). Hence in this study, we look at both the environmental uncertainty and the need for global integration dimensions as important factors to consider in terms of environmental dimensions.

Environmental Uncertainty: Environmental uncertainty refers to three categories of environmental imperatives, i.e. the economic, the technological and the political imperatives (Prahalad and Doz 1987). Although there are many ways to measure the degree of environmental uncertainty most studies based on the contingency perspective (e.g. Lawrence and Lorsch 1967; Miles, Snow and Pfeffer 1974; Snow 1976) use perceptual measures because different firms may perceive the same environmental conditions differently and thus respond with different organizational changes (Sawyer 1993: 290).

In relation to the control style of an organization, it is believed that more uncertain environments require more complex control mechanisms while more stable environments require less complex control mechanisms (Lawrence and Lorsch 1967). Thus, we propose that more complex control styles (i.e. professional clan control or broad bureaucratic control) are suitable for higher environmental uncertainty while less complex control styles (i.e. family clan or narrow bureaucratic control) are suitable for lower environmental uncertainty.

Global Integration: Global integration refers to the centralized management of geographically dispersed activities on an ongoing basis. Managing shipments of parts and sub-assemblies across a network of manufacturing facilities in various countries is an example of integration activities. Global integration arises because of the need to reduce costs and optimize investment. There are different ways of measuring the degree of global integration. However, it is widely agreed that the need for global integration in electronics MNCs is one of the strongest among the MNCs from different industries (e.g. Bartlett and Ghoshal 1989; Kobrin 1991). Hence it is reasonable to assume that the need for global integration for Korean electronics companies has increased as they developed from a domestic company to MNCs.

When an MNC is operating in an industry like electronics which requires strong global integration, it should strengthen the unified and formalized rules to integrate the global operations. Therefore, bureaucratic control, either narrow or broad, seems a suitable style. On the other hand, when the need for local responsiveness is strong, the formalized rules may be limited in their ability to control the subsidiary. Hence, in this case, HQ needs to decentralize decision making to respond to local circumstances. Instead, the HQ should strengthen the socialization processes of the local managers. Thus, clan control, either family clan or professional, should be a better

Environmental
uncertainty

high	*Professional clan control*	*Broad bureaucratic control*
low	*Family clan control*	*Narrow bureaucratic control*

local responsiveness   global integration

Figure 11.2 Environmental dimensions and suitable control styles

control style. From the above discussion, the fit between environment and control styles can be diagrammed as in Figure 11.2.

THE INTERNATIONALIZATION PROCESS AND CONTROL STYLES

So far, we have described a typology of four control styles and proposed that these control styles are suitable for certain environmental circumstances. To test the proposition, we need to know how the business environment and control styles of Korean electronics companies have been changed. Based on such observations, we can determine whether the control styles of Korean electronics companies fit the environment.

Internationalization process of Korean electronics companies

To understand how the business environment and control styles of Korean electronics companies have changed, it is imperative to know how the Korean electronics companies have been developed into the present form of MNCs. Thus, we briefly describe the internationalization process of those companies from their domestic firm stage to the MNC stage (see Kim 1995, for a more detailed description).

The description of the internationalization process of Korean electronics companies given in this chapter is based on the Uppsala model illuminated by Johanson and Wiedersheim-Paul (1975)[3].

Stage 1: No regular export activities (domestic firm stage). There were no regular export activities at this stage. Exporting, if there was any, did not comprise a significant part of the firm's total turnover. This stage began in 1958 when GoldStar was established and lasted till the early 1970s. Since SEC was established in 1969, eleven years later than GoldStar, on the condition that it should export the majority of its products for the first few years, SEC skipped the domestic firm stage which GoldStar had experienced. As the business was a monopoly and the domestic market was strongly protected, the environmental uncertainty was low. On the other hand, the business produced solely for the domestic market and thus, there was no need for global integration.

Stage 2: Export via agents (limited export firm stage). Korean electronics companies at this stage exported mainly through independent agents. Export activities were very much focused on the US market and most exports were OEM based. In their limited export firm stage which lasted from the early 1970s till the late 1970s, GoldStar and SEC adopted a similar strategy and structure. Both companies adopted the strategy focused on OEM-based export to the using agents. In terms of IB structure, both companies adopted a functional structure. Hence, they had an export department attached to the marketing division. At this stage, GoldStar exported about 30% of its product lines while SEC exported almost 70% of its production. However, almost 100% of these exports were OEM based.

Since both companies had secured stable customers (e.g. a big US retailer such as K-Mart), the environmental uncertainty was low. And as the export operations were administered by agents, there was no need for global integration.

Stage 3: Establishment of overseas sales units (export firm stage). Korean electronics companies started to build their own global marketing networks from the late 1970s. At this stage, their export markets were diversified into other developed countries and they began to make efforts to export own-brand products. At their export firm stage which lasted till the early 1980s, both companies adopted a similar strategy. They started to establish their own sales subsidiaries and promoted own-brand exports. However, the majority of exports was still handled by agents and the proportion of own-brand exports was less than 30%. In terms of IB structure, both GoldStar and SEC adopted an international division structure. Since both companies enjoyed a comfortable duopoly in the protected domestic market while a majority of their exports went to the based on OEM, the environmental uncertainty was still quite low. But as the export market diversified and both companies began to build their own overseas sales subsidiaries, the need for global integration increased significantly.

Stage 4: Establishment of overseas manufacturing units in developed countries (early MNC stage). Korean electronics companies started to build production facilities abroad from the early 1980s. But at this stage, their FDIs were limited to only a few developed countries so as to minimize the possibility of trade conflict in these countries. Thus, the motives for the FDI were more political than economic or technological.

At their early MNC stage which lasted till the late 1980s, both Gold-Star and SEC started to build their manufacturing subsidiaries in the USA and the EC, which were still their main export markets. At this stage, the proportion of branded exports of both companies reached about 50% of their total overseas sales. In terms of IB structure, both companies adopted an international structure. Hence, the internationalization process of both companies at this stage was almost identical. As the trade conflict between Korea and the developed countries intensified from the early

1980s, the environmental uncertainty for Korean electronics companies increased significantly. At the same time, as the Korean electronics companies started to build their own production plants abroad, the need for global integration was also high.

Stage 5: Establishment of overseas manufacturing units all over the world (MNC stage). Korean electronics MNCs invested massively all over the world and economic and technological imperatives drove the FDI decision making. This stage started in the late 1980s. Since then both companies have built manufacturing subsidiaries not only in developed countries, but in LDCs too. At this stage, their export markets were considerably diversified and the proportion of branded exports rose to 55% (GoldStar) and 60% (SEC) by the early 1990s. In terms of IB structure, both companies changed their structure from an international structure to a global product-division structure. Therefore, the internationalization process of both companies at this stage was also almost identical. Competition in the global consumer electronics industry became very intensified while the Korean market was being liberalized. Thus, both the environmental uncertainty and the need for global integration became very high.

As described so far, the internationalization processes and IB structures of GoldStar and SEC have been broadly similar except for the very early stage and thus the desirable control style at each stage was also identical. Table 11.2 summarizes the internationalization process and the desirable

Table 11.2 Internationalization process and desirable control styles of the Korean electronics companies

Stages	Internationalization process	Environmental uncertainty	Global integration	Suitable control style
Domestic firm	– focused on domestic sales – no regular export – functional structure	low	low	family clan control
Limited export firm	– OEM based export via agents – export mainly to US – functional structure	low	low	family clan control
Export firm	– brand export by own sales subs – export to US and EC – international structure	low	high	narrow bureaucratic control
Early MNC	– FDI to developed countries – export mainly to US and EC – international structure	high	high	broad bureaucratic control
MNC	– FDI all over the world – export to diversified market – global product division structure	very high	very high	broad bureaucratic control

* Domestic firm stage applies to GoldStar only.

control style of each stage in the Korean electronics companies based on the above discussion.

Fit between environment and control styles

We described the internationalization process of Korean electronics companies and the suitable control style at each stage. Thus, we propose that if a company has adopted suitable control styles as the environment changes, it should have performed better than a company which failed to adopt suitable control styles consistently. To examine this proposition, we need to know how Korean electronics companies have performed throughout their internationalization processes.

Table 11.3 briefly summarizes the performance of GoldStar and SEC for the past twenty years. Sales, on the growth of which Korean companies focus most, have grown by a factor of 680 in the case of SEC, while GoldStar's figure is 137. The total assets of SEC have grown by a factor of almost 660, compared with GoldStar's 170. The net profit of SEC has also grown far faster than that of GoldStar. In 1974, SEC was less than a half the size of GoldStar in terms of total assets, sales and net profit. However, SEC overtook GoldStar in terms of gross sales and net profit in 1984, and total assets in 1988. And the gap between the two companies has increased ever since. Therefore, we can safely say that overall, SEC has performed better than GoldStar for the past twenty years. SEC's consis-

Table 11.3 The growth of GoldStar and SEC (thousand million won)

	GoldStar			SEC		
	Total assets	*Net profit*	*Sales*	*Total assets*	*Net profit*	*Sales*
Stage 2						
1974	21.5	2.0	31.5	10.0	0.6	13.4
1976	58.9	2.6	69.2	38.0	1.4	41.0
Stage 3						
1978	140.0	5.7	170.7	112.4	4.4	159.1
1980	257.6	−9.1	253.0	255.8	−5.5	233.6
Stage 4						
1982	355.1	9.6	454.3	387.4	5.1	426.4
1984	718.0	10.5	1,295.6	607.7	**25.1**	**1,351.6**
1986	1,124.1	20.7	1,539.6	872.7	31.6	1,958.9
Stage 5						
1988	2,228.6	18.2	2,825.3	**2,462.0**	101.8	3,028.3
1990	2,614.6	33.3	2,984.0	4,057.2	73.0	4,511.7
1992	3,436.7	26.5	3,787.4	6,326.6	72.4	6,102.7
1993	3,652.1	65.6	4,323.5	6,659.4	154.6	8,154.8

Source: Company documents, GoldStar and SEC.

tently better performance is also documented in other studies (Kim and Campbell 1995; Bloom 1994).

Applying our proposition, we can posit that SEC's control styles have attained a better fit with the environment than those of GoldStar for the past twenty years. To test the proposition, we compared the actual control styles of GoldStar and SEC with the desirable control style as their internationalization processes deepen.

At the domestic firm stage which applies only to GoldStar, the company's control style was one of family clan control. Since GoldStar was established by two families, the Koos and the Huhs, members of both families became massively involved in management and thus its control style was a family clan control[4]. Since both environmental uncertainty and the need for global integration were low, the family clan control style was the viable one for GoldStar.

At the limited export firm stage which lasted till the late 1970s, the family clan control style was still viable because environmental uncertainty and the need for global integration were still low. In GoldStar, large family groups were still involved in management, while the bureaucratic control processes were not well developed. Hence its control style was still one of family clan control[5]. SEC started its business at this stage. As a newcomer, SEC also appointed family members as CEO and to some senior positions. SEC's control style at this stage was also a family clan type. Hence, the control style of both companies did fit the environment. At the export firm stage which lasted till the early 1980s, the desirable control style was shifted to a narrow bureaucratic control. However, GoldStar had yet to introduce a well-established feedback control system. The change which happened in GoldStar was that it emphasized socialization processes and recruited a large professional management group. Thus its control style moved closer to a professional clan control. However, since the top management were still family members, while the bureaucratic control system was not yet well established, it was still classified as a family clan control company[6]. On the other hand, as the company grew bigger and the need for professional management increased, SEC quickly appointed professional managers to top management and family members were withdrawn[7]. In addition, it introduced strong feedback control processes. SEC was the first company in Korea which introduced advanced management techniques (e.g. management information system (MIS), profit centre and management by objectives (MBO)). By establishing strong budgeting and feedback control systems, SEC's control style was shifted to a narrow bureaucratic control which was a good fit with the environment at this stage.

At the early MNC stage which lasted till the late 1980s, the desirable control was a broad bureaucratic control style. However, GoldStar still kept its family dominated control style and failed to establish strong bureaucratic control systems. Thus, its control style was still a family clan control, while SEC was strengthening its feedback control systems. The control style of SEC at this stage was still a narrow bureaucratic control, while the desirable style has been shifted to a broad bureaucratic control. Thus, neither company has the suitable control style at this stage although SEC's control style was closer to a broad bureaucratic control.

At the MNC stage which began in the late 1980s, the desirable control is a broad bureaucratic control. Since the late 1980s, GoldStar has been decentralizing its decision making, while emphasizing formalization and socialization. However, since many family members are still involved in management, its control style is still of the family clan control variety[8]. On the other hand, SEC centralized its strategic decision-making process to cope with the need for global integration whilst still keeping strong feedback control processes. Hence, its control style is now a broad bureaucratic control which better fits the environment. The changes of control styles of GoldStar and SEC following their internationalization processes are summarized in Table 11.4.

Our findings show that although GoldStar and SEC have been experiencing a similar internationalization process, they have adopted different control styles since their export firm stage before eventually converging in terms of control styles. Our findings also show that although both companies have grown very rapidly compared to electronics companies from other parts of the world (see Campbell and Kim 1994), SEC's growth rate has been much higher than that of GoldStar. As a relative latecomer, SEC was far behind GoldStar till the mid-1970s, but started to catch up in the late 1970s and overtook GoldStar in 1984. Since then SEC has outperformed GoldStar. Then why has the performance of SEC been consistently better than GoldStar for the last twenty or so years? Can we explain the reasons as other than their control styles? Factors generally regarded as affecting the performance of a firm are: strategy and organizational form, product portfolio, financing, technology and size. Thus we also look at these factors in both companies.

Table 11.4 The internationalization process and changes of control styles of Korean electronics companies

Stages	Changes in control style	
	GoldStar	**SEC**
Domestic firm	family clan (v)	–
Limited export firm	family clan (v)	family clan (v)
Export firm	family clan	narrow bureaucratic (v)
Early MNC	family clan	narrow bureaucratic
MNC	family clan	wider bureaucratic (v)

* Domestic firm stage applies to GoldStar only.
** (v) denotes 'suitability to environment'.

Factors affecting performance

(a) *strategy and organizational form*: it is widely agreed that the strategy and structure of GoldStar and SEC have been very similar for the last twenty or so years (Bloom 1994; Kim and Campbell 1995).

(b) *product portfolio*: both companies have had almost identical product lines. They have produced home appliances, industrial electronics and now they are broadening their product lines into computers, telecommunications equipment and semiconductors.

(c) *financing*: GoldStar and SEC belong to two of the largest chaebol, the LG group and the Samsung group respectively. Both groups have had similar business portfolio and financing patterns, and thus the way they financed their strategic businesses in groups such as electronics has been broadly similar for the last twenty or so years.

(d) *technology*: in terms of technology development, GoldStar had technological advantages as the first comer, which somehow eroded in recent years.

(e) *size*: GoldStar was twice as big as SEC twenty years ago, but is now only about half the size.

All these factors shows that GoldStar was originally in a better position or at least similar position compared to SEC. Thus, they do not explain SEC's superior performance. The above discussion strongly suggests that the performance difference between GoldStar and SEC is due to the fact that both companies have different control styles. In other words, SEC's consistently better performance can be explained by its control style which has been generally a better fit to the environment in recent years.

SUMMARY AND DISCUSSION

In this chapter, we tried to fulfil two aims. The first aim was to try to provide a new framework for control mechanisms in the MNC context and the second aim was to give a better and fuller understanding of control by describing the longitudinal changes of control styles and their suitability to the environment. To do so, we developed a typology of control styles. Each control style is posited to be a good fit to a particular environmental circumstance and the suitable control style changes as the environmental circumstance changes. To describe the changing patterns, we investigated and compared desirable control styles and actual control styles of two Korean electronics companies, GoldStar and SEC, as their internationalization process evolved. In terms of a new framework of control styles, we proposed a typology of four control styles; a family clan control, a professional clan control, a narrow bureaucratic control and a wider bureaucratic control style.

Having set up a new typology of control styles, we investigated the longitudinal changes of control styles and their suitability to a constantly changing environment. From the investigation on the changes of control styles in Korean electronics companies, we found that SEC has been willing to change its control style to respond to environmental changes, and its control style has been generally more suitable for the environment if not always than GoldStar's. On the other hand, GoldStar for a long time stuck with family clan control and proved unable to shift its control style even though the environmental circumstance had changed. As GoldStar and SEC have adopted a broadly similar strategy and structure (Kim and Campbell 1995) for the past twenty or so years, it seems that SEC's better performance should be explained by the close fit between its control style and the rapidly changing environment in which it continues to internationalize.

The most enduring theory in organization studies in recent years is the contingency theory which emphasizes that there is a strong relationship between the environment, organizational strategy and/or structure and performance. Thus, contingency theorists argue that if an organization's strategy and/or structure fits its environment, the organization should perform better than other organizations whose strategies and/or structures do not fit the environment. However, this theory does not explain the performance difference between companies like GoldStar and SEC which adopt similar strategy and structure in similar circumstance.

We believe that the best way to address this issue was to investigate and compare the changes of control styles as those companies internationalized. By doing so, we could understand how their control styles have changed, whether their control styles fit closely with the environment and thus, why one company's performance is better than another.

NOTES

1 Changed its name into 'LG Electronics Co.' in early 1995. However, the company still uses 'GoldStar' as its brand name.
2 Korean-type conglomerates which, by Korean Law, have total assets of more than 300 billion Korean won ($\approx$ US$370 million).
3 The Uppsala model depicts internationalization of a firm as a four-stage process: no regular export activities (stage 1, domestic firm stage); export via independent agents (stage 2, limited export firm stage); establishment of overseas sales subsidiary (stage 3, export firm stage); establishment of overseas manufacturing units (stage 4, MNC stage). However, since Korean electronics companies have two distinctive FDI stages, stage 4 is divided into two in this study (i.e. early MNC stage and MNC stage).
4 Seven out of eleven founding members of GoldStar were from the Koos and the Huhs.
5 Four out of eight founding members of SEC were the owner's family members and SEC's first CEO was the owner's in-law.
6 Although the majority of executive managers were professional managers at this stage, the chairman and president were still family members.
7 Since its establishment, only two out of nine past CEO's of SEC were family

members including the first CEO. And no other family members have ever occupied a significant position in the company.
8 In 1993, five out of seventeen GoldStar board members were the founder's of family.

BIBLIOGRAPHY

Alvesson, M. and Lindkvist, L. (1993) 'Transaction Costs, Clans and Corporate Culture', *Journal of Management Studies* 30: 427–52.

Anthony, R.N. (1965) *Planning and Control Systems: A Framework for Analysis*, Boston: Graduate School of Business Administration, Harvard University.

Ashby, W.R. (1963) *An Introduction to Cybernetics* (3rd edition), London: Chapman & Hall Ltd.

Bartlett, C.A. and Ghoshal, G. (1989) *Managing across Borders: The Transnational Solution*, Boston: Harvard Business School Press.

Beechler, S. (1990) *International Management Control in Multinational Corporations: The Case of Japanese Consumer Electronics Subsidiaries in Southeast Asia*, unpublished doctoral thesis, University of Michigan.

Beechler, S. and Yang, J.Z. (1994) 'The Transfer of Japanese Style Management to American Subsidiaries: Contingencies, Constraints and Competencies', *Journal of International Business Studies* Fall: 467–91.

Beer, S. (1967) *Cybernetics and Management* (2nd edition), London: The English Universities Press Ltd.

Berry, A.J., Loughton, E. and Otley, D. (1991) 'Control in Financial Service Company (RIF): a Case Study', *Management Accounting Research* 2: 109–39.

Binberg, J.G. and Snodgrass, C. (1988) 'Culture and Control: A Field Study', *Accounting, Organizations and Society* 13: 447–64.

Bloom, M. (1994) 'Globalisation of the Korean Electronics Industry: A Chandlerian Perspective', in Helmut Schutte (ed.), *The Global Competitiveness of the Asian Firm*, London: Macmillan Press.

Campbell, N. and Kim, Y.H. (1994) 'Korea's Electronics Giants: The Case Against National Management Style', paper presented at 14th Strategic Management Society conference, Paris.

Doz, Y.L. and Prahalad, C.K. (1984) 'Patterns of Strategic Control in MNCs', *Journal of International Business Studies*, Fall: 57–72.

GoldStar Co., internal documents and Annual Reports.

Goold, M. and Campbell, A. (1987) *Strategies and Styles*, Oxford: Basil Blackwell.

Green, S.G. and Welsh, G. (1988) 'Cybernetics and Dependence: Reframing the Control Concept', *Academy of Management Review* 13: 287–301.

Jaeger, A.M. (1982) 'Contrasting Control Modes in the Multinational Corporation: Theory, Practice and Implications', *International Studies of Management and Organisation* 11: 59–77.

—— (1983) 'The Transfer of Organisational Culture Overseas: An Approach to Control in the Multinational Corporation', *Journal of International Business Studies* Fall: 91–105.

Johanson, J. and Widersheim-Paul, F. (1975) 'The Internationalization of the Firm: Four Swedish Cases', *Journal of Management Studies* 12: 305–22.

Kim, Y.H. (1995) *Strategic Control in Multinational Corporations: The Case of Korean Electronics Companies*, unpublished doctoral thesis, University of Manchester.

Kim, Y.H. and Campbell, N. (1995) 'Strategic Control in Korean MNCs', *Management International Review*, Special Issue 1: 95-108.

Kobrin, S.J. (1991) 'An Empirical Analysis of the Determinants of Global Integration', *Strategic Management Journal* 11: 17–31.

Lawrence, P.R. and Lorsch, J.W. (1967) *Organization and Environment*, Boston: Harvard Business School.

Lebas, M. and Weigenstein, J. (1986) 'Management Control: The Roles of Rule, Markets and Culture', *Journal of Management Studies* 23: 259–72.

Lorange, P., Scott Morton, M.F. and Ghoshal, S. (1986) *Strategic Control Systems*, St Paul: West Publishing Company.

Maanen, J.V. and Schein, E.H. (1979) 'Towards a Theory of Organizational Socialization', *Research in Organizational Behaviour* 1: 209–64.

Martinez, J.I. and Jarillo, J.C. (1989) 'The Evolution of Research on Coordination Mechanisms in MNCs', *Journal of International Business Studies*, Fall: 489–514.

Miles, R.E., Snow, C.C., and Pfeffer, J. (1974) 'Organisation-Environment: Concepts and Issues', *Industrial Relations* 13: 385–404.

Ouchi, W.G. (1981) *Theory Z: How American Business can Meet the Japanese Challenge*, Reading, MA: Addison-Wesley Publishing Co.

Prahalad, C.K. and Doz, Y.L. (1987) *The Multinational Mission*, New York: Free Press.

Samsung Electronics Co., internal documents and Annual Reports.

Sawyer, O.O. (1993) 'Environmental Uncertainty and Environmental Scanning Activities of Nigerian Manufacturing Executives: A Comparative Analysis', *Strategic Management Journal* 14: 287–99.

Simons, R. (1990) 'The Role of Management Control Systems in Creating Competitive Advantage Perspectives', *Accounting, Organization and Society* 15: 127–44.

Snow, C.C. (1976) 'The Role of Managerial Perceptions in Organisational Adaptation: An Exploratory Study', *Academy of Management Proceedings*, pp. 249–55.

12 The recent changes in PRC's economic development strategy and their impact on Foreign Direct Investment in China[1]

Chen Changzheng

INTRODUCTION

Attracting and utilizing foreign investment has become the key issue in China's open-door policy since the early 1980s. Foreign direct investment (FDI) is one of the most important and effective ways for China to develop trading relationships. China has already taken the lead in the South-east Asian developing countries in absorbing FDI with an accumulated total FDI of over US$95 billion by the end of 1994.[2] The role of FDI in China's economic development and in China's economic development strategies is of considerable importance and significance for foreigners with interests in China's market: a trade mission[3] with both money and goods in hand is more likely to achieve its goals than one with intentions only of selling to China.

This chapter will look at the formation of and changes in China's economic development strategy since the early 1980s, in relation to the role of FDI in China's economic development. These changes and the new industrial policy will be highlighted through an analysis of China's open-door policy and recent efforts to build a socialist market economy under a market-oriented legal system. The focus of the chapter is a discussion of the impact of these changes on FDI in China.

CHINA'S ECONOMIC DEVELOPMENT POLICY AND FDI THROUGH THE 1980s

The 1978 national congress of the CPC (the Communist Party of China) ushered in a new era in reform and, in particular, the open-door policy. China set itself the goals of transforming the country into a powerful, modern, socialist state by the year 2000 and of quadrupling its GNP. In pursuing these goals, reform of the macro-economic control system and opening up to the outside world have been the most significant instruments. One of the concrete embodiments of reform was the growth of inward FDI through preferential treatment since the early 1980s.

Reforming the macro-economic control system

The disadvantages of a highly centralized planned economic control system were revealed during the rapid economic development of the early 1980s. Therefore, reform of the traditional planned-economy became the key issue for China. However, during the first ten years of reform, mainly because of political disputes within the CPC, final goals and methods for reforming the economic control system were not clearly defined. As a result, reform during this period was under tight control but characterized by regional differences and experimentation.

The major policy issues and achievements in economic reform during this period included:

- Gradual decentralization of the planned-economy control system;
- Encouragement of market forces;
- Development of forms of ownership other than state and collective;
- Construction of a new legal system.

While certain measures of reform achieved great success and brought obvious benefits to the Chinese people, some deep-rooted problems in macro-economic control emerged, forcing the CPC finally to give up the planned-economy system and adopt the market concept in the early 1990s.

Opening-up to the outside world

China's open-door policy, by its nature, is a policy regarding the degree of freedom of resources, services and exchange of information across China's border, with the issue of foreign investment at the centre. Under the control of the planned-economy system, the open-door policy was characterized by experiment during 1980s. The total influx of foreign capital, including foreign loans and FDI, was under tight control of the Chinese central government.

Table 12.1 shows the schedule of the opening of China's market in order to attract and absorb FDI since the early 1980s. The initial pattern was established in 1980: four small Special Economic Zones (SEZ) were established along the southern coast. For the first time FDI was encouraged and quickly replaced foreign indirect investment as the major means of attracting foreign investment.

The year 1984 witnessed the acceleration of this process. The open areas spread first from south to north along the coast-line during the late 1980s, and since 1990, from east to west along the Yangtze River corridor, changing in nature from a series of small zones to vast areas with large-scale development.

Table 12.1 The process of opening China's market to inward FDI

Time	Economically opened areas
1980	Establishing Shenzhen, Zhuhai, Shantou, and Xiamen Special Economic Zones along the south China coast
1984	Opening 14 port cities along the whole coast, namely Tianjin, Shanghai, Dalian, Qinhuangdao, Yantai, Qingdao, Lianyungang, Nantogn, Ningbo, Wenzhou, Fuzhou, Guangzhou, Shanjian, and Beihai
1985	Opening the Yangtze River delta, Pearl River delta, and Xia-Zhang-Quan Triangle; partly open the East Liao Peninsula and East Jiao Peninsula
1988	Enlarging the open areas in the East Liao and East Jiao Peninsulas
1990	Establishing Pudong New Area Special Economic Zone in Shanghai
1992	Opening 13 frontier cities along the north-east and south-west borders, all the provincial capitals, and 5 more cities along the Yangtze corridor

Table 12.2 China: the growth of GNP since 1980
(RMB 1 billion yuan, current price)

1980	1985	1988	1989	1990	1991	1992	1993	1994
447.0	855.7	1,406.8	1,599.3	1,769.5	2,023.6	2,437.8	3,134.2	4,380*

* See note 3.
Source: *1994 Statistical Yearbook of China*.

FDI and China's continuing development miracle

In the 1980s, China began an era of rapid economic modernization and steady expansion of its international economic activities. As a result of reform and the open-door policy, notable gains in economic development were achieved, reflected in the fast upgrading of technologies in manufacturing industries and in high growth rates of both foreign trade and the economy as a whole.

From 1980 to 1990, China's real gross national product (GNP) expanded from RMB 447.0 billion yuan to RMB 1,769.5 billion yuan[4], an average annual increase of more than 10% (Table 12.2).

During the decade, the role of FDI in economic development changed significantly. In the early 1980s, the scale of inward foreign investment was very limited. The major volume of foreign investment came from foreign loans which had been tightly controlled by government at different levels to restrict the scale of foreign borrowing. However, the Chinese government faced problems with insufficiency of foreign loans accompanied by a rapid increase in demand for foreign investment capital. The initial success of the SEZs showed the worth of FDI. Continued efforts to improve the investment environment, adjusting the open-door policy, and enlarging the scale of opportunities have resulted in a dramatic increase in inward FDI, and an increasingly important role of FDI in China's economic development. Since the mid-1980s, actively attracting and utilizing FDI has been a major plank in China's development strategy.

Shenzhen SEZ: achievements and problems in miniature

As one of the four SEZs established in the first phase of opening-up, Shenzhen is a perfect miniature reflecting the whole picture of achievements and problems in China's development in the 1980s.

Radical economic reform and special region-oriented preferential treatment caused Shenzhen's economy to develop with leaps and bounds. Within fourteen years, Shenzhen grew from a small town of 200 factories and a mere annual industrial output of RMB 70 million to a prosperous modern city with more than 10,000 enterprises and an annual industrial output valued at RMB 48 billion, an 800-fold increase.[5] The engines of successful economic development can be summarized as follows:

- radical reform of the economic control system;
- open-door policy;
- influx of FDI lured by preferential treatment.

However, the above-mentioned achievements were not achieved without the sacrifice of economic benefits in other regions in the country. In fact, the fast development of Shenzhen was largely based on a substantial inflow of economic resources from not only overseas but also domestic markets. It can be argued that some of the privileges should be reviewed: for example, preferential treatment of foreign exchange and currency holding caused many existing companies previously outside Shenzhen to relocate their export/import businesses to take advantage of flexibility and lower transaction costs. Overall the experiment brought incredible business benefits to the coastal SEZs in south China, but in so doing revealed a striking contrast between the old and new systems illustrating most of the major problems in China's economic development since reform:

- conflicts between the low efficiency of the planned economic control system and the demands of quick response from the market;
- conflicts between the old legislative systems based on a highly centralized economic control system and the requirements of a market-oriented system;
- a striking contrast between the poor performance of the state-owned enterprises and the performance of enterprises under other types of ownership;
- unbalanced development between the opened and unopened regions.

Some of these problems are illustrated by Figure 12.1 and Tables 12.3 and 12.4.

(GNP per head 1991, China = 100)

	0	50	100	150	200	250	300	350	400
Shanghai									
Beijing									
Guangdong									
China									
Sichuan									
Guangxi									
Guizhou									

Figure 12.1 The unbalanced development between different regions in PRC
Source: *1992 Statistical Yearbook of China.*

Table 12.3 1988–93: indices of gross output values of industry showing the unbalanced development between four groups of enterprises with different ownership in PRC
(Preceding year = 100)

	1988	1989	1990	1991	1992	1993	Average
National Total	120.8	108.5	107.8	114.8	127.5	128.0	117.9
State-owned	112.6	103.9	102.9	108.6	112.4	105.7	107.7
Collective-owned	128.2	110.5	109.0	118.4	139.3	135.9	123.6
Individual-owned	147.3	123.8	121.1	125.3	152.9	167.9	139.7
Foreign-funded* and other ownership	161.5	142.7	139.3	150.1	164.9	186.5	167.1

* Including Hong Kong-, Macao- and Taiwan-funded enterprises.
Source: *1994 Statistical Yearbook of China.*

Encouraged by the success of the SEZs but noting the warnings of the new problems, the Chinese government realized that there was no way to achieve further success without complete reform of the economic control system and full implementation of the open-door policy.

THE NEW INDUSTRIAL POLICY AND FDI IN THE 1990s

Background to the new policy

The political tragedy and a sharp economic decline in 1989 put pressure on the Chinese government to redouble its efforts to reform and liberalize.

Table 12.4 Values of industry output (enterprises with independent accounting systems), 1993. Grouped by ownership (RMB 1 billion yuan)

	1993	*Percentage*
National total	3,969.30	100
State-owned enterprises	2,208.79	55.6
Collective-owned enterprises	1,188.84	29.9
Stock ownership enterprises	146.06	3.7
Foreign-funded enterprises*	361.41	9.1

* Including Hong Kong-, Macao- and Taiwan-funded enterprises.
Source: 1994 Statistical Yearbook of China, p. 378.

Radical reform and further opening in the early 1990s

The years 1990 and 1992 stood as two milestones in the development of China's new strategy. In 1990 the opening took place of Pudong in Shanghai, a key step in opening the Yangtze corridor – the most important economic belt in the country. In 1992, the former CCP leader Deng Xiaoping made an inspection tour to south China, and launched a campaign for further reform and liberalization. In the same year, the 14th National Congress of CPC made it clear that the goal for the reform of the country's economic system was to establish a socialist market economy. Theoretically and practically, it was a great breakthrough. The shift to the market economy laid the cornerstone for restructuring the frame of economic legislation and development policies, and for reformation of the whole economy and society. Since then, a campaign has been sweeping across the entire country to speed up reform and reconstruction. The channels for foreign capital have been widened and a foreign investment surge has taken place. China's economy has been roaring ahead at double-digit figures. GNP expanded from RMB 1,769.5 billion yuan in 1990 to RMB 4,380 billion yuan in 1994.

1991–3: the great breakthrough of FDI

The reforms in the early 1990s resulted in a great leap forward in China's utilization of FDI. Adoption of the concept of the market economy has paved the road for a large scale of influx of FDI, associated with various Western business concepts and practices. Within 1992 alone, foreign investment increased tenfold to that of the 1980s. Both the number of newly-approved foreign-funded enterprises[6] and the amount of contractual FDI surpassed the total of the thirteen years before 1992, and for the first time, the amount of actually-utilized FDI in 1992 exceeded foreign loans[7].

Foreign-funded enterprises have made a great breakthrough in terms of the scale of investment and the scope of management. For the country as a whole in 1993, foreign investment in China reached its highest level ever with an increase of 91.5% over 1992. During the year actually-utilized FDI took a 12.5% share of total investment in fixed assets for the whole country, compared with 7.7% in 1992 and 4.2% in 1991. By the end of 1993, more than US$60 billion of accumulated FDI had been poured into China[8].

FDI: contributions vs. growing problems

In the fourteen years since reform, FDI has played an important role in:

- bringing in foreign capital to support fast economic growth;
- bringing in high- and new-technologies to help upgrade China's industry;
- changing a self-sufficiency economy into an export-oriented one.

Foreign-funded enterprises have become one of the main forces in China's economic reconstruction, and have made considerable contributions to Chinese economic development. The obvious social and economic benefits of foreign-funded enterprises are manifested in various sectors, and their contributions to modernization and internationalization of capital are growing constantly.

For example, up to the end of 1993, among 167,500 approved foreign funded enterprises, 83 thousand in operation have created an industrial output valued at more than RMB 360 billion yuan, and a total volume of import and export valued at US$ 67 billion, accounting for 11% of national industrial output and one third of the volume of imports and exports in the PRC, respectively[9].

In Beijing, by the end of May 1994, 2,236 foreign-funded enterprises employed 234,000 local people. The total output value of these enterprises reached 10.64 billion yuan, representing 15.6% of the city's total. They paid RMB788 million yuan in taxes, excluding tariffs, or 18.8% of the city's total industrial and commercial taxes[10].

In recent years, there have been increasing concerns about the inadequate inflow of high and new technology into the country. For example, while China has been advancing in the international market with remarkable trading growth, her main exports are non-capital goods such as native products, light industrial goods and textiles. Machinery and electronics account for only one-fourth of the country's average annual export volume.

In addition, strengths of foreign-funded enterprises have been exerting additional pressure on the state-owned enterprises, many of which lack the strength to meet the challenge of the market, because of, for example inefficient management, a heavy burden of higher taxation and social security responsibilities.

Therefore, there is an urgent need to re-examine and adjust the country's development policy, taking into account not only the need for rapid expansion but also the need for sustainable, balanced development with adequate considerations for stable social development and protection for the growth of national industries.

The new industrial policy of the 1990s

In 1994 a critical change took place in Chinese FDI policy from regional preference to industrial preference.

The State Planning Commission (SPC) accelerated its work on formulating a nationally unified industrial policy to guide the restructuring of industries within the whole country. In April 1994, the first version was approved and announced by the State Council. One of the main aims of the policy was to adjust the role of FDI in economic development. The main points include:

- continuous strengthening of agriculture as a foundation for expansion of the rural economy;
- building of more basic industry, so as to ease the serious lack of basic industrial products and infrastructure;
- acceleration of the development of the mechanical and electronic engineering industries, the petrochemical industry, the automobile industry and the construction industry, so as to promote all-round revitalization of the national economy;
- rational readjustment of the structure of foreign economic relations and trade, so as to increase China's competitiveness in world markets;
- quickening the pace of development of high- and new-technology industries, so as to support the development of newly-emerging industries and new products;
- continued development of the service sector, at the same time optimizing industrial structure and location with respect to distribution;
- the coastal areas in the eastern part of the country should vigorously develop an export orientation, concentrating on the development of industries and products that yield high added value, earn more foreign exchange, use advanced technology, consume less energy and raw material, and make use of more foreign capital and resources.

National industrial policy is export-oriented with balanced development of labour-intensive products and technology- and capital-intensive products. It is also clear that development of the Yangtze River corridor will stress financial, technological and large-scale industries rather than labour-intensive industries.

Since the strategy was announced, the Chinese government has been accelerating its work on formulating complementary policies. Policies for several major industries were developed. For example, on 19 February 1994, the SPC issued a series of government policies for the automotive industry, which were further approved by the State Council and published on 3 July 1994.

Policy guidelines for overseas investment in China were also announced, first in the form of provisional regulations, then approved by the State

Council and published in June 1995. These will reinforce Chinese governmental control over FDI in the coming years.

Government priorities for inward foreign investment will be agriculture, infrastructure, communications, energy, transportation and raw materials. Encouragement will also be given to projects which:

- improve produce performance and quality;
- save energy and raw materials;
- manufacture equipment and new materials that are clearly in demand;
- develop new techniques and equipment for the more efficient use of resources or renewable resources, and prevent and control pollution;
- produce raw materials and components for current products;
- speed up the technical upgrading of large state-owned enterprises; and
- make good use of labour and resources in western China in line with the state industrial policies.

Foreign investment in finance, foreign trade, transportation and service will also be gradually introduced and expanded on a trial basis. To implement the policy governing overseas investment, China will take the following measures:

- Build a market-oriented legal system and provide incentive measures, such as favourable tax policy (see Table 12.5 below).
- Financial support. In terms of domestic bank loans, mature FDI projects in above-mentioned sectors will receive priority treatment.
- Comprehensive compensation assessment. Since the investment required is large and the payback period long, the Chinese Government will allow foreign investment projects in railways, roads and bridges to widen their scope in order to undertake some high-return projects.

Building the market-oriented economic legislative system

The Second Session of the 6th National People's Congress adopted the 'Law of the PRC on Joint Ventures Using Chinese and Foreign Investment' on 1 July 1979. This was the first law of its kind on the use of foreign

Table 12.5 Part of new laws passed or coming into effect in 1994

Name	Passed	Came into effect
Foreign Trade Law		1 July
Labour Law	5 July	
Urban Real Estate Management Law		5 July
Company Law		1 July
Audit Law	31 August	
Arbitration Law	31 August	
Advertisement Law	27 October	

investment. Since then, China's use of foreign capital and legislation on foreign economic activity have been moving forward, hand in hand. China has made considerable progress in this legislation over the past fifteen years and has developed a whole series of laws and regulations from scratch. The package of reforms since the end of 1993 are summarized below.

(A) The taxation system reform

To establish a new system of 'tax sharing' between central and provincial governments, and to reform the old taxation system, a series of new tax laws were issued towards the end of 1993. Several main points of the reform concerning FDI are as follows:

● The reform has cut the number of tax categories affecting foreign-funded enterprises and foreign employees to eleven. For example, VAT has eliminated double taxation associated with the former industrial and commercial consolidated taxes.

● The new system also retains preferential policies related to turnover tax, including no VAT levies for machinery, equipment and components imported by foreign-funded enterprises for production within the total amount of their investments, and no VAT and consumption tax levies for export products produced by foreign-funded enterprises, with the exception of items covered by specific government stipulation.

● Most of the former preferential policies on income tax for foreign-funded enterprises remain unchanged under the new system. The Income Tax Law stipulates that enterprises with foreign investment will be subject to a 30% income tax rate and a 3% local surcharge for assessed income. However, it can be reduced or partially exempted under the following conditions:

1. On those established in SEZs and those of a production nature in economic and technological development zones in coastal port cities, or those in coastal economic open zones, or in other regions defined by the State Council within the scope of projects encouraged by the state, it shall be levied at the reduced rate of 15%.

2. On those of a production nature established in coastal economic open zones or in the old urban districts of cities where the special economic and technological development zones are located, it shall be levied at the reduced rate of 24%.

3. Those of a production nature scheduled to operate for a period of not less than 10 years of profit making, be exempted from income tax in the first and second years and allowed a 50% reduction in the third to fifth years.

Various further preferential income tax treatments are also granted to Chinese-foreign equity joint ventures engaged in the construction of infrastructure projects, or in the development of agriculture, forestry or animal husbandry, those established in remote underdeveloped areas, or in the SEZs and engaged in service industries, or the export-oriented enterprises and technologically advanced enterprises with foreign investment.

(B) The foreign exchange rate system reform[11]

Most foreign investors would be aware of the previous dual exchange rate system under which an official exchange rate, fixed at about 5.8 yuan per US dollar, co-existed with market rates which were determined by supply and demand at the various swap centres around China. The rate hovered around 8.7 yuan per US dollar, diverging substantially from the official market rate. The dual exchange rate system had been in place for more than ten years, since the early 1980s when China began to open its door to the outside world.

On 1 January 1994, the Chinese government introduced a managed floating of the Renminbi under which the daily foreign exchange rates published by the central bank in China (the People's Bank of China) were based on average prices among the major swap centres. This arrangement prevailed until the introduction of the interbank foreign exchange market.

Two Foreign Exchange Trading Centres have been set up, and the operation of inter-bank hard currency trading markets has created a mechanism under which exchange rates are set according to market demand. It enables the central bank to intensify its macro-economic control.

(C) Government financial system reform

To overcome ever-increasing financial problems such as deficits, China has introduced a new system of tax distribution to replace the former responsibility system of fixed quotas for revenue and expenditure. Major targets and measures include:

- drawing a clear distinction between financial revenues of the central and local governments by distributing revenues through different tax channels;
- establishing a new tax-collecting system, which consists of two independent taxation authorities, one for the central government and one for local government;
- increasing financial resources for central government.

(D) Banking and investment system reforms

Investment decisions have always been one of the major responsibilities and activities of government at all levels in China. The Chinese saying 'governments dig holes and banks plant trees' is a vivid expression of the fact that banks usually have not had the power to make investment decisions in the past.

To narrow the gap between China's banking system and that of developed countries, to clarify the different responsibilities between government and enterprises, and to encourage enterprises into the market, a banking system reform package was introduced in early 1994. A major step was made in separating policy-lending banks and commercial banks. Three policy banks – the State Development Bank, Import and Export Bank of China and Agriculture Bank of China – were phased in and have acted as the basic tools to implement government policy. At the same time, under the supervision of the central bank, all other banks were transformed into commercial banks responsible for their own business behaviour with less and less intervention from governments.

(E) The foreign trade system reform

The Foreign Trade Law of the PRC, which was promulgated on 12 May 1994, went into effect on 1 July of the same year. The adoption of the first national foreign trade law in China shows the determination to further reform the foreign trade system to make it more compatible with the international practices. The law includes the following aspects:

- The General Provision clearly stipulates that China has introduced a unified foreign trade system;
- The importation and exportation of prohibited or limited goods and technologies can only be carried out on the basis of the conditions and methods outlined in the law. Conditions prescribed by the law are in full compliance with the stipulations prescribed by the GATT;
- Domestic industries are provided with appropriate protection. The law abandons past systems, such as import substitutions and administrative examination and approval, while at the same time adopting common international systems such as anti-dumping, anti-subsidies and protective measures;
- The law abandons various foreign trade subsidies systems practised in the past, and explicitly stipulates that foreign trade managers should engage in independent management, and should assume sole responsibility for their own profits and losses according to law. Government policies for encouraging the development of foreign trade will be carried out by adopting universally accepted promotional measures, such as the establishment of special financial institutions to enhance the development of foreign trade, establishing foreign trade development and risk funds, and introducing export refunds.

Governed by the Foreign Trade Law, foreign trade reform has abolished the mandatory plan for foreign trade and adopted a guidance system for total import volume, foreign currency income from exports and expenditures for imports. The quota management system for imports and exports has been improved. China has also made further readjustment to the tariff rate structure, lowering the total levels of tariffs, and improving the export rebate system.

Implications of the new FDI policy

On the one hand, the new reforms of 1992 and 1994 have fuelled China's recent economic development: GNP in 1994 reached RMB 4,380 billion yuan, an increase of 11.8% over 1993. The total volume of imports and exports reached US$236.7 billion, a 29.9% increase. The amount of foreign capital actually used was US$45.8 billion, a 17.6% increase. Of this amount, US$33.8 was in the form of FDI.

On the other hand, it seems that the reforming measures also fuelled inflation and brought about some new problems in economic development. Whilst GNP shot up, and industrial production and exports scored sustained and fast growth, inflation also went up, and bottlenecks in capital, energy, raw materials and transport further tightened.

The new pattern of liberalization has resulted in a diversified inflow of FDI and has necessitated the formulation of a new strategic focus on the areas for foreign investment.

The opening of Pudong in Shanghai and the Yangtze River corridor represented a great change in China's liberalization strategy. It is a key step, following on from the development of the country's coastal areas. In 1990, Deng Xiaoping commented on the open-door policy: 'if there is any mistake in our strategy of opening to the outside world, it is that we did not decide to open Shanghai to the world earlier'. This view indicated the vital importance to the country of opening Shanghai, backed by the mighty Yangtze River Valley.

As the largest river in China, the Yangtze River, with twenty-three open cities within its valley, is the only inland river in the country which has all its major ports open to the outside world, and is a perfect route into the vast Chinese market.

Different from the four SEZs initially opened along China's southern coast which are far from most of the major markets of the country, the Yangtze River corridor is the country's major resource centre and is a developed area of regional industrial concentration following years of investment. Its output makes up one third of the country's total and it is also one of the major financial sources for the central government.

The strategic importance of the Yangtze River also lies in its comprehensive industrial structure, enjoying very close cultural and economic relationships with other areas of the country.

Shanghai, known as the head of the dragon, enjoys incomparable superiority in the new pattern of China's globalization. The opening of Pudong in Shanghai in 1990 put Shanghai at the cross-over of two strategic economic belts: the coastline and the Yangtze River. Shanghai has launched a campaign to restore its international position as an economic centre, as a trade centre, and as a financial centre. It is widely believed in Chinese business circles that Shanghai, backed by the Yangtze River Valley, has an excellent chance of surpassing Hong Kong to become the number one international trade and finance centre in China.

Spreading along the Yangtze River corridor, FDI in China has begun to move from the coast to the central and western parts of the country. From 1979 to 1991, more than 90% of FDI was made along the coast. Since 1992, the growth of FDI in the inland areas of China has surpassed that in the coastal areas, and FDI in the inland areas now accounts for more than 20% of total FDI.

After the radical change of policy to prioritize certain areas and industrial sectors, pledged foreign investment as a whole has drifted down since the end of 1993. Although the Chinese government declares that this is a natural reaction to anti-inflation policies, and a result of competition for investment from other developing countries, many observers believe that there are other important reasons for the decline. For example, it is suggested that potential investors may be more cautious because they perceive the investment environment to be less stable. Another suggestion is that the Chinese government has tightened control over some of the high-return industrial sectors, such as commercial real estate development projects.

Whilst preferential treatment of certain regions will be retained, selective industrial policy will play an increasingly important role in directing the channels and directions of inward FDI.

The investment environment in China has substantially improved through the new package of reforms and the establishment of a market-oriented legislative system. For example, the foreign exchange rate has stabilized after a short period of violent fluctuation at the beginning of 1994. The stability of the yuan has provided a financial environment to help China expand trade and economic co-operation with other countries. This stability has also made it possible for Chinese enterprises to improve their management capability and for the country to engage more closely with the world economy. It also, of course, offers encouragement to more overseas firms to invest in China.

The new tax system, designed to eliminate anomalies and create fair, and generous conditions for foreign-funded enterprises, retains most of the preferential policies whilst reducing the overall tax burden (according to a high-ranking official of the State Administration of Taxation)[12].

Whilst more and more foreign investors are lured into China, they are now more likely to face intensive competition in the marketplace.

Major competitors include not only other investors from abroad, but also the state-owned enterprises, remotivated and re-activated by the market and gaining strength. As a result of a relatively fair competitive environment, the performance of many state-owned enterprises has improved considerably and will continue to improve.

Recent trends in FDI in China

First, Shanghai, backed by the Yangtze Valley, has become the new hot spot for inward FDI. In the first half of 1994, contractual foreign investment in Shanghai increased by 16% over the same period in 1993, ranking Shanghai second in the country. It is a great leap forward compared with sixth place in 1993.

Second, more and more transnational corporations and internationally renowned enterprises have invested in China. Nearly fifty transnational corporations opened for business in Beijing in the first half of 1994, double the 1993 figure.

Third, the number of large-scale projects is increasing and FDI is shifting from manufacturing industry into various others such as the tertiary industry sector. The focus of FDI has, in many regions, shifted to infrastructure projects and other forms of large-scale development.

The Singapore-Suzhou Township, recently launched in the Yangtze corridor, is one of the biggest projects. Established in February 1994 on the approval of the State Council, this project requires US$ 20 billion in investment over a dozen years of development. The goal is to build a modern industrial garden city which meets a high standard of international economic development with high and new technology as the priority, modern industries as the mainstay, and supported by tertiary industry and various social welfare undertakings. Never before has China attracted overseas investment through government agreement at such a high level.

China's vast potential for the tertiary sector is attracting considerable attention. Eight major Japanese Banks have established branches in Shanghai. Standard-Chartered Bank, Hong Kong based, has opened more than ten representative offices and branches in the country. Another recent development includes the establishment of the first investment bank formed on the basis of a Sino-foreign joint venture. It was announced in November 1994, and the major partners are the Construction Bank of China and Morgan-Stanley.

Fourth, the number of wholly-foreign-owned investment projects has been increasing. Both the Chinese government and foreign investors are searching for new methods of introducing foreign capital to China. New forms of utilizing foreign capital, such as BOT (build-operate-transfer), joint-venture investment companies, stock investment and security investment have been introduced. Most recently, the Chinese government has stated explicitly that it welcomes foreign investment funds to help State-owned enterprises renovate their technologies.

Business risks and opportunities in China's dynamic market

(A) Risks

Political risks have been significantly reduced since 1990, due to a constant process of reform of the political system, including a shift of administrative power and authority from the CPC to the government and the market, and the transfer from planned to market economy.

However, certain business risks do exist.

First, contradictions between the old and new economic control systems may cause confusion. The internationalist role of the Chinese government has not been clearly defined. One problem is where, when and how the government will intervene in the market. From a foreign investor's point of view, the government is a double-edged sword. In many cases, government cannot resist the temptation to interfere in the market. Foreign businesses may also welcome intervention if this reduces business risk, but frequent government intervention is most likely to hinder the development of the market system.

Second, the legal system still needs to be perfected in order to reduce conflicts within the existing system. For example, the newly issued 'Enterprise Law of the People's Republic of China' allow enterprises, under certain circumstances, to reduce their registered capital. But 'Sino-Foreign Joint Venture Law of the People's Republic of China' prohibits enterprises partly funded by foreign investment to do so.

Third, there is a high risk of lack of local capital, deriving from the country's huge investment in fixed-assets in recent years. Financial support for projects is extremely difficult to obtain. Rapid growth also exacerbates the bottlenecks in energy, raw materials, and transport. Projects and businesses that require large inputs of these resources are very likely to encounter problems.

Fourth, the double-digit rate of inflation will continue to be the biggest headache during the next few years, because investment in fixed-assets will increase sharply with strong industrial growth. During the first ten months of 1994, fixed asset investment by State enterprises increased by 40.4%. According to a projection of the State Information Centre (SIC), the retail price index is expected to show a year-on-year rise of 21%. In the period January–September 1994, the money supply increased by 32%.

Finally, before the foreign exchange market is fully established, there is considerable risk of exchange-rate control and of violent fluctuations in rates. The exchange rate between RMB and USD has been strangely stable while the inflation rate in the PRC has been about five times of that in the US. The yuan was quoted at 8.70 against the US dollar at 1 January 1995. After a short period of fluctuation, the exchange rate at December 1995 was about 8.50 RMB. Bearing in mind that the appreciation of the yuan co-existed with a rate of inflation of over 20%, it is clear that foreign exchange risk has increased considerably. Explanations for the phenomenon include the huge demand for RMB in expanding production and investment in fixed-assets, and the fact that the foreign exchange market is still subject to intervention and control.

Many foreign investors have also expressed concern over further reform of the foreign exchange system, affecting the repatriation of profits.

(B) Opportunities

While new geographical areas are opening to FDI, new industrial sectors are also queuing for foreign investment. There are many business opportunities for European and other foreign companies in China.

Further reform and liberalization of the vast and dynamic Chinese market will continue to provide investment opportunities to foreign investors. As many EU companies are 'new and late-comers' to China, they are fortunate to have emerging markets in central and western parts of the PRC, together with newly-opened industrial sectors.

Certain economic and cultural linkages still exist along the Yangtze River and Western countries due to the relationship established during the mid-nineteenth century.

A huge demand for foreign capital will continue to the turn of the century. For example, at the Roundtable on Policy Aspects of Promoting FDI in China's infrastructure, held in November 1994 in Beijing, the Chinese government announced that it had designated 210 key projects for the period 1993–2000 with a total investment volume of $30 billion, and foreign investors are being encouraged to compete for these projects. The Ministry of Posts and Telecommunications has proposed to invest $42.35 billion over the next six years intended for a massive expansion in facilities and service.

Outside Beijing, most of the provincial capitals have also set targets for internationalization of their metropolitan areas. Guangzhou alone, the capital of Guangdong Province, needs about 300 billion RMB to finance investment projects.

A huge new market for inward FDI has developed recently – the Chinese government is encouraging FDI into state-owned enterprises to finance technical renovation. It is estimated that of more than 5,000 large and medium state-owned enterprises in east and north-east China, one-third need such renovation.

China will continue to press ahead with liberalization of the financial services industry. It is reported that China is considering further opening up its finance sector to foreign investors. The expected reforms call for more Chinese cities to develop financial services focused on insurance, securities, trusts and investment funds.[13]

There are already thirteen cities open to overseas bank branches. The number of operational foreign bank branches and financial corporations on the Chinese mainland reached 101 by the end of March 1995, with capital assets totalling US$14 billion – a 40% increase over the previous year, according to PBC figures. Unpaid loans from these institutions to enterprises in China, most of which are foreign-funded ventures, amounted to US$8.8 billion, up 78% over the same period a year previously. Recently, the State Council has approved the opening of foreign financial institutions in ten more provincial capitals and regional economic centres. In addition, it is also considering allowing more foreign insurance firms to set up branches or joint ventures in China.

CONCLUSION

- Foreign investments will play an increasingly important role in China's economic development, as long as China sticks to its stance of reform and opening-up to the outside world. Foreign direct investment is and will be one of the major forms of absorbing foreign investment in China.
- As a result of the continuing efforts in opening to the outside world, reforming the political system, and improving the legal system and the investment environment, the gap between international standards and Chinese practice has been narrowed significantly, reducing the political and economic risks of investment in China.
- China is becoming more aware of the need for balance in growth and economic development. Industrial policy directives will become increasingly important in the selection and approval of projects, co-operators and partners. However, as a result of decentralization, it may be that the Chinese government lacks the power to guarantee implementation of all aspects of the new industrial policy.
- The Yangtze River delta and corridor will become both more competitive and more attractive to foreign investors.
- Clarification of business risks, such as inflation and exchange rate instability, is vital for successful investment in China. Even so, markets are dynamic and exciting, providing excellent returns in certain sectors.
- During the expansion of the liberalization process a completely new and comprehensive pattern of investment opportunities has emerged. Although foreign direct investment will continue to be the major mode of attracting foreign capital, new methods, such as build-operate-transfer (BOT) and investment trust funds, will in future account for a significant share of total investment.

NOTES

1 Acknowledgement should be made first and foremost to Mr J.R. Slater, whose efforts in organizing an EU–East Asia Business Research Group in 1993 has provoked the ideas for my thesis at the beginning, and who, throughout the process of my writing the thesis, has always been very helpful in giving me

sincere advice and encouragement. He has also provided me with direct financial support to sponsor my attendance to the first EU–Asia Business Conference. Without his help my thesis would not have been finished.

In addition, I feel very grateful to the co-editor of this book, Roger Strange, who has spent a lot of time to write the comments and given me precious advice, which has been extremely helpful in the process of restructuring and further improving my thesis.

Finally, I want to thank Ms Progson, the programme officer of the British Council, for her encouragement and help to me in passing through the approval procedure within a very limited time, without which I would have not had the chance to attend the conference in Britain.

Thanks to all who have helped me.

2 Source: *1994 Statistical Yearbook of China*, p. 527, and figures from Chen Jinhua's 'Report to the Third Session of the Eighth National People's Congress' on 6 March 1995.

3 Thirteen trade missions representing 150 British companies in 1994 were organized by the China–Britain Trade Group (CBTG), a non-profit-making organization sponsored both by the British government and the industry. Small group and individual business visits were not included.

4 Source: *1994 Statistical Yearbook of China*, p. 20. Figures are at current prices.

5 News reported by Xin Hua, XINMIN WANBAO, 27 September 1994.

6 Foreign enterprises, enterprises with both Chinese and foreign investments and Sino-foreign co-operative enterprises (including Hong Kong-, Macao- and Taiwan-funded enterprises) hereinafter are referred to as foreign-funded enterprises or enterprises with foreign investment.

7 Source: *1994 Statistical Yearbook of China*, p. 527.

8 Ibid.

9 Ibid.

10 News reported by journalist of The Central People's Radio Station, 4 June 1994.

11 On 6 February 1996 China's State Council announced a relaxation of state controls on foreign exchange, permitting domestic and foreign firms to buy hard currency at selected banks. The measures allow foreign investors to repatriate profits, dividends and interest earnings from the forex accounts or by selling their yuan earnings at designated banks. *Reuter*.

12 Chen Jinhua, 'Report to the Third Session of the Eighth National People's Congress' on 6 March 1995.

13 *China Daily*, 19 June 1995, Foreign financial institutions growing.

BIBLIOGRAPHY

Beijing Review (1994) Report: 'New Tax System Benefits Investors', 6–12 June.
—— (1995) 'New Policies to Guide Overseas Investors', 22–28 May.
Chuan, H. (1994) 'Guangzhou Focuses its Strategy of Attracting Foreign Capital on Big Firms Abroad', *Economic Express*, 25 July, Beijing.
Hu, S. (1994) 'Phenomena of Chinese Strategies: Analyses and Thinking', *Reform* 4.
Ji, C. (1994) 'China: Foreign Trade Strategy', *Intertrade*, June.
Li, H. (1994) 'Introducing Foreign Fund into China: 1993's Review and 1994's Forecast', *Reform*.
Liu, W. (1994) 'Year-end Growth on Right Track', *Business Weekly, China Daily*, 13–19 November.
Wang, Y. (1995) 'Drop in investment dismissed', *China Daily*, 22 June.

Wu, Y. (1994) Minister of the Ministry of Foreign Trade and Economic Relations of China, 'Basic Framework', *Intertrade*, June.
Zhang, J. (1994) 'Speech at the Roundtable on Policy Aspects of Promoting FDI in China's Infrastructure', November, Beijing.
Zhou, P. (1994) 'China Adopts Common International Practices', *Beijing Review*, 6(12) June.

13 The economic restructuring of the state-owned enterprises in China and the implications for European investment

Weihwa Pan and David Parker[1]

INTRODUCTION

After 1949 the new Communist Government transformed China into a socialist planned economy (Selden and Lippit 1982). By the end of the 1950s private ownership had been largely eliminated in favour of state-owned enterprises (SOEs) and collective firms and farms (Li 1960).[2] Since the death of Mao Zedong in 1976 and under the leadership of Deng Xiaoping, however, China has introduced important market reforms. Whereas between 1949 and 1978 economic performance was lacklustre, since the reforms began the country has sustained close to double-digit economic growth (Lardy 1994, ch. 1). Industrial output is expanding by well over 20% per annum and the share of manufactured goods in total exports has increased from about 49% in 1980 to 82% in 1993. Amongst developing economies China is now the world's largest recipient of foreign investment.[3]

Compared with the 'quick fix' policies pursued in a number of Central and Eastern European countries since 1989, China has carried out its reform programme on a gradual and experimental basis (Overholt 1993; Fan and Nolan (eds) 1994; Naughton 1994). This gradualism has resulted first from the Government's concern not to fuel the conditions for social unrest – a policy reinforced by the Tianamen Square revolt of June 1989 – and second from the continuing absolute control of the Chinese Communist Party (CCP). Within the CCP the political initiative has swung backwards and forwards between pro-reformers and neo-conservatives, but even the pro-reformers have advocated a 'socialist market economy', not full-blooded capitalism. The objective has been described by Deng Xaioping as 'socialism with Chinese characteristics'.

Despite the clear economic success of the reform programme, the future poses important challenges (Shirk 1994). In particular, over 100,000 state-owned enterprises (SOEs) still account for about one half of China's economic activity. The SOE sector is associated with price distortions, chronic misinvestment, over-manning and continued financial losses. Current estimates suggest that between 30% and a half of all of the SOEs are loss-making. This imposes a major burden on the economy and in particular on the public finances and the financial system.

This chapter details the organization and control of China's SOEs, the steps taken since 1978 to reform them and current policy towards them. The chapter also considers the implications for European investment in China of the current state of reform of the SOE sector.

THE ORGANIZATION AND CONTROL OF CHINA'S SOEs

Studying the SOEs in China is complicated by the complex and sometimes differing ways in which they are organized and controlled (Thomas 1993). Principally, however, very large and strategic industries, such as major defence firms, are accountable to government in Beijing, while the vast number of small-and medium-sized SOEs are usually accountable in the first instance to provincial or municipal governments, under the guidance of plans formulated in Beijing. Figure 13.1 provides a guide to the structure of control.

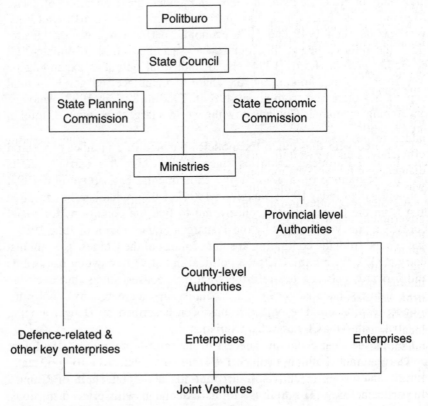

Figure 13.1 Chinese SOEs: structure of control

Source: Developed from S. Jackson (1992) *Chinese Enterprise Management: Reforms in Economic Perspective*, Berlin: de Gruyter, p. 17.

During the 1950s the formation of the planned economy led to a dual party-state administrative structure. Rules relating to the nature and management of the SOEs were laid down by the CCP and SOE management were accountable to the appropriate government department. Experiments in decentralization did occur from time to time, but they were not pursued with sufficient consistency or rigour to have much effect (Walder 1981).[4]

In more recent years central control has diminished. In part this has been the result of a policy decision to decentralize and in part it has been a *de facto* product of increasing regional autonomy. Economic development has been highly uneven across China with the coastal regions, especially Guangdong, having the fastest growth rates. Governments in these regions have asserted a degree of independence from Beijing over the last decade.

Up until the 1980s central government set targets for production, allocated labour, appointed management, arranged raw material supplies and managed sales. Administered pricing meant that market signals were either non-existent or highly distorted. Wages and salaries were based on national wage scales and were not related to enterprise productivity or demand and supply in the local labour market (Walder 1986; Fan and Nolan (eds) 1994). A number of aspects of this control process remain.

Management and the authorities both planned and operated in a vacuum regarding true market demand and the economic cost of inputs. In 1978 97% of retail commodities, 94% of agricultural produce and 100% of capital goods were sold at state-fixed prices. Also, the SOEs provided 'the iron rice bowl'. Instead of centrally financed welfare services, housing, education and health care were provided by the SOEs for both current and former employees. This may have been socially meritorious but it greatly added to production costs and complicated assessment of true operating efficiency. Linking welfare services to employment also acted as a major disincentive for workers to change jobs. Labour turnover in Chinese SOEs was very low and over-manning endemic.

A system of production in which all outputs and inputs are controlled by government departments leaves little scope for managerial initiative. The management of the SOEs carried out the policies of government. The control of the CCP was enforced through political appointments to managerial positions and until 1983, the local party secretary was in charge of internal structure and operations in each factory. Each department in the firm was accountable to the appropriate government department for its actions; for example, the finance department would be accountable to the local or central finance bureau, the personnel department to the labour bureau, and so on.

The planning system in China, as in other communist countries, provided little in the way of incentives for management to use resources efficiently. In particular, after the output target under the plan was achieved there was no incentive to produce more. The SOEs were expected to remit all of their residual revenues ('profits'), if any, to the state budget. The state budget in

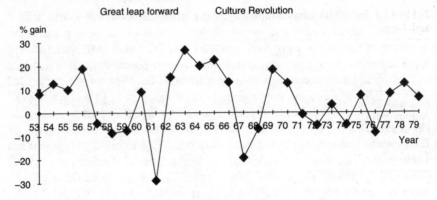

Figure 13.2 Productivity in state-owned enterprises
Source: Figures from *1992 China Statistical Yearbook*: 832.

return financed all losses. Unsurprisingly productivity languished (Chen *et al.* 1988; Ginneken 1988). According to official statistics the growth in labour productivity in the 1970s was a miserly 1.6% per annum. Economic performance was also affected by the political ferment which swept across China from time to time during the 1950s and 1960s. Figure 13.2 shows a steep decline in labour productivity during the Great Leap Forward (1958–60) and the Cultural Revolution (1966–9).

Centrally planned economies are prone to management hiding capabilities and hoarding resources (Ericson 1991; Shleifer and Vishny 1992). This was true of China. Convincing the planners to set low production targets meant that the management was less likely to fail to meet target and therefore less likely to attract criticism. Hoarding resources was an understandable reaction when planned inputs might fail to be delivered and therefore achievement of the target output might be put at risk.

The amount of funding provided to firms for expansion was determined by the central plan. There was no necessary link between the cost of capital, risk and potential returns from the investment. Moreover, investment funding did not depend upon the SOE generating the necessary revenues. Funds for both fixed investment and working capital came largely from government grants. Also, all plant and machinery belonged to the state not the enterprise and therefore incentives to maintain the capital stock were weakened.

A further problem was the uneconomic scale of production in the state sector. Under Communism specialization according to regional comparative advantage was discouraged (Singh 1992: 14). Instead, regional self-reliance was practised, under which regional bodies determined where production could be sold and each province was encouraged to be economically independent. This policy resulted from poor communications combined with enduring regional loyalties within China, but also from a

Table 13.1 Industrial concentration by major industrial sectors in China, USA and Japan

Sector	China		USA		Japan	
	Large firms	Sales %	Large firms	Sales %	Large firms	Sales %
Iron and Steel	38	46.7	7	83.7	20	84
Automobiles	7	35.6	13	94.6	10	74.1
Chemicals	7	10.2	19	84.9	15	48
Engineering	6	2.9	9	58.4	10	53.9
Textiles	2	1.5	5	40.7	10	68.4

decision to disperse industrial production around the country to minimize the threat from military attack.

The result was a large number of small, duplicated production facilities with few plants able to reap scale economies. This makes China's economy different to the economies of Central and Eastern Europe where, under Communism, generally large-scale state-monopolies were favoured. The Industrial Concentration Index confirms that many Chinese SOEs remain small in scale compared with their counterparts in the main industrialized countries (Table 13.1). At the same time, the fact that the government purchased all planned outputs left little scope for competition between the SOEs.

In summary, the result of state ownership and planning was both static and dynamic economic inefficiency. The static inefficiency was composed of: (a) *allocative efficiency*, in the sense that prices did not reflect marginal costs of production; and (b) *productive efficiency*, in the sense that in the absence of market signals incentives to minimize production costs for any given output were generally absent. Dynamic efficiency is concerned with innovation and the seeking out of new production processes and products. In the absence of competition and in the presence of guaranteed markets there was little incentive for managers to innovate.

THE FIRST TWO STAGES OF REFORM: 1978–1993

Since 1978 China has adopted a series of reforms with the objective of improving both allocative and productive efficiency. In studying the reform of the SOEs it is possible to divide the period since 1978 into three. The first period lasted until 1984 and included the first, tentative steps towards introducing market forces. The second stage ran from 1984 to 1993 and was concerned with introducing further market incentives and fiscal reform. The third stage was announced in 1993 and is associated with official recognition of the case for some privatization. (For a summary of the main features of all three stages of reform, see Appendix, pp. 197–8.)

The first stage of reform

The first stage of reform was announced at the Third Plenum of the Central Committee of the CCP in December 1978. The objective was a modernized economy but still 'regulated mainly by planning mechanisms and [only] supplemented by market forces'.[5] There was no question at this stage of abandoning the primary role of central planning. The Central Committee simply accepted the need for limited reforms but firmly *within* the planning mechanism.

In line with socialist principles, at first the idea seemed to be to base reform on decentralized decision-making at the factory level. Workers congresses had been formed after the Communist take-over in 1949 but had always played a minor role. Now they were given powers to elect management within the SOEs. The management were to account for their actions to the worker congresses. In practice, however, the reform had little effect since management side-stepped the congresses (Thompson 1992: 236).

More important were the reforms introduced from the late 1970s aimed at increasing management autonomy within the plan. One important aspect was the decision to allow enterprises to retain a fixed proportion of any surplus revenues. Whereas all profits had previously been paid over to the state, now some of the profit could be retained within the SOE to replace equipment, pay bonuses or provide further welfare services for employees. Another change was the decision to allow management to produce outputs above the planned levels and generate surplus revenues. In 1981 a limited degree of price flexibility was introduced for certain products.

Measures were also adopted to encourage foreign capital (see also Chapter 12 in this volume, by Chen Changzheng, and Chapter 14, by Xiaohong Wu and Roger Strange). In the past the CCP had condemned foreign investment as Western imperialism. Now the government acknowledged that outside investment would be needed if Chinese industry was to obtain hard currencies and at the same time gain the necessary management skills, international distribution channels and technology to compete effectively in world markets. A joint venture law was passed in 1979 and the first special economic zones (SEZ) were established from 1980. Investment in a SEZ brought tax and regulation concessions for foreign investors. During the 1980s the restrictions on the terms of joint ventures with SOEs were eased, though only after 1986 were wholly foreign-owned businesses allowed (Brown 1993).[6]

This early stage of reform also included the first steps to encourage private property. Private ownership was formally recognized in 1978; previously it had been actively discouraged. As a result, private enterprise began to expand. For example, the state's share of retailing fell from 91% in 1978 to 46% by 1985 (Lockett 1988: 14). In agriculture farm collectivization was reversed so that by 1984 the commune system had effectively disappeared.

It is important, however, not to exaggerate the impact of the reforms. They were important more for what they signalled about the change in Chinese politics than for their immediate effects. The vast bulk of production remained centrally planned, as did foreign investment (Steidlmeier 1992: 71; Yusuf 1994: 76). Only a very limited degree of managerial autonomy had been granted.

The second stage of reform

During the second stage of reform, as profit incentives and market prices became more firmly established, management autonomy increased. The second stage was heralded by the promulgation of the 'Temporary Regulation on Further Enlarging the Autonomy of State-owned Enterprises' by the State Council in May 1984 (Fan 1994: 142).

One key feature of this Regulation was the granting to the SOEs of the right to sell certain products at 20% above or below the planned prices. This meant that a dual-track pricing system was created involving both planned and market prices for outputs and inputs (Rajaram 1992: 5–7). Production to meet planning quotas continued to be sold at planned prices, but production above quota could be sold at higher prices, that is to say at prices much closer to market-clearing levels. This was quickly followed by further reform.

From January 1985 the 20% ceiling was gradually removed, permitting the first decontrolled pricing. Now a growing number of firms that fulfilled their output quotas could raise profits by selling excess production in the market or to each other at free or 'floating' prices. Floating prices were allowed to fluctuate around an officially determined base price. By 1987 around 65% of all prices in agriculture, 55% of consumer goods and 40% of production prices were either free or floating (Minami 1994: 20). Later in the decade planned prices for most capital goods began to be abolished, though it was only in 1992/93 that energy and transport prices were freed. By 1993 only 5% of retail commodities, 10% of agricultural goods and 15% of capital goods were sold under planned prices (Lardy 1994: 11).

A limited amount of labour market restructuring paralleled the price reform. In 1986 the payment of wage supplements based on experience, training and achievement over and above the basic state wage was permitted. Also, government allocation of workers and lifetime employment were reduced by the introduction of contract workers. Begun as an experiment in some industries in 1980, it was now extended across the country, though it applied only to new employees (Thompson 1992).

In addition to liberalized prices and employment, the second stage of reform included greater autonomy for firms to export and import. By the end of 1987 more than 1,400 large firms had received permission to engage in foreign trade. Also, although all land remained state-owned, more land could now be transferred, at first under short leases. This meant that while most land was still officially allocated, a market in the use of land began to develop (Deliusin 1994: 32). In the early 1990s the buying and selling of long-term land leases in urban areas was permitted to facilitate business expansion (Perkins 1994: 29).

Moreover, the SOEs were now encouraged to take more control of their outputs and investment. By the end of 1986 the number of key products under the direct control of the State Planning Commission had fallen from 120 to 60; the share of industrial products with output targets from 40% to 20%; the number of goods and materials distributed by the state from 256 to 20; and plan-controlled commodities administered by the Commerce Ministry from 188 to 25. The share of total investment financed by the state budget also fell sharply (Minami 1994: 165–8).

Along with more autonomy to set outputs and prices the SOEs were now expected to raise more of their working capital from the banks rather than by direct grants from government. By the early 1990s most investment in the SOEs was financed from retained earnings and bank loans rather than direct state grants. State budgets were now mainly used to finance infrastructure schemes and very large manufacturing projects.

The banking sector remained state owned but separate commercial banks were set up with the right to control their own funds, manage their personnel and decide how to use any residual income. The fact that the banks faced political pressure to continue to dispense loans liberally to the SOEs, however, blunted the impact of this change (*Financial Times* 7 July 1994: 21). Until the late 1980s bankruptcy of SOEs was not permitted, which meant that the banks had little choice but to extend credit. In 1988 a Bankruptcy Law was introduced, but in practice few bankruptcies were allowed. Where they did happen, management and labour were usually transferred to other SOEs, which stymied the incentive effect.

A product of the early reforms was a growing spread in the profits earned by different SOEs. In addition, less profit was paid over by the SOEs to the authorities. The Government's response was to introduce a new tax system, including an Enterprise Income Tax (EIT) and an Enterprise Income Adjustment Tax from October 1984. Tax rates under the EIT were set at between 7 and 55% and were defined in terms of fixed asset values. The Enterprise Income Adjustment Tax (EIAT) was introduced to compensate for the different profitability of enterprises arising from extraneous factors, such as price distortions and capital endowments. Hence, while previously SOEs had turned over all but a tiny fraction of their profits to the government in return for funding, in principle, they now paid taxes, retained post-tax profits and conducted financial dealings with the banks. In practice, however, the new taxes were negotiable which led to a softening of the intended budget constraint (Perkins 1994: 38).

Another major aspect of the post-1984 reforms was the Contract Responsibility System (CRS). In 1983 the roles of the party secretary and the SOE manager had been legally separated. The manager was now supposed to have full management responsibility, but in practice intrusive planning processes ensured continued political intervention (Liu 1992). The purpose of the contract system was to increase productivity within the framework of continued state-ownership by formally separating the ownership of assets by the state from the management of the enterprises. The contract was expected to strengthen the budget constraint facing SOE management, especially those in firms that had suffered losses for years. It was implemented in late 1987 and covered 70% of the SOEs by 1988 and 95% by 1992 (Fan 1994: 149; *Brightness Daily* 2 August 1992: 1).

Under the contract each SOE agreed to pay a certain percentage of its profits in taxes and to maintain and modernize equipment. In return, the authorities agreed to restrict their intervention in the day-to-day management of the firms. In practice, the contract system was not especially successful. Party officials were still tempted to intervene in management directly and through the approval of banks loans. Within firms short-termism proved to be a problem. The contracts covered only three to five years, when they were to be renewed through the normal bargaining process. Management could boost profits in the short-term to their own advantage by decreasing depreciation charges and by neglecting asset maintenance (*Cheng Ming Monthly* February 1993: 32).

The second stage of reform consolidated the earlier and very limited movements towards introducing market incentives into the SOEs. However, the objective was still market reforms within a planned economy or a 'socialist market economy'. Also, it is unclear how far the reforms were successful in improving SOE performance. A number of studies have found evidence of improved industrial productivity in the SOEs during the 1980s (e.g. Jefferson, Rawski and Zheng 1992; Groves *et al.* 1993).[7] But the extent to which this improvement resulted from the reforms remains unclear; the economy was expanding quickly in this period largely as a result of agricultural reforms, new private production and foreign joint ventures. Our own estimates based on official data suggest that the value added per employee (in constant prices) rose by an average of 139% in the SOE sector between 1985 and 1992. But this compares with a growth of 229% amongst collective enterprises and 364% in what is described in Chinese statistics as 'other' firms (stock ownership, foreign enterprises and equity joint ventures) (Parker and Pan 1996).

Also, a recent study of 769 SOEs from 10 manufacturing industries covering the period 1980 to 1990 suggests that improvement within the SOEs was very uneven. Growth seems to have been especially rapid in electronics, machinery and chemicals, but stagnant in the textiles, lighting and energy industries. The study also found that productivity growth in the SOEs peaked in 1982, well before most of the reforms were introduced (Liu and Liu 1994: 9).

Table 13.2 Share of SOEs in the Chinese economy

Year	SOEs	Collective	Others
1979	78.47	21.53	n/a
1980	75.97	23.56	0.48
1981	74.76	24.66	0.58
1982	74.44	24.88	0.68
1983	73.36	25.86	0.78
1984	69.09	29.90	1.01
1985	64.86	33.93	1.21
1986	62.27	36.27	1.46
1987	59.73	38.26	2.02
1988	56.80	40.49	2.72
1989	56.06	40.49	3.44
1990	54.60	41.01	4.38
1991	52.94	41.40	5.66
1992	48.42	44.98	6.60
1993/94#	43.00	47.00	10.00
2000*	27.20	61.10	11.70

Source: 1992 China Statistical Yearbook and *China Economic System Reform Yearbook 1993.*
* From National Information Centre. *Economic Daily* (Beijing) 14 January 1993, p. 5.
# From *1994 China Statistical Yearbook.*
Note: 'Collectives' includes the township and village enterprises.

What is indisputable is the *relative* decline of the SOE sector within the Chinese economy (see Table 13.2). For example, between 1985 and 1993 the SOEs' share of gross output fell from around 65% to under 45%. The share of output accounted for by the collectively-owned firms and town and village enterprises rose from around 32% to 47%. The growth of both the 'others' sector and the town and village enterprises (local co-operatives, municipally-owned firms and some private businesses) seems to have occurred entirely at the expense of the SOEs (the figures for the year 2000 in Table 13.2 are official estimates and confirm a continuing relative decline for the SOE sector).

Turning to specific reforms, the gradual spread of the double-track pricing system allowed two prices, planned and market, to co-exist, but the profitability of a SOE depended crucially upon the relative bargaining power of management and government departments regarding production quotas, planned prices and inputs. SOE management pressed for low output quotas to maximize production at market prices, and high input quotas since then more inputs were obtained at planned prices, which were generally far below market levels. Table 13.3 provides examples of the huge gap that continued to exist between planned and market prices.

Following the 1980s reforms, management had more freedom from central controls but still lacked much discretion over the employment of capital and labour inputs (World Bank 1990; Boisot 1995). The assets

Table 13.3 Prices in 1988 under the dual pricing system (price in Renminbi)

Items	Planned	Market	Gap
Coal	60	200	140
Crude oil	100	500	400
Timber	119	636	517
Wire rod	610	1,680	1,070
Thin plate steel	870	4,602	3,732
Med. thick plate	570	1,804	1,234
Pig iron	293	752	459
Aluminium ingots	4,000	16,077	12,077
Cement	90	193	103

Source: Date from Rajaram, 1992: 32–3.

under the control of the SOEs were still the property of the state and this meant that problems of low utilization of capital and asset neglect continued. Also, the 1980s reforms may have exacerbated the scale problem in Chinese industry by encouraging more local rather than central control. After 1984 the regional bodies, which until then had determined where industrial firms could sell their products, were abolished. This led management to expand local capacity. Certainly, the reforms did nothing to integrate production.

A degree of wage flexibility had been introduced and market wages spread in the new township and village enterprises that sprang up, but official pay scales still dominated in the SOEs.[8] By 1988 10% of workers in SOEs were on contracts ranging from one year to over five years, but this still left the vast majority of employees with life-time employment.[9] Most workers were still assigned by the state and management freedom to lay-off workers remained severely restricted. It is only recently that the authorities have loosened their tight political control over the allocation of skilled labour, such as university graduates. The Government was reluctant to sanction a wider right to 'hire and fire' because of the conflict with Communist principles on employment and, more pragmatically, because the Government feared the social and political consequences of large redundancies and resulting unemployment. In consequence, the SOEs remained grossly over-manned. The continued use of labour rather than capital was encouraged by the EIT. The tax was levied according to the value of assets and therefore favoured those enterprises with low asset values.

Although the 1980s reforms meant that SOEs began to seek markets for their products, market signals were still distorted and because of the easy access to bank finance a soft-budget constraint continued. Almost all investment by the SOEs was financed by bank credit and some financing leaked into paying revenue expenses, including wages. When bank credit

Table 13.4 The restructuring of China's SOEs, 1988–91

	Number of firms
Closed	39
Stopped production or under partial production	427
Assets transferred to other SOEs	229
Bankrupted	2
Merged	400
Total	1,097

Source: *Almanac of the Reform of the Chinese Economic System*, 1992: 792.

failed to arrive, the SOEs ran up debts with each other, amounting to a sum equivalent to 30% of China's industrial output by 1993.

The new private sector firms and joint ventures with foreign investors introduced competition in some of the SOEs' markets, notably in consumer goods and textiles, and for materials and labour (Zhang 1990) and in the face of this the finances of many SOEs worsened further. By the early 1990s the SOE sector still absorbed 70% of all of China's investment funds.

As financing directly from the state switched to more reliance on bank funding, the growing financial losses in the SOE sector increased indebtedness to the banks. By 1993 non-performing loans to the SOEs threatened the entire banking system. The 1988 law on bankruptcy was used very sparingly, mainly because of official fears that the closure of large numbers of SOEs would lead to high unemployment.

By 1993 changes in China's economy had also put at risk the government's finances. In 1992 total subsidies paid by the state amounted to Renminbi (RMB) 72.2 billion of which around 16% went directly to maintain SOEs. A large part of the remainder was spent on price subsidies which indirectly benefited the sector. Growing state subsidies were paralleled by an increasing reluctance to pay taxes. Tax revenues from the SOEs fell from 20% of GDP in 1978 to only 4% by 1992. Over the same period the ratio of central government tax revenues to GDP fell from over 30% to around 19% (*The Economist* 4 June 1994: 25). In the absence of adequate tax revenues, monetary expansion to finance the losses of the SOE sector became an important contributory factor to rising inflation.

In summary, the reform programme after 1984 led to some freeing of prices and wages, more profit retention at the enterprise level and more management freedom to manage. It also led to more competition amongst SOEs and some restructuring and closures (Table 13.4). At the same time, however, the reforms created new frictions, particularly in the state finances and the banking system. The Contract Responsibility System could have marked a significant change in the relationship between government and the enterprises, but continued state subsidies of industries and prices, soft bank loans and a largely ineffective bankruptcy law meant that

Table 13.5 Profit retention by enterprises in 1987

Country	Proportion retained %
Yugoslavia	60
Czechoslovakia	30–7
Hungary	30
Romania	20
USSR	20
China	14.5

Source: Liu 1992.

while SOE managers took the credit for exceeding targets and profited accordingly, they took much less responsibility for financial losses.

The reforms from the mid-1980s were aimed at increasing management autonomy from political control with the intention of raising productive efficiency in the SOEs (Hua and Du 1990). They did not, however, tackle effectively the real sources of inefficiency, namely over-manning, the failure to match demand and supply, the biased input and output prices, asset neglect, and the extensive welfare system provided by the SOEs. Also, compared with other communist countries in the late 1980s, Chinese SOEs still retained a surprisingly small percentage of their profits (Table 13.5).

In an important respect the reforms may have been misguided. Increasing the separation of ownership by the state from management of the industries was understandable to reduce political meddling, but research has pointed to the potential agent-principal problem that exists when management achieve operating autonomy without adequate accountability to owners (e.g. Vickers and Yarrow 1988, ch. 2). The Chinese reforms gave management more scope to set outputs and prices and to employ inputs, but did not couple this with an effective incentive mechanism to ensure that resources were managed efficiently. Greater autonomy along with a soft budget constraint was a recipe for managers to pursue their own utility. There is evidence that SOE management pursued output expansion from the late 1980s leading to considerable over-capacity in many industries; for example, currently China has more than 100 refrigerator plants with a total capacity to produce more than 16 million refrigerators per annum. More than half of the production lines are idle (*People's Daily* 26 April 1994).

Perhaps not surprisingly, therefore, although the centre abdicated some power over the management of the SOEs, the reforms encouraged a movement of control to the local party level. SOEs generating 80% of total SOE output are now controlled by local authorities.[10] This can be seen as a reaction to the void in management accountability created by the decline of central control. It is, however, unclear whether accountability to the local party is more desirable than accountability to Beijing. What it did produce was a greater variety in the degree and form of control of the SOEs. Also, planned economies are prone to 'cronyism' and the reforms of the

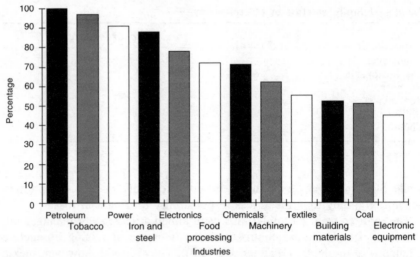

Figure 13.3 State control of China's top twelve industries: % of output contributed by SOEs

Source: Merrill Lynch, *Far Eastern Economic Review*, 7 July 1994: 60.

mid-1980s seem to have exacerbated the problem at the local level (Lockett 1988).

The third stage of reform

The 1980s reforms were an attempt to combine managerial autonomy and a system of market pricing with continued state ownership and planning. A programme of privatization was specifically rejected. In effect, a market system was grafted uneasily onto a continuing Soviet-style command economy (Lin 1989). The share of output accounted for by the SOEs fell but mainly because of the development of a separate and parallel private sector of industries. In absolute terms the SOEs continued to dominate industrial production, accounting for around a half of all production and 61% of total fixed investment in the early 1990s. These are average figures and the SOEs' share of the output of industries such as petroleum, tobacco, power and iron and steel was much higher (Figure 13.3). In terms of employment, between 1978 and 1991 the numbers working in the SOE sector actually rose by 33% to around 107 million.[11] By comparison, in June 1994 only around 5 million worked in the private sector (excluding township and village enterprises).

In terms of raising efficiency the 1980s reforms were at best only partially successful. Compared with the rapidly developing private sector, boosted by foreign investment, the performance of the SOE sector remained unimpressive. In addition, the pace of economic change in China was such that it was proving increasingly difficult for the Government to permit their continuing financial losses.

The November 1993 CCP Third Plenum announced the start of what seems to be an important third stage of reform. Private property was specifically endorsed and for the first time ,he possibility of privatization was officially acknowledged; albeit, somewhat ambiguously, still within the context of a socialist market economy (Goldstein 1994). The Plenum approved a 50-point blueprint for further economic liberalization, including market reforms, new forms of ownership, freer competition between state, collective and private enterprises and reform of the monetary, legal and social security systems.

The decisions of the Third Plenum involved ending the dual exchange rate system and a revamping of the tax system. The dual exchange rate weighed against foreign investment and in January 1994 it was replaced by a single unified exchange rate, an important step towards eventual full convertibility of the Chinese currency. This was followed by the introduction of a single tax system and the effective ending of negotiation over tax rates. Reform of the financial system, however, in particular the intended transformation of debt-burdened banks into commercial entities, by consolidating bad debts into three 'policy banks', is proceeding much more slowly.

The main reforms specifically concerned with restructuring the SOE sector, developing since the Third Plenum, involve control and asset use:

Control

The Chinese Government now seems to favour all SOEs becoming corporations with issued shares (though the official position on the form and pace of change of the SOEs continues to fluctuate reflecting the shifting political balance in Beijing between reformers and conservatives). The shares in centrally controlled SOEs are to be held by the state in the first instance, but the intention is to distribute them to provincial and local governments, other state firms, banks and asset management companies. Sales to the private sector are to be encouraged.

China plans to earmark some 10,000 SOEs for early corporatization with perhaps 100 SOEs becoming important share-holding companies. State-holding companies in petrochemicals, aviation and non-ferrous metals have already been chosen.[12] The Government now seems to favour the SOEs having legal autonomy from the state and hence full responsibility for profits and losses, taxes, and responsibilities to any shareholders. The Government acknowledges that it should no longer intervene directly in the SOEs, which should operate according to market requirements. Enterprises which cannot pay their debts are to be made bankrupt. Banks will no longer be required to make loans to failing enterprises, though political pressures may well limit the effects of this set of decisions, especially at the local CCP level.

There are signs that the Government is at last serious about closing

Table 13.6 Recent steps towards privatization

Heilongjiang Province	Built 18 ownership exchange markets and 'transferred' ownership of 290 enterprises.
Shanghai Enterprise Exchange market	329 businesses put up for sale but mainly township and village enterprises. SOEs expected to follow.
Sichuan Province	Decided to sell 33 enterprises employing 77,000 to overseas bidders in industries such as machinery, electronics, metallurgy and pharmaceuticals.
Shaoguan City	Three-day trade and investment fair. 41 SOEs offered for sale.
Shanghai Lantern Factory	Management buy-out early 1994.
Shunde City	Privatization programme announced to reduce the city government's stake in local manufacturers to an average of about 30%. However, foreign investors appear not to be favoured this time. Already sold control of 164 enterprises, most of them small, through a mixture of equity sales to foreigners, discounted stock offerings and management buy-outs.

Source: *Central News Daily*; *Financial Times*; and IMI, *International Marketing Insight*, Commerce Department, The American Embassy, Beijing.

loss-making firms – 159 SOEs in larger cities were allowed to go bankrupt in 1994. In January 1995 the Government announced that it intended to rehabilitate 1,000 of the 14,000 large and medium-sized SOEs through financing for plant modernization. It appears that the rest may be left to fend for themselves. The State Statistical Bureau has suggested that 43% of China's SOEs may need to be liquidated (*Central News Daily* 3 September 1994: 4). Recently a number of city and provincial governments have taken steps to sell some of their SOEs and management and employee buy-outs are occurring; examples are given in Table 13.6.

Asset use

The ownership of the assets of the SOEs will still be invested in the state, but the firms will now have full legal control over their use. The SOEs are also to be encouraged to install modern forms of management systems and organization with an aim of improving asset utilization (Wu 1993).

PROSPECTS FOR EUROPEAN INVESTMENT

Prior to 1993 private capital had already begun to make inroads into the SOEs. As early as 1979 some SOEs had been permitted to fund investment by selling corporate stock, though at this time only to their employees.

After 1984 stock could be offered to the Chinese public, though progress in issuing public stock was restricted by the lack of a capital market. Only in the early 1990s were the first stock exchanges established, in Shenzhen and Shanghai. By the end of 1993 over 4,000 joint stock companies had been formed in the state-owned sector, but most had unlisted shares which traded informally, if at all, in kerb-side markets (*Financial Times* 5 October 1994). Only just over 280 'A' shares were quoted on the mainland exchanges and a mere handful of companies had shares listed on stock markets outside China.[13]

Foreign capital had made some inroads into the SOEs through direct investments and joint ventures. By the end of 1993 there were around 167,000 foreign-owned firms and joint ventures in China, accounting for less than 5% of GDP though two-thirds of exports (*Financial Times* 15 June 1994: 22). Majority foreign equity stakes were permitted, but most ventures with SOEs involved minority investments in jointly-owned companies. Also, in terms of investing in the shares of the corporatized SOEs, foreigners were limited to owning 'B' shares denominated in US dollars and by the end of 1993 only 42 companies had issued 'B' shares.

It is important, therefore, not to exaggerate the degree of involvement of private capital in the SOEs. By 1993 only 4,000 of the over 100,000 SOEs had become corporations and very few of these had quoted shares. Similarly, only a small minority of mainly larger SOEs had arranged important joint ventures with foreign firms. Even in the small number of cases of SOEs with listed shares, the state often held a minimum 50% holding, which meant that government retained an effective veto over managerial decisions. The state's continued control was often, in fact, much greater because typically a large proportion of the remaining shares were made available to institutional investors. Within China the institutional investors are state-owned.

Trade between China and the EU countries has risen 14-fold over the past fifteen years to ECU 35 billion (£29 billion) in 1994. China is now the EU's fourth largest market and fourth largest supplier. Yet in terms of investment in China, the EU states have lagged well behind certain other countries, notably the USA, Taiwan and Japan (Tables 13.7a–c) – though some of the investment through Hong Kong may involve European capital. Foreign investment offers a means by which under-capitalized SOEs can obtain the necessary funds for new plant and machinery, new management skills and access to export markets. But investment, both in terms of investing directly in a SOE or through an equity joint venture, is high risk. The implications of the economic restructuring of the SOEs for European investors are essentially the same as for all foreign investors. They can be summed up as uncertainty about property rights and about management competence and independence from the state.

In the past, because China officially rejected privatization, the opportunities for foreign investment in the SOE sector were limited to joint

Table 13.7a Top ten foreign investors in China, 1979–93
(in US$ bn)

Country	No. of projects	Contracted investment
Hong Kong/Macao	114,147	150.90
USA	5,296	78.47
Taiwan	20,982	18.40
Japan	7,180	8.90
France	242	6.84
Singapore	3,122	4.80
Britain	616	3.00
Thailand	1,399	2.10
Canada	1,540	1.80
Germany	569	1.50
Total	155,093	276.71

Table 13.7b China's actual Foreign Direct Investment in 1994
(in US$ m.)

Hong Kong/Macao	20,174
Taiwan	3,391
USA	2,491
Japan	2,075
Singapore	1,180
South Korea	723
Britain	689
Germany	259
Italy	206
Canada	216
Total	33,767

Table 13.7c China's contracted Foreign Direct Investment in 1994
(in US$ m)

Hong Kong/Macao	48,692
USA	6,010
Taiwan	5,395
Japan	4,440
Singapore	3,778
Britain	2,748
South Korea	1,806
Germany	1,233
Canada	890
Australia	849
Total	82,680

Source: Ministry of Foreign Trade and Economic Co-operation (MOFTEC), Beijing.

ventures and, more recently, small-scale shareholdings. The opportunities for foreign investment in the SOEs will now almost certainly rise as SOEs are corporatized and seek foreign capital. For example, SBIC Finance Asia, a Hong Kong investment bank, and Arthur Andersen and Co. have obtained one of the largest consultancy deals in the world involving a restructuring of China's entire iron and steel industry (*Institutional Investor* 1993).

European investment in China's SOEs poses, however, special problems, in addition to the usual ones associated with the transition to a market economy, namely macro-economic and micro-economic reforms to support market trading, such as effective competition laws, sound fiscal and monetary policies and an end to bureaucratic regulations (for a review of these reforms see Kornai, 1990; Kaser and Allsop 1992; Kikeri, Nellis and Shirley 1992).

China still lacks adequate commercial laws. Effective corporate governance requires well-defined, private property rights (Alchian 1965), but property rights are not fully protected in China. For example, land leased on long-term contracts with city and provincial governments is still liable to be compulsorily re-acquired (as the American fast-food company, McDonald's, discovered to its cost, when its site in Beijing was compulsorily acquired despite a twenty-year lease). A new company law took effect on 1 July 1994 but is weak in adequately defining ownership and leaves the maximum proportion of any company an individual may own unclear.

The last decade has seen considerable change but nevertheless the money and capital markets are in their infancy. Outside financiers take a particular risk when investing in the shares of China's SOEs because of the degree of continued state ownership and associated cronyism. Insider trading is a particular problem, though a new securities law is expected shortly (*Legal Daily* 16 September 1994). The currency is not convertible and regulations relating to foreign-exchange balancing and profit repatriation continue to hamper investment (Plasschaert 1993). Foreign investors are required to seek approval from the Chinese authorities to convert Renminbi earnings into hard currencies.

The state retains and will continue to retain directly and indirectly a dominant control over the SOEs for quite some time, at least, while new state-holding companies as a vehicle for private capital raise continuing questions about governance and accountability. Management in the SOEs and officials in the various tiers of government presently adopt rent seeking behaviour, which is likely to be curtailed only when management is legally separated from political control, at both the central and local levels, and is replaced by an effective system of corporate governance. Non-accountable management is not an attractive proposition, especially where product competition is restricted. Experience elsewhere in the world suggests that incentives to manage enterprises efficiently are best achieved when state enterprises are made accountable to private shareholders (Parker 1994a).

In China, however, privatization is likely to be gradual and often partial in nature. This distinguishes China's economic transition from that of a number of former Communist states, including Russia, where complete sales to the private sector have occurred. The Chinese road appears to be similar to that of certain other South-east Asian countries, such as Malaysia, where privatization has been associated at first with minority sales to the private sector and sales to financial institutions controlled by the state or the ruling political party (Parker 1994b). Continued political control and ineffective corporate governance will blunt the incentive effects of private investment.

China shows no signs of adopting an Anglo-American style of free-market capitalism, like that found in Hong Kong (Redding 1990: 234–5). The decision in 1994 not to approve any more foreign joint-venture car plants until after 1996 is evidence of a continued high level of planning. Even where privatization occurs, government is still likely to regulate economic activity heavily (Howell 1992). Again, the Malaysian (or South Korean) example of state leadership in development seems to be a more appropriate model than the Anglo-American one.

In an environment of the 'socialist market economy' it is unclear to what extent private-sector management introduced with foreign investment will be allowed to close down factories and slim down manning. Whereas, for example, the collective and mixed public-private enterprises cut around 2.5 million jobs in the first half of 1994, only 159,000 were made redundant by state firms. Also, the recent resurgence of neo-conservative forces within the CCP acts as a warning not to take China's market reforms for granted. Concern has been expressed in government circles about exploitation of labour by foreign enterprises in China (*Financial Times* 21 March 1994: 2). The imminent death of Deng Xiaoping adds to inherent political uncertainties.

In the past the government has used revenues generated by the SOEs to finance state spending. The decline in payments from the SOEs has placed severe strains on central government finances which the new tax reform may not alleviate. Beijing's revenues in 1994 amounted to as little as 5.1% of GDP compared with over 9% in 1986. The future tax regime for foreign investments, therefore, remains unclear, particularly since central government spending is likely to rise. In particular, as the welfare system at the firm level shrivels so more responsibility will fall on the state's finances, inevitably with adverse budgetary effects (*China Statistical Yearbook* 1992).

To add to the uncertainty, the SOEs lack reliable balance sheets and it can be unclear what assets an investor is buying. Until recently there were no agreed accounting standards in China and asset valuations are particularly suspect. New general accounting practices designed by a US consultancy firm appeared in 1994 and where implemented have exposed even more SOEs as loss-makers than official estimates previously suggested (Wang 1994).

It can be difficult to identify the true ownership of assets. For instance, the China Jialing Group, a producer of car parts in Sichuan province, has ten factories each owned by different combinations of local and provincial governments and the People's Liberation Army (*The Economist* 27 August 1994: 56).

As always in China, decentralization continues to conflict with a need to maintain order from the centre. Relations between central government and China's 22 provinces, 3 metropolitan areas and 5 autonomous regions remain troublesome. In the recent past Guangdong has paid little tax to the centre and continued friction over state finances between local officials and Beijing increases the chance of political upheaval (Overholt 1993).

Despite fifteen years of economic reform China lacks a developed market economy. Markets are often protected from both foreign and domestic competition through extensive import duties and other controls and by regionalism and poor communications, which hamper the distribution of imports. Although opportunities will continue to develop for establishing wholly-owned foreign firms in competition with SOEs, and more especially for creating joint-ventures with SOEs, progress will be restricted by the lack of a competitive product market. Cash injections from the state and generous credit facilities from the state-owned banking sector add further uncertainties when competing with SOEs.

Another important obstacle to development is China's infrastructure, which has been neglected and is in urgent need of large-scale investment. Energy, telecommunications, water and transportation, all state-owned, are major bottlenecks in the economy.

Moreover, there is still a lack of an appropriate state-level welfare system to act as a social safely net, especially during the transition period.[14] Some municipalities, such as Shanghai, have experimented with introducing welfare provision and in November 1994 Beijing announced sweeping reforms based on national insurance (*Financial Times* 15 November 1994: 5). But until the financing of welfare is removed from industries, considerable uncertainty will surround their finances.

Finally, in China, as in many other countries, investment is complicated by cronyism and corruption. Standards of business probity may not match those expected in developed economies. 'Trust' has been identified as an important aspect of a successful economy (Casson 1991), but can only develop given experience. In the meantime, outside investors need to research their potential partners carefully.

In sum, over the next few years joint ventures and direct investment in the SOEs will offer possibilities for European investment. The prospects should not be exaggerated, however, since investing in China involves considerable risk and uncertainty. In particular, buying into one of the SOEs or its assets is only for the brave-hearted. Recent estimates suggest that up to a third of current foreign ventures in China are failing to generate profits for outside investors (*Financial Times* 7 November 1994). A recent legal dispute, involving a US investment bank and three of China's biggest trading companies over a failure to pay debts, emphasizes the need for a sober assessment of the investment prospects in China. Capital injected into the SOE sector should generally be viewed as high risk with, hopefully, long-term returns.

CONCLUDING REMARKS

This study has charted the reform of the SOE sector in China since 1978 and has looked in general terms at the implications for European investment. The SOEs are seeking more foreign capital and many more are likely to be put up for sale. This creates opportunities for European investors both in the form of directly-owned enterprises and joint ventures. But there are many potential pitfalls. High subsidies, a lack of effective market disciplines and opaque accounts are just some of the traps for the unwary investor.

Moreover, China is not like central and eastern Europe, where for the most part central planning has been abandoned. State planning is less prominent but China remains 'socialist' with all the attendant uncertainties and ambiguities for private capital. The 'socialist sector' still dominates industrial production. The SOEs account for around 43% of China's industrial output and the collectives for a further 38%. Around 100,000 SOEs are still the backbone of the Chinese economy and many have been little affected by the reforms. An uncertain number have been sold-off or made bankrupt (perhaps around 1,500), a few have been floated on the stock markets in China or abroad. But the vast majority continue largely as before, consuming vast quantities of resources, including over 60% of all fixed-asset investment in China. Also, there are no signs of a mass privatization programme. It still seems unlikely that the CCP, as currently constituted, will sanction the ending of state ownership of large-scale industries, especially the utilities (water, gas, electricity and telecommunications – notwithstanding the recent decision to permit some outside investment in telecommunications) and defence-related industries.

Moreover, the reform programme is subject to shifts in the political balance within the CCP. At present high inflation is producing a period of uncertainty regarding the direction and pace of reform. In March 1994 price controls were reimposed on certain foodstuffs and services and the phasing out of subsidies to public utilities, such as gas and electricity, was postponed. The Government has also slowed down the introduction of the restructuring reforms for the SOEs announced in November 1993. The Fourth Plenum of the CCP, in September 1994, emphasized stability and consolidation rather than reform.

Such periods have occurred before in China, however; for example, in 1988 price decontrol was temporarily reversed in the face of a similar rise in inflation and fears of social unrest. The reforms outlined in November

1993 will shape the direction of change in the SOEs over the next few years even if the pace of reform may vary. By the end of the decade not only should China's new private sector have greatly expanded but many of the moribund SOEs are likely to have been privatized, liquidated or allowed to wither on the vine.

NOTES

1 We would like to thank participants at the first EU-East Asia Research Group conference in January 1995, an anonymous referee and Professor Roger Sugden for their helpful comments on an earlier draft of this chapter.

2 The literal translation of the term used in China for SOEs is 'whole people-owned'. It equates with the term in English 'public ownership'. Collective firms are typically owned by local governments but have tended to have harder budget constraints and less bureaucratic controls than the SOEs.

3 It has been suggested recently that these growth statistics may exaggerate the actual performance (e.g. Wolf 1994; Lardy 1994). Whatever the correct figures, indisputably China's economy has expanded rapidly since the late 1970s. In Chinese statistics 'industry' includes mining and utilities as well as manufacturing.

4 However, Chinese planning was always less comprehensive and centralized than planning in the USSR. More responsibility was delegated to the provincial and local levels (Hua, Zhang and Luo 1993).

5 The report of the Third Plenum is taken from: Lu Gao (1993):136.

6 The number of contracts signed to set up wholly-owned subsidiaries by foreign investors rose from 18 in 1986 to 2,795 in 1991 (Tsang 1994: 105). The actual number of subsidiaries created, however, will have been much smaller. The number of contracted schemes always greatly exceeds the number of actual investments over the same period.

7 There are also in-depth studies which confirm more commercial attitudes and behaviour in the management of the SOEs in the 1980s, e.g. Tidrick and Chen 1987; Granick 1990; Byrd 1992; Child 1994.

8 Township and village enterprises were started by individuals and local governments and therefore are a mixture of public, private and collective ownership. They make profits for their owners and unlike the SOEs are not heavily subsidized (Byrd and Lin 1990).

9 Just under 28% of SOEs had adopted contract labour by the middle of 1994 (*Financial Times Survey: China* 7 November 1994: 5).

10 Local political control will prevail as long as party officials continue to appoint and dismiss managers.

11 This is about 18% of the total workforce. The largest percentage of workers still work in agriculture. As few as 11,000 of the SOEs account for 34% of total output and 52% of tax payments.

12 Space precludes a detailed discussion of the growing role of state-holding companies in China. In addition to the new ones just mentioned, important is the China International Trust and Investment Corporation (Citic) which was set up in 1980. Citic invests in both projects and firms, including SOEs, and today has more than thirty subsidiary companies.

13 By November 1994 eleven mainland companies had shares quoted on the Hong Kong stock exchange and six mainland companies had listed on Wall Street.

14 A very limited form of unemployment benefit was introduced when contract labour was established in 1986.

BIBLIOGRAPHY

* Indicates published in the Chinese language (English translation of title).
Alchian, A.A. (1965) 'Some Economics of Property Rights', *Il Politico* 30: 816–29.
* *Almanac of the Reform of the Chinese Economic System* (1992) Beijing.
Boisot, M. (1994) 'The Lessons from China', in M. Boisot (ed.) *East–West Business Collaboration: The Challenge of Governance in Post-Socialist Enterprises*, London: Routledge.
* *Brightness Daily*, 2 August 1992: 1.
Broadman, H.G. (1995) *Meeting the Challenge of Chinese Enterprise Reform*, Washington DC: World Bank Discussion Paper 283.
Brown, R.C. (1993) 'The Role of the Legal Environment in Doing Business in the People's Republic of China', In L. Kelley and O. Shenkar (eds) *International Business in China*, London: Routledge.
Byrd, W.A. (1992) *Chinese Industrial Firms under Reform*, Oxford: Oxford University Press.
Byrd, W.A. and Lin, Q. (1990) 'China's Rural Industry: an Introduction', in W.A. Byrd and Q. Lin (eds) *China's Rural Industry: Structure, Development and Reform*, New York: Oxford University Press.
Casson, M. (1991) *The Economics of Business Culture: Game Theory, Transaction Costs, and Economic Performance*, Oxford: Clarendon Press.
* *Central News Daily*, Taipei, 3 September 1994: 4.
Chen, K. *et al.* (1988) 'Productivity Change in Chinese Industry, 1953–1985', *Journal of Comparative Economics* 12 (December): 570–91.
* *Cheng Ming Monthly*, Hong Kong, February 1993: 32.
Child, J. (1994) *Management in China During the Age of Reform*, Cambridge: Cambridge University Press.
* *China Statistical Yearbook*, Beijing, 1992, 1994.
Deliusin, L. (1994) '"Chinese Capitalism" or "Socialism with Specific Chinese Features"?', *Problems of Economic Transition* 37 (July): 24–44.
* *Economic Daily*, 14 January 1993: 5.
* —— 23 October 1994: 3.
The Economist (1994) 'China's Communists: the Road from Tiananmen', London, 4 June: 23–5.
—— (1994) 'China's New Model Army', London, 11 June: 71–2.
—— (1994) 'China Stirs its Sleeping Giants', London, 27 August: 55–6.
Ericson, R. (1991) 'The Classical Soviet-Type Economy: Nature of the System and Implications for Reform', *Journal of Economic Perspectives* 4: 11–29.
Fan, Q. (1994) 'State-owned Enterprise Reform in China', in Q. Fan and P. Nolan (eds) *China's Economic Reforms*, London: St Martin's Press.
Fan, Q. and Nolan, P. (eds) (1994) *China's Economic Reforms: the Costs and Benefits of Incrementalism*, London: St Martin's Press.
Financial Times (1994) 'China Probes Labour Exploitation', London, 21 March: 2.
—— 'Foreign Investment in China Slows', London, 15 June: 22.
—— 'From Abacus to Automation', London, 7 July: 21.
—— 'The Chinese Superlative', London, 5 October: 4.
—— 'China to Overhaul Social Security', London, 15 November: 5.
Financial Times Survey: China, London, 7 November 1994.
Gao, L. (1993) 'The origin of "Socialist Market Economy"', *Reform Yearbook 1993*, Beijing: China Economic System.
Ginneken, W.G. (1988) 'Employment and Labour Incomes in China, 1978–96', *Labour and Society* 13(1): 55–79.
Goldstein, C. (1994) 'Are We There Yet? China Dangles midway between Statism and Capitalism', *Far Eastern Economic Review*, 7 July: 60–2.

Granick, D. (1990) *Chinese State Enterprises: a Regional Property Rights Analysis*, Chicago: University of Chicago Press.

Groves, T., Hong, Y., McMillan, J. and Naughton, B. (1993) *Productivity Growth in Chinese State-run Industries*, San Diego: University of California Working Paper.

Howell, J. (1992) 'The Myth of Autonomy: the Foreign Enterprise in China', in C. Smith and P. Thompson (eds) *Labour in Transition: the Labour Process in Eastern Europe and China*, London: Routledge.

Hua, S. and Duo, H. (1990) 'State-owned enterprise reform in China', in J. Heath (ed.) *Public Enterprise at the Crossroads*, London: Routledge.

Hua, S., Zhang, X. and Luo, X. (1993) *China: from Revolution to Reform*, Houndsmills: Macmillan.

IMI, *International Marketing Insight*, Commerce Department, The American Embassy, Beijing.

Institutional Investor (1993) 'Privatising China's State Sector: another long march?', *Institutional Investor* 27(5): 74–5.

Jackson, S. (1992) *Chinese Enterprise Management: Reforms in Economic Perspective*, Berlin: de Gruyter & Co.

Jefferson, G.H. and Rawski, T.G. (1994) 'Enterprise Reform in Chinese Industry', *Journal of Economic Perspectives* 8(2): 47–70.

Jefferson, G.H., Rawski, T.G. and Zheng, Y. (1992) 'Growth, Efficiency and Convergence in China's State and Collective Industry', *Economic Development and Cultural Change* 40(2): 239–66.

Kaser, M. and Allsop, C. (1991) 'The Assessment: Macroeconomic Transition in Eastern Europe, 1989-91', *Oxford Review of Economic Policy* 8(1).

Kelley, L. and Shenkar, O. (eds) (1993) *International Business In China*, London: Routledge.

Kikeri, S., Nellis, J. and Shirley, M. (1992) *Privatization: the Lessons of Experience*, Washington DC: World Bank.

Kornai, J. (1990) *The Road to a Free Economy*, London: W.W. Norton.

Lardy, N.R. (1994) *China in the World Economy*, Washington DC: Institute for International Economics.

Legal Daily, Beijing, 16 September 1994.

Li, C.M. (1960) 'The First Decade of Economic Development', *China Quarterly* (Beijing), Spring.

Lin, C. (1989) 'China's Reforms caught in No Man's Land', *Guardian* 24 April.

* Lin, S. (1990) *China's Industrial Structure and the Present Industrial Adjustment*, Beijing: Institute of World Economics and Politics, Chinese Academy of Social Science.

Liu, C. (1992) 'The Incentive Structures of China's Enterprises under the Contract Responsibility System', *Journal of Contemporary China* 2(1): 69–81.

Liu, J. (1992) 'The Reform of State-owned Enterprises', in World Bank (ed.) *Case Studies of Chinese Economic Reform*, Washington DC: World Bank.

Liu, Z. and Liu, G.S. (1994) *The Efficiency Impact of Chinese Industrial Reforms in the 1980s*, Discussion Paper no. 94004, London: The Chinese Economic Association in the UK.

Lockett, M. (1988) 'Culture and the Problems of Chinese Management', *Organisation Studies* 9(4): 475–96.

Minami, R. (1994) *The Economic Development of China: a Comparison with Japanese Experience*, Houndsmills: Macmillan.

Naughton, B. (1994) *Growing out of the Plan: Chinese Economic Reform 1978–1993*, Cambridge: Cambridge University Press.

Overholt, W.H. (1993) *China: the Next Economic Superpower*, London: Weidenfeld and Nicolson.

Parker, D. (1994a) 'International Aspects of Privatisation: A Critical Assessment of Business Restructuring in the UK, former Czechoslovakia and Malaysia', *British Review of Economic Issues* 16(38): 1–32.

—— (1994b) 'Privatisation and the International Business Environment', in S. Segal-Horn (ed.) *The Challenge of International Business*, London: Kogan Page.

Parker, D. and Pan, W. (1996) 'Reform of the State-Owned Enterprises in China', *Communist Economies and Economic Transformation* 8(1): 109–27.

* *People's Daily*, Beijing, 26 April 1994.

Perkins, D. (1994) 'Completing China's Move to the Market', *Journal of Economic Perspectives* 8(2): 23–46.

Plasschaert, S.R. (1993) 'The Foreign-Exchange Balancing Rule in the People's Republic of China', in L. Kelley and O. Shenkar (eds) *International Business in China*, London: Routledge.

Rajaram, A. (1992) *Reforming Prices: The Experience of China, Hungary and Poland*, Washington DC: World Bank Discussion Paper 144.

Redding, S.G. (1990) *The Spirit of Chinese Capitalism*, Berlin and New York: Walter de Gruyter.

Roehrig, M.F. (1994) *Foreign Joint Ventures in Contemporary China*, New York: St Martins Press.

Selden, M. and Lippit, V. (1982) *The Transition to Socialism in China*, London: Croom Helm.

Shirk, S.L. (1994) *How China Opened the Door: The Political Success of the PRC's Foreign Trade and Investment Reforms*, Washington DC: Brookings Institution.

Shleifer, A. and Vishny, R. (1992) 'Pervasive Shortages under Socialism', *Rand Journal of Economics* 2: 237–46.

Singh, I. (1992) *China: Industrial Policies for an Economy in Transition*, Washington DC: World Bank Discussion Paper 143.

Steidlmeier, P. (1992) 'China's Most Favoured Nation Status: Attempts to Reform China and the Prospects for US Business', *Business and the Contemporary World* 4(3): 68–80.

Thomas, S. (1993) 'Chinese Enterprise Management Reforms in the Post-Tiananmen Era: the View from Liaoning Province', in L. Kelley and O. Shenkar (eds) *International Business in China*, London: Routledge.

Thompson, P. (1992) 'Disorganised Socialism: State and Enterprise in Modern China', in C. Smith and P. Thompson (eds) *Labour in Transition: the Labour Process in Eastern Europe and China*, London: Routledge.

Tidrick, G. and Chen, J. (1987) *China's Industrial Reform*, Oxford: Oxford University Press.

Tsang, E.W.K. (1994) 'Strategies for Transferring Technology to China', *Long Range Planning* 27(3): 98–107.

Vickers, J. and Yarrow, G. (1988) *Privatization: an Economic Analysis*, Cambridge, Mass.: MIT Press.

Walder, A. (1981) 'Some Traces of Maoist Legacy in Industry', *Australian Journal of Chinese Affairs* 5: 21–38.

—— (1986) *Communist Neo-Traditionalism: Work and Authority in Chinese Industry*, Calif.: University of California Press.

* Wang, Y. *Central New Daily*, 1 August 1994.

Wolf, M. (1994) 'Baffling Questions for China-Watchers', *Financial Times Survey: China*, 7 November: iv.

World Bank (1990) *China Between Plan and Market*, Washington DC: World Bank.

*Wu, J. (1993) 'On Enterprise Institution Reform', *Chinese Industrial Economic Study* (Beijing), December.

Yusuf, S. (1994) 'China's Macroeconomic Performance and Management During the Transition', *Journal of Economic Perspectives* 8(2): 71–92.
*Zhang, Z. (1990) 'Keeping Private Business on the Right Track', *Beijing Review* (Beijing), 8 January: 4–5.

APPENDIX 13.1: MAIN FEATURES OF THE REFORMS IN CHINA: 1978–95

1978–84

Objective: modernized economy but still 'regulated mainly by planning mechanisms and [only] supplemented by market forces'.
Key Points:
- decentralized decision making
- introduction of some profit retention at the firm level
- production of some output above planned levels
- some, tentative decontrol of prices
- encouragement of foreign capital
- legal recognition of private property
- ending of the commune system in agriculture.

1984–93

Objective: continued reform within a 'socialist market economy'.
Key points:
- dual-track pricing system
- wage supplements and contract labour
- beginnings of a land market
- more freedom to export and import
- more dependence on bank finance
- bankruptcy law passed though rarely used
- tax reform
- contract responsibility system
- only foreign-owned firms permitted.

1993–?

Objective: further reform but still without formally abandoning socialism as the official doctrine.
Key points:
- 50-point blueprint for further economic liberalization
- private property officially endorsed
- monetary, legal and social security reforms

- corporatization of more SOEs and the development of state-holding companies
- more bankruptcies amongst SOEs
- privatization of some SOEs now a possibility.

14 FDI policy and inward direct investment in China

Xiaohong Wu and Roger Strange

INTRODUCTION

The People's Republic of China (PRC) was established in 1949, and the new government took control of the industrial enterprises belonging to the previous government of the Republic of China.[1] Private enterprises were tolerated for a brief period, but soon became joint ventures with the owners and managers forced to surrender control to the government. Methods of central planning were adopted for key industries,[2] and the government managed various state-owned enterprises through some twenty Ministries of the State Council. A State Planning Commission was established to co-ordinate and direct the Ministries. Output targets were set; inputs were centrally distributed; products of the state-owned enterprises were distributed by the State at predetermined prices; profits were mostly surrendered to the State; funds for capital construction and expansion had to be approved by the State. Agriculture too was operated essentially on central planning principles.

Two very serious political disturbances disrupted the functioning of the Chinese economic system in the ensuing years. The first was the Great Leap Forward Movement from 1958 to 1961. The second was the Cultural Revolution of 1966 to 1976. By the mid-1970s, the economic system was in some disarray. By Chinese official statistics, national output is divided into the five sectors of agriculture, industry, construction, transportation and commerce.

> In 1978 when reform began, these five sectors accounted respectively for 32.8, 49.4, 4.2, 3.9 and 9.8 percent of national income . . . . Collective farming prevailed in agriculture under the Commune system which had been introduced in 1958 during Chairman Mao's Great Leap Forward Movement. Of the total labour force of 401.5 million in 1978, 306.4 million or 76.3 percent were labourers in rural areas while 95 million were classified as staff and workers. Of the latter, 74.5 million or 78.4 percent worked in state enterprises and the remaining 20.5 million worked in collective enterprises in cities and towns . . . . In 1978,

77.6 percent of the gross output value of industry was from state enterprises. Thus most of industry and other nonagricultural sectors consisted of state enterprises which were not operated for profit and were under the control of central planning, although the degree of control was not necessarily complete. In sum, in 1978 most of China's productive units in agriculture, industry and the other sectors were not operating for profit as in a market economy.

Foreign trade was directed by central planning in 1978. When construction projects were included in a five-year plan, some required imports of foreign capital goods and materials. Certain consumption goods in the plan had to be imported, including food grain, when domestic supply was inefficient. All these projected imports required the use of foreign exchange, which has to be earned by the planned export of domestic goods. Exports, imports and the demand for and supply of foreign exchanges were incorporated in a foreign trade plan which was part of China's economic plan. In the State Council, the Ministry of Foreign Trade directed the affairs of foreign trade, supervising the Bureau of Import-Export Control and the General Administration of Customs, assisted by the State Administration of Exchange Control. The official exchange rate was set below market rates; at the official rate of 1.9RMB per US dollar, the Chinese people could not obtain US dollars without the approval of the government. Imports were restricted and exports were managed by the government. In 1978 foreign trade totalled 27.25RMB, with 13.97 billion exports and 13.28 billion imports, and accounted for 10.3 percent of national income of 164.4 billion.[3]

The decade of the 1980s saw the progressive liberalization of much of the domestic Chinese economy and the opening-up of the economy to foreign trade and investment. The incidents in Tiananman Square in June 1989 brought a temporary halt to the development of Sino-foreign economic relations, but the process has regained much of its early dynamism by the mid-1990s. This chapter[4] focuses on the development of FDI policy within China since 1978, and the effects of the policy changes on the pattern of inward investment. We outline in the section below the economic reforms that have taken place in China since 1978, focusing in particular on the implementation of the 'open-door policy'. Following this section we trace the changes in China's policy towards FDI (pp. 202–6) and highlight various important trends in the data (pp. 206–12). Finally, we speculate on likely developments through the late 1990s (pp. 212–14).

ECONOMIC REFORM IN THE PEOPLE'S REPUBLIC OF CHINA

Mao Zedong died in September 1976, and this led to a period of political struggle culminating in the downfall of the so-called 'Gang of Four' and the rise to power of Deng Xiaoping. Economic reform officially began in December 1978 at the Third Plenary Session of the Eleventh Congress of the Communist Party, when the decision was taken to move towards a more market-oriented economy.[5] The 'Four Modernizations' programme (Science and Technology, Agriculture, Defence, Industry) was put forward, and placed great emphasis on the transfer of technology from the more advanced economies in a reversal of the xenophobia of the Cultural Revolution.

The first step[6] in the reform process was the revision of the Commune system and the adoption of a responsibility system in agriculture. The second was to allow the development of small private enterprises and private markets. The third was the progressive reform of the state enterprises. The fourth was to allow more prices to be determined by the market forces of supply and demand. The fifth was the decontrol of the supply of consumer goods. The sixth was the expansion of foreign trade and the encouragement of foreign investment through an 'open-door policy'. And the seventh step was to change the government planning process to suit the more market-oriented economy.

Notwithstanding considerable progress in many areas, the reform process was initially rather piecemeal and unco-ordinated. On 20 October 1984, however, the Third Plenary Session of the Twelfth Central Committee of the Chinese Communist Party agreed a proposal for overall reform of the economic structure. Implementation of the proposal was to be effected largely during the Seventh Five-Year Plan of 1986 to 1990. The seven key elements of the proposal[7] were to:

- give individual state enterprises autonomy in decisions regarding production, supply, marketing, pricing, investment, and personnel as independent profit-seeking economic units;
- reduce the scope of central planning and, except for certain major products, change the method from mandatory planning to guidance planning;
- allow prices of more products to be determined by the forces of demand and supply rather than by central control;
- develop macro-economic control mechanisms through the use of taxes, interest rates, and monetary policy under an improved financial and banking system;
- establish various forms of economic responsibility systems within individual enterprises to promote efficiency and encourage differential wage rates to compensate for different kinds of work and levels of productivity;
- foster the development of individual and collective enterprises as supplements to state enterprises; and
- expand foreign trade and investment as well as technological exchanges.

As Chow notes, the essential characteristics of the reform were captured by the slogan, 'Invigorate the micro-economic units. Control by macro-economic means.'

It is the 'open-door policy' and the ensuing series of reforms with regard to foreign investment that are of most concern in this chapter:[8] in particular, the reforms to encourage new forms of trade, notably compensation trade and export processing, were linked to various incentives to attract foreign direct investment (see pp. 202–6 for details).

In January 1992, Deng Xiaoping made a highly publicized visit to the south, and this marked the symbolic start of a series of more intensive economic reforms. In October 1992, the Fourteenth Congress of the Communist Party endorsed the adoption of a market economy as a means to practising 'socialism with Chinese characteristics'. As Pomfret has noted,[9] the Congress was generally interpreted as having emphasized the *market* rather than *socialism*. An integrated package of fiscal and financial reforms was put together for approval at the Third Plenum meeting in November 1993, and many of the new Laws came into effect at the beginning of 1994. These reforms have been far-reaching, and have concerned the taxation system, the exchange rate system, the banking system, and the foreign trade system (see Chapter 12), as well as the state-owned enterprises (SOEs) – see Chapter 13 – and the regulations governing the treatment of FDI.

POLICY REGARDING FOREIGN DIRECT INVESTMENT IN THE PEOPLE'S REPUBLIC OF CHINA

A key element of the economic reform process in the People's Republic of China has been the encouragement of an inflow of foreign direct investment. On 1 July 1979, the Second Session of the Fifth National People's Congress adopted and promulgated *The Law of the People's Republic of China on Joint-Ventures using Chinese and Foreign Investment*. The Law laid down the general principles for the establishment of joint ventures in China, but did not provide the well-defined legal environment that was essential for long-term inflows of foreign capital. The State Council also awarded rights of autonomy in foreign economic trade to Guangdong and Fujian Provinces and, in 1980, set up four Special Economic Zones (SEZs) in Shenzhen, Zhuhai, Shantou, and Xiamen. Despite steady growth in the numbers of joint ventures in the early 1980s, there was still a need to liberalize and clarify the environment regarding profit repatriation, technology transfer, and foreign exchange. This was the purpose of the 1983 *Regulations for the Implementation of the Law of the People's Republic of China on Joint Ventures using Chinese and Foreign Investment*, and the pace of FDI in joint ventures increased dramatically in 1983 and 1984, stimulated also by the domestic economic reforms outlined above. On the basis of the experience with the SEZs, fourteen coastal cities[10] were designated as 'Open Cities' in 1984,[11] and granted many of the special privileges accorded the SEZs. Twelve of the fourteen cities (the exceptions were Beihai and Wenzhou) were designated Technology Promotion Zones (TPZs) in 1985 to expedite the transfer of technology.

The rate of growth of FDI in joint ventures slowed in 1985 and 1986. Import liberalization, together with inadequate control over credit creation and an overvalued exchange rate, had led to an import boom and large trade deficits. The government reacted by restricting private spending of foreign exchange, and this had an immediate impact on joint ventures both in terms of the need to pay for imported materials etc. and the requirement to repatriate profits. Furthermore, there was growing competition for international investment in the 1980s throughout Asia.

A series of detailed subject laws and regulations[12] were put forward during the early 1980s to clarify the operational environment for joint ventures, but these were too general to promote specific industrial sectors, with the result that a substantial proportion of the early FDI was in 'unproductive' sectors such as hotels and amusement parks. In order to direct FDI towards the 'productive sectors', especially those involving advanced technology and being export-oriented, the State Council promulgated on 11 October 1986 the *Provisions of the State Council of the People's Republic of China for the Encouragement of Foreign Investment*. These '22 Article Provisions' provided foreign joint ventures with preferential tax treatment, the freedom to import inputs such as materials and equipment, the right to retain and swap foreign exchange with each other, and simpler licensing procedures.[13] Additional tax benefits were offered to export-oriented joint ventures and those employing advanced technology. The government also attempted to guarantee further the autonomy of joint ventures from external bureaucratic interference, to eliminate many 'unfair' local costs, and to provide alternative ways for joint ventures to balance foreign exchange. Privileged access was provided to supplies of water, electricity and transportation (paying the same price as state-owned enterprises) and to interest-free RMB loans. The 1986 Provisions thus provided incentives for FDI rather than merely permitting it, and this more proactive approach was furthered by the adoption on 12 April 1986 of the *Law of the People's Republic of China on Enterprises Operated Exclusively with Foreign Capital*[14] at the Fourth Session of the Sixth National People's Congress. This explicitly linked (Article 3) the establishment of wholly foreign-owned enterprises to the development of China's national economy, and required such enterprises either to be export-oriented or to use advanced technology and equipment. The more liberal approach was furthered by the April 1990 Amendments to the 1979 Joint Venture Law.[15] These amendments permitted non-Chinese to act as Chairman of the Board of Directors, allowed extensions to the terms of operation of joint ventures, and removed the upper limit to the proportion of the registered capital (minimum not less than 25%) contributed by the foreign partner.

Since 1984, China has also moved to open up more of the country to FDI. Certain SEZ concessions were extended to Hainan Island in the South China Sea in 1985. Open economic development zones were established from January 1985 in the Yangtze River Delta, the Pearl River Delta, the south-eastern Fujian Delta (Xiamen-Zhangzhou-Quanzhou), the Liaodong and Shandong Peninsulas, and the Bohai Sea Coastal Region. In March 1988, Hainan Island was separated administratively from Guangdong Province to form a Super-SEZ. In 1990, the Pudong District of Shanghai was designated as a new development zone to lead development along the Yangtze River. By 1994, China had opened up all provincial capitals in the interior, 13 cities bordering neighbouring countries, approved 27 economic and technological development regions, and 52 new and high-tech industrial development zones.[16]

The huge inflows of foreign capital in the late 1980s and, in particular, in the early 1990s (see pp. 206–9 for data and further discussion) have allowed the Chinese Government to be more discriminating in its attitude to inward investment. Furthermore, the scale of the investment, particularly that in real estate, was partly blamed for the high rates of price inflation that beset the Chinese economy in 1992–93. FDI policy since 1994 has thus been aimed at ensuring that any inflow of investment is consistent both with China's domestic industrial policy and its wider economic objectives.

In April 1994, the State Council outlined new proposals to attract FDI into the agriculture, hydropower, communications, energy and raw material sectors through favourable tax policies and selective financial support. On 3 November 1994, the State Administration for Industry and Commerce (SAFIC) and the Ministry for Foreign Trade and Economic Co-operation (MOFTEC) issued a *Circular on Issues relating to Strengthening the Examination and Approval of Foreign-funded Enterprises.*[17] This tightened the procedures regarding the approval of contracts and the registration of foreign enterprises, and enhanced the penalties if agreements were not fulfilled. Investors were thereafter required to pay in their registered capital within a prescribed time limit. Failure to do so (Article 10) might result in the revocation of the approval documents and/or the business license of the enterprise. If no time limit was specified in the contract or Articles of Association, then (Article 6) approval/registration would not be provided. The terms of the contract/Articles would strictly involve the sharing of interests and risks by the Chinese and foreign partners, and should not involve guarantees by the Chinese partner for the paid-up capital of the foreign firm, or for guaranteed rates of return on loans and/or bonds. Failure to observe these conditions would result in non-approval or non-registration. Confiscation of approval documents, revocation of business licenses, and various penalties might also be applied to phoney ventures set up to take advantage of favourable tax/investment incentives.

The *Provisional Guidelines for Foreign Investment Projects* took effect on 27 June 1995,[18] and were aimed at linking FDI projects more closely to domestic industrial objectives. Priority was to be given to FDI in the agriculture, energy, transportation, telecommunications, basic raw materials, and high-technology industries, and FDI projects which could take advantage of the rich natural resources and relatively low labour costs in the central and north-west regions were to be vigorously encouraged. The Guidelines stipulated that the *Guiding Catalogue of Foreign Investment Projects*[19] was to provide the basis for the examination and approval of FDI projects, which were to be classified to one of four categories: Encouraged, Restricted (Division A and Division B), Prohibited, and Permitted.

'**Encouraged**' projects were those in infrastructure or underdeveloped agriculture; those with new/advanced technology which could upgrade product function, save energy and raw materials, improve economic benefits, or manufacture under-supplied new equipment/materials to satisfy market demand; those which were export-oriented; those which involved new technology/equipment which made full use of natural/regenerative resources and prevented/controlled pollution; those which were in line with industrial policy and which could take advantage of inland human/natural resources; and those other activities encouraged by national laws and administrative regulations. 'Encouraged' projects would be allowed to sell up to 100% of their output in the domestic market. Long-term energy and infrastructure projects (coal, electric power, railway, roads, ports) would be allowed (Article 8) to expand into related business when permission was sought. And 'encouraged' projects would retain certain tax advantages.

'**Restricted**' projects were sub-classified into those whose technologies had been developed or transferred, and those where production exceeded domestic demand (Division A); and those under experiment or monopolized by the State, those engaged in the exploration of rare and valuable mineral resources, those subject to State planning, and those activities restricted by national laws and administrative regulations (Division B). 'Restricted' projects were required to specify a fixed term of operation, and the Chinese partner (Division A projects) was not allowed to use borrowed capital for its investment (Article 9). Approval for 'restricted projects' might only be granted by provincial/municipal or higher-level planning authorities. Preferential tax policies were to be phased out for most 'restricted' projects. The restrictions on Division A projects would be relaxed if they permitted the development of the resources of the central and north-west regions, and if the projects were in line with industrial policy.

'**Prohibited**' projects included those which jeopardized national security or harmed the public interest; those which damaged the environment, natural resources or human health; those which used sizeable amounts of arable land or were detrimental to the protection and development of land resources, or endangered the security and functioning of military facilities; those which applied technologies unique to China; and those other activities which were prohibited by national laws and administrative regulations.[20]

Those FDI projects that were not deemed to be 'encouraged', 'restricted' or 'prohibited' were classified (Article 4) as **'permitted'**, but were not explicitly defined in the *Guiding Catalogue*. Division A 'restricted' projects which derived more than 70% of their sales from export were also deemed 'permitted' and were not subject to Article 9. Most Division A 'restricted' projects concerned investments by Overseas Chinese from Hong Kong, Macao, and Taiwan, and the *Guidelines* thus declared that special treatment was not accorded the Overseas Chinese with regard to inward investment.

FOREIGN DIRECT INVESTMENT IN THE PEOPLE'S REPUBLIC OF CHINA

More than 210,000 foreign-funded ventures had been approved from 1979 to the end of 1994 – see Figure 14.1 – with cumulative pledged (contracted) investment of US$275 billion, and cumulative actual (utilized) investment of US$85.1 billion – see Figure 14.2. In 1994, the amount of actual investment reached US$33.8 billion, which represented about half of total FDI to developing countries worldwide, indicating the strength of China's appeal to international investors. Optimistic Chinese government officials and other commentators believe that these trends are set to continue.

The major international investors in the Chinese market are, not surprisingly, from Hong Kong, Taiwan, US and Japan – see Figure 14.3. Britain is only number six in the list of top investors, but British investment is quite impressive in comparison to FDI from other EU countries – see Figure 14.4 – and exceeds that from Germany, France and Italy. From 1979 to 1994, at least 1,017 British FDI projects were approved, with pledged investment and utilized investment amounting to US$6 billion and US$1,267 million respectively. In 1994 alone, contracted British investment in China was worth about US$2,129 million from 401 projects.[21]

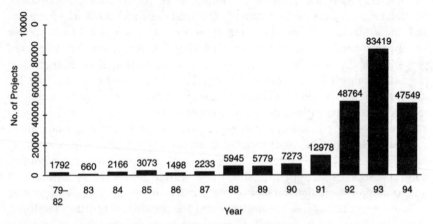

Figure 14.1 Number of FDI projects in China, 1979–94
Source: Almanac of China's Foreign Economic Relations and Trade; Statistical Yearbook of China.

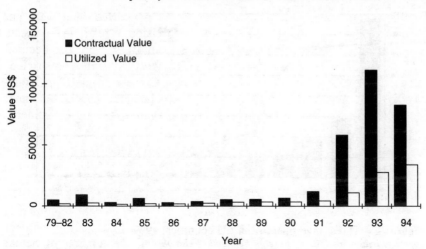

Figure 14.2 Pledged and utilized FDI in China, 1979–94
*Source: Almanac of China's Foreign Economic Relations
and Trade; Statistical Yearbook of China.*

Although foreign investors continued to pour funds into China, the number of new foreign-funded projects and the value of contracted investment declined after the frenzied activity of 1993 in which pledged funds exceeded those for the previous fourteen years combined. This slowdown coincided with attempts by the authorities to calm the overheating domestic economy. Moves to clamp down on real estate speculation were a major factor in the 43% and 26% fall-off in the number of contracts approved and the value of contracted FDI in 1994. In the first quarter of 1995, the value

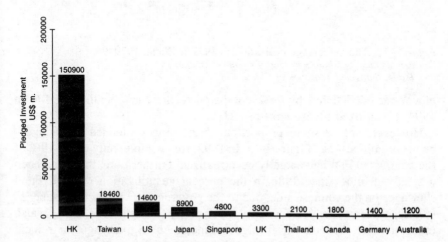

Figure 14.3 The top ten investors in China, 1979–93
Source: Almanac of China's Foreign Economic Relations and Trade;
MOFTEC Foreign Investment Administration.

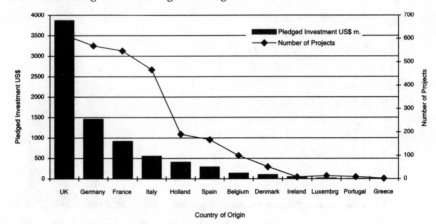

Figure 14.4 Direct investment from EU countries, 1979–93
Source: Almanac of China's Foreign Economic Relations;
MOFTEC Foreign Investment Administration.

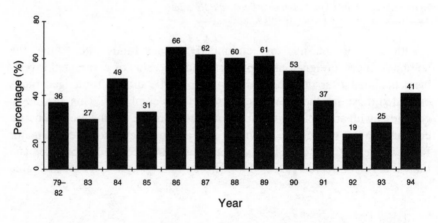

Figure 14.5 The percentage utilization of FDI in China, 1979–94
*Source: Almanac of China's Foreign Economic Relations
and Trade; Statistical Yearbook of China.*

of contracted FDI fell by 25% compared to the corresponding period in 1994, but utilized investment rose 21%.

However, only a small proportion of the money pledged has actually been committed – see Figure 14.5. In 1992, for example, only about 19% of the contracted FDI had actually been realized. Furthermore, there had been a steady decline since 1986 in the percentage utilization of FDI. Fund shortages on the Chinese side, due to the government's tight credit squeeze to control the overheated economy, were partly to blame. The squeeze also made it more difficult for foreign businessmen to exchange their local earnings into foreign currency. In addition, many of the announced projects were actually fraudulent: an acknowledged fact that should not be under-estimated. Phoney joint ventures were set up to take advantage of favourable tax incentives on offer,[22] with bribes paid to the relevant authorities to turn a blind eye to these activities. Finally, unexpected risk exposures may also be partly to blame for the decline. Even though China did make great efforts to improve its investment environment, the so-called 'China factors'[23] did still discourage many foreign investors from making a whole-hearted commitment. It is nevertheless worth noting that the gap between utilized and contracted capital narrowed significantly between 1992 and 1994. The percentage of utilized capital to contracted capital in 1994 was 41%, almost double the proportions in 1992 and 1993. The policy measures introduced in 1993–94 should ensure that this percentage continues to rise (the ratio in the first quarter of 1995 was 45%). A number of other trends may also be identified in the pattern of FDI in China, namely:

- a growth in the average size of projects
- the penetration of FDI to the inland provinces
- increasing investment in tertiary industry
- the increasing importance of FDI in the total inflow of foreign capital
- an increasing number of investing countries/regions

A growth in the average size of projects

The average size of projects has been changing as the industrial composition of FDI in China has been changing – see Figure 14.6. The average size of projects in the early 1980s was quite large due to the predominance of 'non-productive' projects such as hotels and amusement parks. However, the average size declined quite dramatically from US$3 million in 1984 to about US$0.9 million in 1988 as a result of the establishment (mainly by Hong Kong and Taiwanese investors) of large numbers of small-scale

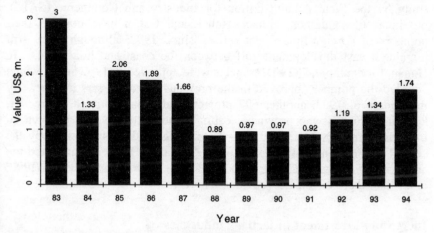

Figure 14.6 The average size of FDI projects, 1983–94
Source: Almanac of China's Foreign Economic Relations and Trade; Statistical Yearbook of China.

labour-intensive manufacturing operations. But the average size has since started to rise again to US$1.7 million in 1994. These figures reflect China's new emphasis on capital intensive, high-tech and infrastructure investments. The figures also reflect the movement into China of large Western multinational enterprises (MNEs), particularly in infrastructure investment and other key industrial projects. In the telecommunications sector, for example, Motorola, AT&T, Ericsson, Northern Telecom, Alcatel, Siemens, NEC, and Hong Kong Telcom all have ambitious investing plans. Motorola, for instance, invested US$300 million by the end of 1994 in factories producing cellular phones, paging systems and semiconductors. And Hong Kong Telcom will invest US$260 million in a fibre optic link from Hong Kong to Beijing and a mobile telephone network in Beijing. Moreover, in such core industries as petrochemicals, agrochemicals and automobiles, large MNEs are stepping up their efforts to secure a foothold. Car giants such as Toyota, Ford and General Motors are fighting for market share, attracted by the prospect of China becoming a major new market for passenger cars and commercial vehicles. At the same time, the list of active investors in the petrochemical and agrochemical sectors is getting longer and longer, including such renowned companies as Aramco, the Saudi Arabian State Oil Company, Shell, ICI, BP, Zeneca and Du Pont.[24]

The penetration of FDI to the inland provinces

Apart from a trend towards larger scale projects, foreign investment has also became more widely distributed geographically within China, with the inland provinces showing bigger percentage increases (though from lower bases) in new investment than the coastal regions. This is a direct result of China's policy of opening up the whole country to FDI. According to a study by the State Administration for Industry and Commerce (SAIC), provinces like Guizhou, Hunan, Hubei, and Gansu have doubled their numbers of foreign-funded enterprises since 1992, although there still remains a vast development gulf between the coast and hinterland.[25] In Hunan, for example, 782 FDI projects were approved in 1992 alone, which doubled the number approved in the previous thirteen years together. By the middle of 1993, another 697 projects had been approved. Moreover, key cities such as the provincial capitals and ports have also shown an immediate rush of FDI, after they were designated as open cities by the central government in 1992. In Wuhan, capital of Hubei Province and the cross-roads of central China,[26] 300 FDI projects were approved in 1992, more than the total for the previous ten years.[27]

Increasing investment in tertiary industries

There has been a marked jump in the value of FDI in real estate, public utilities and services – see Figure 14.7. Investment in these sectors was

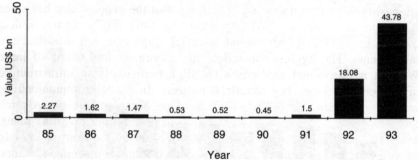

Figure 14.7 The value of FDI projects in Chinese real estate, public utilities and services, 1985–93
Source: Almanac of China's Foreign Economic Relations and Trade.

fairly constant at about US$0.5–2 m. each year over the period 1985 to 1991, but there was a twelvefold increase in both the value and the number of projects in 1992, and a further doubling in the value to US$44 m. in 1993. These developments have meant that real estate, utilities and services accounted for almost 40% of total FDI in 1993 (compared with 5% in 1990), whereas manufacturing only accounted for 46% of total FDI in 1993 (compared with 84% in 1990). These trends are likely to continue as China upgrades its industrial structure and as it liberalizes its service sector in preparation for entry to the World Trade Organization.

The increasing importance of FDI in the total inflow of foreign capital

One immediate result of the 1986 policy adjustments regarding FDI has been to stimulate a steady annual increase in the proportion of the total capital inflow to China provided through direct investment – see Figure

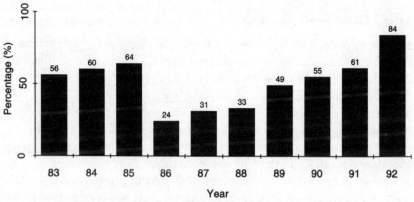

Figure 14.8 FDI as a proportion of total capital inflow in China, 1983–92
Note: Percentage refers to FDI as a percentage of total Foreign Capital (including FDI and Foreign Loan).
Source: Almanac of China's Foreign Economic Relations and Trade.

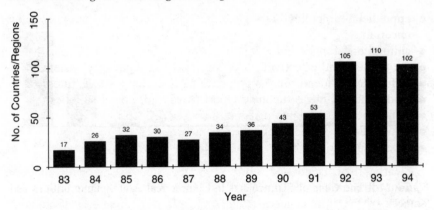

Figure 14.9 The numbers of countries/regions investing in China, 1983–94
*Source: Almanac of China's Foreign Economic Relations and Trade;
Statistical Yearbook of China.*

14.8. In 1986, FDI only accounted for 24% of the total inflow of capital, but this proportion had increased to 84% by 1992. This trend highlights the increasing importance of FDI for the economic modernization programme in China.

The increasing numbers of investing countries/regions

The numbers of investing countries/regions has increased dramatically since the introduction of the 'open-door policy', reflecting China's growing appeal to international investors. Over the period 1983 to 1993 – see Figure 14.9 – the numbers of investing countries/regions increased from 17 to 110.[28]

CONCLUDING REMARKS

The past two decades have seen remarkable changes in policy towards inward direct investment in China. Four distinct stages can be identified. Before 1979, the policy was essentially one of prohibition. The 'open-door policy' then ushered in a period of participation between 1979 and 1986. The '22 Article Provisions' of October 1986 amended the policy to one of active promotion of foreign investment. And the *Provisional Guidelines* of June 1995 would appear to be moving towards more selective permission of foreign enterprises in the Chinese economy.

China in the mid-1990s offers attractive growth prospects and extraordinary opportunities for foreign investors yet there are – as in many other emerging markets – many practical difficulties. The authors' fieldwork in August–November 1994 suggested that the following issues were of widespread concern:

- unpredictable policy changes, including political and economic uncertainty;
- cultural differences and communication;
- the fairness and effectiveness of the legal and regulatory systems;
- difficulties in identifying appropriate partners for joint ventures;
- inadequacy of infrastructure support (road, rail, power supplies);
- difficulties in setting up distribution networks;
- availability and quality of senior managers;
- accessibility to raw material supplies and to market information.

Clearly, there is no one 'correct' strategy for dealing with all these various difficulties, and much will depend upon the particular circumstances of the firm concerned and the industry. Some brief comments may, however, be useful in demonstrating how some of the more 'enlightened' British companies have coped.[29]

The far-reaching economic reforms have contributed to the uncertainty of doing business in China. The inevitable temptation is to insist upon complete management control of any Chinese affiliate, and to have an 'easy exit' strategy – and many foreign investors have succumbed to this temptation. Yet a long-term commitment is essential for understanding Chinese business culture, for building-up meaningful business relationships and, ultimately, for success in the Chinese market.

Investment in a wholly-owned subsidiary is an attractive option for foreign firms not wishing to spend time etc. arranging a suitable Chinese partner for a joint venture. But wholly-owned subsidiaries may be subject to a number of requirements (export targets, advanced technology) or restrictions (non-entry to certain industries) that make this mode of investment impractical. One possible solution is to establish a joint venture with a 'silent' Chinese partner who provides local know-how and political contacts, but has no involvement in the venture's management control. The foreign firm may thus take advantage of many of the opportunities available to a joint venture, whilst essentially running a wholly-owned subsidiary.

Cultural difficulties are an oft-cited source of frustration for foreigners attempting to do business in China, particularly when combined with the seemingly – to Western eyes – arbitrary nature of the Chinese legal and regulatory systems. The key is to understand the historical roots of the problem. As Lee Kuan Yew has pointed out:[30]

During periods of strong rule, imperial power reached into the furthest corners of the Chinese Empire. The exercise of this power was arbitrary and brutal: the Mandarin was both prosecutor and judge. A separate judiciary was never established and hence the ordinary person never looked to the law to settle his grievances. Traditionally, he would take the law into his own hands. The modern equivalent of this situation is that the bureaucrat interprets central regulations to suit the conditions of his own province and city. Family ties and closely-knit peasant society have lent value to personal relationships. Where there is not enough to eat, not enough room on the bus or not enough steel for the factory, personal relationships are vital. They provide the lubricant which smoothes away anarchy. *Guanxi* is the asset value of personal relationship built up from family, village schoolmates and so on. In short, Chinese law is flexible and open to interpretation by officials, whilst Western law is rigid and can be interpreted only by the courts . . . . What ethnic Chinese from Hong Kong, Macau and Taiwan did was to demonstrate that guanxi through the same language and culture can make up for a lack in the rule of law and the transparency in rules and regulations. This guanxi capability will be of value for the next twenty years at least, until China develops a system based on rule of law and with sufficient transparency and certainty to satisfy foreign investors.

The solution is thus not to expect Western methods and standards in China, but to adapt to the Chinese contemporary reality. One common strategy is to employ well-connected (perhaps Western-educated) Chinese senior management to facilitate mutual understanding between partners, and other local managers not only to provide prompt notification of policy changes but also to allow effective resolution of practical difficulties.

Bureaucratic delays, changing administrative regulations, restricted market access may also plague the foreign investor. One way to deal with theses difficulties is to design a corporate strategy that encompasses the aims of the Chinese authorities. One successful British company in a service industry under tight central control has made progress by offering intensive training to the staff of local competitors, by providing these companies with up-to-date market information, and by offering assistance in international markets. By so doing, it has established its long-term commitment to the Chinese industry. As a result, it has built up particularly good relations with the industry regulator and its major local competitors, and was the first foreign firm in the industry to be granted a nationwide operating license. This privileged position has enabled the British firm to capture a good deal of business in the short-term from foreign enterprises in the Chinese market.

It is of course too early to see the impact of the 1994–95 reforms on trade with, and investment in, the People's Republic of China. Given the more industry-specific nature of the new FDI policy towards projects in power generation, transportation, oil and gas exploration, telecommunications, and heavy machinery, it would seem likely that more and more Western companies will become involved and that the average size of FDI projects will continue to grow. Such a prediction is reinforced by the fact that Chinese FDI policy appears to be moving towards fairer 'national treatment' of foreign companies. Indeed, it is anticipated that tax reforms in the coming years will include the introduction of a unified enterprise income tax, applicable to both domestic and foreign firms, regardless of location.

Thus foreign companies in the future will pay rather more attention to infrastructure and market proximity in selecting investment locations, and will be less likely to be guided by tax incentives etc. on offer in designated zones. If the dominant form of Sino-foreign business in the 1980s was the straightforward sales of goods and/or equipment, the most popular form in the late 1990s is likely to be direct investment.

NOTES

1 See Chow (1994: 8–9) for a more extensive discussion.
2 Though not for all Chinese industry as many smaller enterprises were operated by local and provincial governments.
3 Chow (1994: 27–9).
4 See Strange and Wu (1995) for a fuller discussion of the impact of the Chinese reforms on British trade and investment with the People's Republic.
5 The policy was endorsed at the Second Annual Session of the Fifth National People's Congress in June 1979. See Chow (1994: 19).
6 The following description of the reform process is taken from Chow (1994: 30–6).
7 See Chow (1994: 33).
8 See Lardy (1992: 38–82) for an extensive discussion of reform over the period 1978 to 1990.
9 Pomfret (1995: 21).
10 Dalian, Qinhuangdao, Tianjin, Yantai, Qingdao, Lianyungang, Nantong, Shanghai, Ningbo, Wenzhou, Fuzhou, Zhanjiang, Guangzhou and Beihai.
11 Preferential treatment was provided to the SEZs and fourteen coastal cities mainly through tax concessions. For details, see the *Provisional Regulations on Reduction and Exemption of Income Tax and Industrial and Commercial Consolidated Tax for Enterprises in the Special Economic Zones and 14 Port Cities*.
12 The subject laws on joint ventures are such as the *Detailed Rules for the Implementation of the Regulations of the People's Republic of China on Labour Management in Joint Ventures Using Chinese and Foreign Investment*, the *Regulations for Providing Loans to Joint Ventures Using Chinese and Foreign Investment by the Bank of China*, the *Provisional Regulations of the General Bureau of Industrial and Commercial Administration of the People's Republic of China on the Standard of Registration fees to be paid by Joint Ventures Using Chinese and Foreign Investment*, the *Income Tax Law of the People's Republic of China Concerning Foreign Enterprises*, and the *Rules for the Implementation of Foreign Exchange Controls Relating to Individuals*.
13 See *The China Investment Guide* (fifth edition), pp. 172–6. The preferential treatment included: (a) 100% refund of income tax already paid on the rein-vested portion when profits are reinvested in export-oriented or high-technology enterprises for an operation of no less than five years. (b) Export enterprises and technologically advanced enterprises may enjoy a list of special treatments: the exemption of various subsidies granted by the state to the staff; the reduction of land renting charges; bills for water, electricity, means of transport and communication facilities needed by the enterprises being calculated at the same rate as for local state enterprises; priority in receiving loans for short term circulation funds for production and other needed credits, after examination by the Bank of China; the exemption of income tax on investors' profits when remitted abroad. (c) 50% reduction of income tax at the current

rate for export enterprises with a more than 70% export ratio, and a 10% of income tax for export enterprises that already pay a 15% income tax to local authorities; three-year extension of income tax payment at a 50% reduction rate for technologically advanced enterprises after the expiration of the period for the reduction or exemption of enterprise income tax in accordance with state provisions.

14 See *The China Investment Guide* (fifth edition), pp. 151–4. See also Article 3 of the *Detailed Rules for the Implementation of the Law of the People's Republic of China on Wholly Foreign-Owned Enterprises*, approved by the State Council on 28 October 1990. *The China Investment Guide* (fifth edition), pp. 155–72.

15 The 'Decision on Amendment of "The Law of the People's Republic of China on Chinese-Foreign Equity Joint Ventures"' was passed on 4 April 1990 at the Third Session of the Seventh National People's Congress. See *The China Investment Guide* (fifth edition), pp. 115–18.

16 *The China Investment Guide* (fifth edition), pp. 573–6.

17 MOFTEC. *International Business* 4 (April 1995): 63–4.

18 *People's Daily (overseas edition)* (1 July 1995).

19 Drafted by the State Planning Commission.

20 The prohibited list thus applies to projects in agriculture, forestry, husbandry, fishery and associated industries, light industry, petrochemical/chemical, and pharmaceutical industries which are related to valuable natural/mineral resources and/or unique traditional technologies; to projects extracting and processing radioactive mineral resources; to projects in futures trading, electrified wire netting construction/management, city water supply/drainage construction/management, city gas/heating power network construction/management, postal and network telecommunications operations, aviation management, journalism, newspaper publishing, broadcasting, film producing and releasing, and video showing; to projects in military weapon manufacturing; to other industrial activities which jeopardize the security/functioning of military facilities, which process raw materials which can cause cancer, deformity and mutation, or which engage in gambling and pornography; and to other industrial activities which are prohibited by agreements between China and relevant countries, or by international treaties of which China is a signatory.

21 Authors' estimates.

22 See also Pomfret (1995: 23).

23 These include the parlous state of much of the country's infrastructure; difficulties of arranging distribution and supply due to a crumbling transport system; lack of convertibility of the yuan; bureaucratic strictures that complicate personnel management; opaque rules and regulations; and an unreliable legal system whose dispute-setting mechanisms are loaded heavily against the foreign party. See pp. 212–14 for further discussion.

24 *Financial Times* (7 November 1994).

25 Ibid.

26 Wuhan lies half-way up the Yangtze, and halfway between Beijing and Guangzhou on the main north–south railway line.

27 *Beijing Review* (15 February 1993).

28 The reasons for the apparent fall in the number to 102 in 1994 are unclear, and may reflect problems of data collection.

29 More extensive case studies of the companies involved have been prepared, but have not yet been approved for publication. Please contact the authors for further information.

30 In addressing the Second World Chinese Entrepreneurs Convention in Hong Kong (22 November 1993).

BIBLIOGRAPHY

Chow, G.C. (1994) *Understanding China's Economy*, Singapore: World Scientific Publishing.

Lardy, N.R. (1992) *Foreign Trade and Economic Reform in China, 1978–1990*, Cambridge: University Press.

Pomfret, R. (1995) 'Chinese Economic Reform, 1978–1994', *MOCT-MOST: Economic Policy in Transitional Economies* 5(1): 13–27.

Strange, R. and Xiaohong, W. (1995) *British Trade and Investment Relations with the People's Republic of China*, Report prepared for the British Chamber of Commerce in Hong Kong, July.

Taylor, R. (1990) *China, Japan and the European Community*, London: Athlone Press.

Yue, X.Z. (1993) *The EC and China*, London: Butterworth & Co.

15 Financial centres in the Asia Pacific Region: the prospects for Taipei

Yi-Cheng Liu and Roger Strange

INTRODUCTION

The Asia Pacific Region includes a number of national economies which have, over the past few years, experienced, and are still experiencing very high rates of economic growth. Concomitant with this economic development, there has not only been a substantial inflow of foreign capital in search of lucrative investment opportunities, but also many governments in the region have taken a series of measures to deregulate their financial sectors during the 1980s. As a result, the financial markets in these countries have expanded rapidly, in terms of the range and variety of financial instruments, the volume of financial transactions, and the efficiency of the financial systems.

Development in the region has emphasized export-oriented industrialization and the improvement of domestic infrastructure, and these objectives have created a substantial demand for capital throughout the region. Taiwan is eager to play a more active and important role in regional development in the future, and its government has been encouraging Taiwanese industrialists and financial institutions to diversify their investments from mainland China to the other South-east Asian countries for both political and economic reasons. The Taiwanese Government has also been promoting an industrial upgrading policy.[1] One of the goals of this policy is to establish Taipei as a major Financial Centre for capturing the new international financial business generated from trade emanating in the Asia Pacific Region.

However, there are already three well-established Financial Centres in the region, namely: Hong Kong, Singapore and Tokyo. Furthermore, a successful financial reform programme during the 1980s has led to the emergence of Sydney as an important new Financial Centre. In addition, at the beginning of the 1990s, the benefits of being a Financial Centre have attracted the governments of various other countries (e.g. Indonesia, Thailand, and PRC) to set up their own initiatives. Besides these external challenges, Taiwan's financial sector has long been criticized for being outdated and inadequate.

This chapter examines the prospects of Taipei becoming a major Financial Centre in the Asia Pacific Region, and suggests how the process of financial liberalization and internationalization should be pursued to aid the further development of the Taiwanese economy. The structure of the chapter is as follows: The first section (pp. 219–22) considers the definition and classification of various types of Financial Centre. We shall then consider previous empirical work on the ranking of Financial Centres, and identify the financial variables that are of most significance (pp. 222–4). The next section presents a statistical ranking (using cluster and factor analysis) of twelve Financial Centres in the Asia Pacific Region (pp. 224–30). And, finally, we shall discuss the future prospects of Taipei in the light of the statistical analysis and of recent institutional developments (pp. 230–1).

THE DEFINITION AND CLASSIFICATION OF FINANCIAL CENTRES

Notwithstanding their significance for world economic development in the past few decades, there are very few economic studies of Financial Centres. Indeed, there is little agreement on what constitutes a Financial Centre (FC), and even the most comprehensive financial/banking dictionaries lack a formal definition.

The definitions of Nadler *et al.* (1955), Kindleberger (1974), and Dufey and Giddy (1978) are quite similar, and may be summarized as follows: A Financial Centre is a city with a high concentration of financial institutions that clear the financial transactions for a country. In the words of Kindleberger:

> Financial centers are needed not only to balance through time the savings and investments of individual entrepreneurs and to transfer financial capital from savers to investors, but also to effect payments and to transfer savings between places. Banking and financial centers perform a medium of exchange function and an interspatial store-of-value function. Single payments between separate points in a country are made most efficiently through a center, and both seasonal and long-run surpluses and deficits of financial savings are best matched in a center. Furthermore, the specialized functions of international payments and foreign lending are typically best performed at one central place that is also (in some instances) the specialized center for domestic interregional payments.[2]

Choi, Tschoegl and Yu's definition is more up-to-date, and takes into account the more sophisticated requirements for a contemporary FC. 'A financial center is a marketplace for financial services. For the marketplace to function, the location must have the following characteristics: (i) a stable legal and regulatory environment that permits entry, operation, and ownership, and (ii) an adequate infrastructure, particularly for physical and electronic communication.'[3]

Clearly, however, some FCs are larger both in the scale and scope of their activities than others, and this has led to various attempts at categorization. Thus Nadler *et al.* define an *International Financial Centre* (IFC) as a city that acts as a clearinghouse for a large value and variety of international transactions, and set out seven basic conditions essential for IFC development:

- a sound and stable financial system;
- substantial and constant demand and supply of the country's currency;
- a well-adjusted balance-of-payments;
- the domestic financial institutions must be capable of handling international financial transactions;
- a liberal financial system for foreign financial institutions;
- specialized institutions that supplement the commercial banking institutions in foreign financial transactions;
- the domicile of the country's Central Bank.

Dufey and Giddy suggest that IFCs are those domestic Centres offering the greatest convenience in terms of financial services, geographic location, international communications, etc., and that they exist as IFCs because they are able to realize efficiency gains through specialization and economies of scale. Kindleberger concurs and, in particular, stresses the number, size and internationalization of banks in the formation process of IFCs.

Johnson (1976) distinguished between *Regional Financial Centres* (which derive their role from their geographical proximity to their customers, and from the safety and ease of operation of foreign banks' branches) and *International Financial Centres* (which serve as a magnet for institutions whose financial, banking and insurance activities serve a substantial part of the world). Gorostiaga (1984) attempted to classify IFCs using an imperial/colonial model. On the one hand, the traditional IFCs (London, New York, Frankfurt, Zurich, etc.) are those that have developed on the basis of domestic capital from local savings and/or funds arising from international trade. These IFCs act as banking centres for their colonies and as depositaries for the reserves of those countries dependent upon the metropolis. On the other hand, the new IFCs (Hong Kong, Bahamas, Bahrain, Panama and Singapore) are of more recent origin, and are typically situated in underdeveloped countries. They lack financial autonomy, and are normally extensions of the traditional Centres, but operating in different time zones.[4]

Reed (1981: 58) noted that the activities of a FC were subject to external influences from other FCs and national economies, and suggested that all Centres were IFCs but that some Centres might serve, to a certain extent, as satellite FCs for more important FCs. He posited a taxonomy of FCs on the basis of extensive statistical analysis (see pp. 222–4, 'Previous Empirical

Analyses', for details) of 80 cities in 1980, with five hierarchical levels as follows:

- Supranational Financial Centre
  (London)
- Supranational Financial Centres of the First Order
  (New York, Tokyo)
- Supranational Financial Centres of the Second Order
  (Amsterdam, Chicago, Frankfurt, Hamburg, Hong Kong, Paris, San Francisco, Zurich)
- International Financial Centres
  (Bahrain, Basle, Beirut, Bogota, Brussels, Buenos Aires, Caracas, Dusseldorf, Jakarta, Johannesburg, Kobe, Kuala Lumpui, Los Angeles, Luxembourg, Madrid, Melbourne, Mexico City, Milan, Montreal, Moscow, Osaka, Panama City, Rio de Janeiro, Rome, Sao Paulo, Seoul, Singapore, Sydney, Toronto)
- Host International Financial Centres
  (Alexandra, Antwerp, Augsberg, Bangkok, Barcelona, Belgrade, Berlin, Bergen, Bombay, Cadiz, Cairo, Calcutta, Canton, Cape Town, Copenhagen, Florence, Geneva, Leningrad, Le Havre, Lima, Lisbon, Lyons, Manila, Montevideo, Munich, Nagoya, Naples, Oslo, Rangoon, Seattle, Shanghai, Santiago, Stockholm, Tientsin, Turin, Vancouver, Venice, Vienna, Yokohama).

According to Reed, *Host International Financial Centres* are those which substantially enhance their financial infrastructure and capabilities by attracting foreign financial institutions, but are usually not a headquarter location for large internationally active banks. In comparison to host FCs, the *International Financial Centres* have a relatively larger number of foreign banks from a relatively larger number of foreign countries, and many are headquarter locations for large internationally active banks. *Supranational Centres* are pre-eminent in finance, communications, and management. They are managers of large amounts of foreign financial assets and liabilities; work closely with large numbers of large industrial corporations; and attract and generate information and ideas that eventually establish the operating and organizational norms that govern internationally active organizations.[5]

An alternative approach to classification is to focus on the functions provided by the FC. Park (1989) categorized FCs according to whether they acted primarily as a source and/or as a destination of funds. Thus he distinguished the following:

- *Primary Centres* (e.g. London, New York, Tokyo).
  Worldwide collection and distribution of funds.
- *Funding Centres* (e.g. Bangkok, Brussels, Seoul, Singapore).
  Supply inward financial intermediation.

- *Collection Centres* (e.g. Amsterdam, Jakarta, Kuala Lumpur).
  Supply outward financial intermediation.
- *Booking Centres* (e.g. Bahamas, Cayman Islands).
  Collection and distribution of funds of non-residents.

Abraham *et al.* (1993: 5) comment that this classification focuses on the nature, rather than the volume, of activity in each FC. They point out that the nature of activity is rapidly changing in the major Centres, and that this activity is nearly always a mix of different functions and that this mix is also subject to rapid change. We would concur. If we neglect the special case of Booking Centres, our belief is that differences between FCs are differences of degree rather than kind, and that categorization can be both meaningless and misleading. All FCs deal, to a greater or lesser extent, with inward and outward flows of goods, services, capital and information between their domestic economies and the rest of the world, and are therefore *international*. All supply a greater or lesser range of financial services and instruments. That is not to say that Taipei and Tokyo, for example, are of similar importance as FCs in the Asia Pacific Region – or indeed that they ever will be – but the same basic range of financial activities is undertaken in both cities. Thus we feel that a hierarchical ranking on the basis of chosen criteria, rather than an essentially *ad hoc* categorization, is a more appropriate method of examining the relative positions of different FCs.

PREVIOUS EMPIRICAL ANALYSES

Much of the early literature on Financial Centres was largely historical and descriptive in nature. A more systematic and objective approach to classification was pioneered by Reed in his 1981 study[6] of the organizational structure of FCs, and of the requirements for FC development over time. Reed collated data on nine financial and banking variables for 76 cities,[7] and then used cluster analysis to group the FCs into homogeneous clusters for selected years between 1900 and 1980. Finally he utilized hierarchical discriminant analysis to identify those variables which were most significant for distinguishing between clusters, and to rank the FCs according to their scores as calculated from the discriminant function.

In a subsequent 1987 paper, Reed refined and extended his basic dataset to sixteen variables. Six variables were retained from the 1981 study, while ten new variables were added to take account of new factors. The sixteen variables were:

- Foreign Financial Assets held in the Centre
- Foreign Financial Liabilities residing in the Centre
- Total international currency clearings (daily average) of the Centre
- Size (liabilities) of the Centre's Eurocurrency market
- Total amount of international bonds issued in the Centre during the year
- Stock exchange activity (daily average) of the Centre

- The number of large internationally active banks headquartered in the Centre
- Capital/deposit ratio of the large internationally active banks headquartered in the Centre
- Capital/asset ratio of the large internationally active banks headquartered in the Centre
- Pre-tax earnings/capital ratio of the large internationally active banks headquartered in the Centre
- Pre-tax earnings/assets ratio of the large internationally active banks headquartered in the Centre
- Revenue/asset ratio of the large internationally active banks headquartered in the Centre
- The number of large internationally active foreign banks with offices (agencies, branches or subsidiaries) in the Centre
- The number of foreign Financial Centres with direct links to the local Centre, where the links are provided by foreign internationally active banks
- The Centre's airline passenger traffic (annual total)
- The Centre's airmail/airfreight volume (annual total).

The most significant variables for FC organization were found to be the amount of international currency clearings, the size of the Eurocurrency market, foreign financial assets, and the number of large internationally active commercial banks. Reed then classified the FCs into *Supranational Centres* (New York and London), *International Centres* (Amsterdam, Frankfurt, Paris, Tokyo and Zurich), and *Host Centres* (Hong Kong, Melbourne, Singapore and fifteen other cities).[8]

Choi *et al.* (1986) examined the location pattern of offices of the world's 300 largest banks. They considered fourteen FCs worldwide, and ranked them in 1970 and 1980 according to the number of banks with representative offices in the Centre in question. London, New York and Tokyo were the three most important FCs in both years, with New York displacing London in first place between 1970 and 1980. The Asia Pacific Region assumed more importance through the decade, with Tokyo, Hong Kong and Singapore rising to second, fifth and sixth places respectively in the ranking. The authors then used regression analysis to assess the reasons for the relative attractiveness of the fourteen FCs. They found that the degree of interpenetration had increased substantially through the decade, and that the attractiveness of a FC was related to the size of the economy it represented (measured by *per capita* GNP multiplied by the population of the FC), and to the amount of international financial activity (as measured by the number of banks that were already there). Furthermore some internationally rivalrous behaviour was detected in the sense that foreign bank presence in a Centre was generally associated with an increased propensity by domestic banks to establish a presence in the foreign Centre.

Goldberg, Helsley and Levi (1989) also used regression analysis to predict the size of the financial sector using a number of cross-section and time-series models. Their analysis points to the influence of imports (positive) and exports (negative!), and also suggests that a measure of economic development (e.g. *per capita* GDP) should be included.

Finally Abraham *et al.* used 1990 data to rank thirty-seven FCs according to their importance measured, on the one hand, by the international links of the financial institutions therein and, on the other hand, by the volume of their outstanding foreign assets and liabilities. The general approach is similar to that of Reed but, rather than using cluster/discriminant analysis, Abraham *et al.* use factor analysis to effect their rankings. Nine explanatory variables were used:

- The number of domestic banks with their headquarters in the Centre
- The number of FCs having a link with the Centre via the domestic banks headquartered in that Centre
- The number of FCs having a link with the Centre via a domestic bank having only a representative office in the Centre
- The number of FCs having a link with a given Centre via a foreign bank established in the Centre
- The number of FCs having a link with a given Centre via a foreign bank with only a representative office in the Centre
- The number of foreign banks established in a Centre
- The number of foreign banks with only a representative office in the Centre
- Foreign financial assets of commercial banks in the Centre
- Foreign financial liabilities of commercial banks in the Centre.

FINANCIAL CENTRES IN THE ASIA PACIFIC REGION

In order to examine the possibility that Taipei could emerge as a significant Financial Centre in the Asia Pacific Region, this study has attempted to rank the following twelve Centres on the basis of data for 1992: Bangkok, Hong Kong, Jakarta, Kuala Lumpur, Manila, Seoul, Shanghai, Singapore, Sydney, Taipei, Tokyo, and Wellington. Fourteen explanatory variables have been used (see Appendix, pp. 233–4, for sources), most of which appeared in the earlier studies by Reed, Abraham, etc., as follows:

(i)　Foreign financial assets of domestic deposit banks in the Centre (FFA)
　　FFA not only indicates the performance of the domestic deposit banks but also the wealth of the Centre as accumulated through international financial activities. Reed interpreted FFA as the FC's willingness and capacity to lend abroad and finance the trade activities of foreigners.

(ii)　Foreign financial liabilities of domestic deposit banks in the Centre (FFL)
　　FFL is an important indicator of the creditability and accountability

of the Centre, and is a reflection of the profitability of the financial facilities and environment. Reed interprets FFL as an indicator of foreign confidence in the FC's institutions, and of the economic and political stability of the country. FFL also indicates a willingness of institutions and monetary authorities to accept foreign funds.

(iii) The number of large internationally active banks headquartered in the Centre (LBH)

LBH is an indicator of bank concentration in a Centre. Abraham *et al.* suggest that LBH measures the concentration in a given FC of the decision-making unit in the domestic banking system.

(iv) The number of large internationally active foreign banks with offices in the Centre (FBO)

Foreign banks establish offices in a FC to service trade and to follow their corporate customers. FBO is thus an indicator of a Centre's financial and economic power.

(v) The number of domestic banks ranked in the World Top 1,000 (BANK) (by capital, according to the Banker's Magazine)

Large banks are typically active participants in global financial markets, work closely with large industrial multinationals, are entrusted with large amounts of foreign financial assets and liabilities, and are net suppliers of foreign direct investment capital to the rest of the world. BANK is an indicator of the country's capabilities for participation in international financial activities.

(vi) Capital/asset ratio of the large internationally active banks headquartered in the Centre (CAR)

If a bank has a low capital/asset ratio, depositors will usually direct future funds to other, better capitalized banks. The undercapitalized bank will continue to lose deposits until its capital adequacy rises. CAR is thus an indicator of the soundness and competitiveness of the country's financial institutions.

(vii) Profit/capital ratio of the large internationally active banks headquartered in the Centre (PCR)

Similarly, funds typically flow to banks with higher profit/capital ratios. PCR is thus an indicator of the efficiency and profitability of each country's financial institutions.

(viii) Return/asset ratio of the large internationally active banks headquartered in the Centre (RAR)

As for PCR.

(ix) Total value of shares traded in the Centre's Stock Exchange (annual total) (SHARE)

The stock market is an increasingly important part of the capital market because of the worldwide trend towards securitization. SHARE is a measure of the scale and performance of the stock market, and an indicator of the country's industrialization and capitalization.

(x)   Market capitalization in the Centre's Stock Exchange (end year) (CAP)
       As for SHARE.
(xi)   The number of domestic companies listed on the Centre's Stock Exchange (end year) (COMP)
       COMP presents another dimension of the stock market, which may be a more appropriate measure of size if speculation is a factor.
(xii) Foreign exchange reserves of the country (FOREX)
       FOREX is an indicator of the liquidity and creditworthiness of a FC, and can be a measure of the FC's ability to participate in global financial markets.
(xiii) The country's exports (annual total) (EXPORT)
       International trade is inextricably linked in practice with international financial activities, including various cross-border banking services.
(xiv) The country's imports (annual total) (IMPORT)
       As for EXPORT.

The fourteen variables thus reflect international lending and borrowing (FFA/FFL); international links through financial institutions (LBH/FBO/BANK); domestic banking performance (CAR/RAR/PCR); the size of the domestic stock market (SHARE/CAP/COMP); the availability of foreign exchange (FOREX); and the international trade position (EXPORT/IMPORT). Unfortunately, data was not available for several other pertinent variables (e.g. the amount of international bonds issued, the size of the Eurocurrency market, total international currency clearings) for all twelve FCs, so these variables have had to be excluded from the analysis.

Two statistical techniques were used in the analysis of the data: hierarchical cluster analysis and factor analysis.[9] Cluster analysis was used to

Table 15.1 Agglomeration schedule from cluster analysis of twelve Asia Pacific financial centres

Stage	Number of clusters	Clusters combined		Coefficient
		Cluster 1	Cluster 2	
1	11	Jakarta	Kuala Lumpur	0.815052
2	10	Shanghai	Wellington	3.645181
3	9	Jakarta/KL	Sydney	3.712788
4	8	Jakarta/KL/Syd	Bangkok	4.206362
5	7	Jakarta/KL/Syd/Bkk	Shanghai/Well	6.636519
6	6	Jakarta etc.	Seoul	8.518852
7	5	Hong Kong	Singapore	11.574621
8	4	Jakarta etc.	Taipei	14.037587
9	3	Jakarta etc.	Hong Kong	20.177057
10	2	Jakarta etc.	Singapore	28.242329
11	1	Jakarta etc.	Tokyo	91.290527

group the twelve FCs into homogeneous clusters with similar characteristics so as to provide a preliminary classification. Table 15.1 shows the
results of the cluster analysis in an agglomeration schedule. The first row of
the schedule (Stage 1) represents the eleven-cluster solution. At this stage,
Jakarta and Kuala Lumpur are combined. The squared Euclidean distance
between these two FCs is displayed in the *Coefficient* column. At Stage 2,
Shanghai and Wellington are combined. At Stage 3, Sydney is added to the
Jakarta/Kuala Lumpur cluster, and so on until Stage 11 where all eleven
FCs have been combined in one big cluster. The squared Euclidean distance gives an idea of how dissimilar are the clusters being combined, and
may be used for guidance in deciding how many clusters are needed to
represent the data. A small coefficient indicates that clusters of similar FCs
are being formed. A large coefficient indicates that quite different FCs are
being combined. Agglomeration should therefore stop as soon as the
increase in the coefficient between successive stages becomes 'large' –
but there is no exact definition as to what is 'large'.

The increase between Stages 7 and 8 is fairly large, so it appears as
though the five-cluster solution may be appropriate. Tokyo is in a cluster on
its own; Hong Kong and Singapore are a second cluster; Taipei is a third;
Manila a fourth; and the remaining seven FCs form a fifth. In the four-
cluster solution, Taipei disappears into the pack. These results are consistent with our intuition and the findings of previous studies that Tokyo is a
major FC, while Hong Kong and Singapore are well-established FCs in the
region. That Manila is a separate case comes as no surprise, but what is
interesting is that Taipei appears to have a (slightly) distinctive position.

We now turn to the factor analysis in an attempt to highlight what
determines the status of a Financial Centre. Factor analysis describes the
covariances between the fourteen explanatory variables in terms of a few
underlying, unobservable dimensions (the factors). The objective is to
explain as much of the total sample variance as possible with a small
number of 'meaningful' factors. Table 15.2 shows that principle components factor extraction results in 91.7% of the variance being attributable to
the first four factors (the remaining ten factors account for only 8.3% of the
variance). Each of the four factors, moreover, has an eigenvalue of greater
than 1 (the chosen stopping criterion).

A model with four factors should therefore be adequate to represent the
data. Large factor loadings in the Table suggest that a factor is closely
related to the responsible variable. Thus Factor 1 is highly correlated with
several variables, notably EXPORT, IMPORT, FFA, FFL, CAP, SHARE,
BANK and, to a lesser extent, COMP. The correlations with EXPORT and
IMPORT affirm the significance of international trade. FFA and FFL have
been interpreted as indicators of the willingness of domestic residents and
foreigners respectively to take part in international financial activities.
CAP, SHARE and COMP are all measures of the scale of the stock market,
and indicators of the country's stage of development. And BANK is an

Table 15.2 Factor matrix from principal components analysis of twelve Asia Pacific financial centres

Variable	Factor 1	Factor 2	Factor 3	Factor 4
EXPORT	+0.97856	−0.04659	+0.09068	+0.09871
IMPORT	+0.96923	+0.03954	−0.01938	+0.07005
BANK	+0.93621	−0.12349	+0.27678	+0.04656
FFA	+0.92555	+0.28842	−0.02719	−0.01671
CAP	+0.92191	−0.11395	+0.31281	+0.07276
SHARE	+0.91280	−0.20945	+0.13863	+0.26972
FFL	+0.91246	+0.31513	−0.04572	−0.05205
COMP	+0.82093	−0.12761	+0.26473	−0.11989
LBH	+0.36479	+0.73023	−0.28315	−0.28851
CAR	−0.42938	+0.66891	+0.56581	+0.07891
RAR	−0.43922	+0.57187	+0.55172	+0.41070
FBO	+0.65468	+0.56463	−0.44526	−0.15592
PCR	−0.40968	+0.20162	−0.49720	+0.61691
FOREX	+0.64002	−0.07133	−0.34073	+0.49116
Eigenvalue	8.34	1.95	1.54	1.02
Cumulative % of total variation	59.5%	73.5%	84.5%	91.7%

indicator of the country's capability for participation in international financial activities. Thus Factor 1 may be interpreted as a measure of the *internationalization* (or the extent of international integration) of the economy in which the FC is located, and is related to the size of the economy.

Factor 2 is highly correlated with the variables LBH and FBO, which are both measures of activity by large international banks. Following Abraham *et al.*, we therefore interpret Factor 2 as the *openness to foreign banking* of the Financial Centre. The banking performance ratios, CAR and RAR, are highly correlated with both Factor 2 and Factor 3. This suggests that Factor 3 may be interpreted as the *profitability of domestic banking* in the Financial Centre, but the correlation with Factor 2 is less easy to interpret. Finally Factor 4 is highly correlated with PCR and FOREX, and may be interpreted as a measure of *creditworthiness*. Thus variations in these dimensions accounts for over 90% of the total variation in the sample: Factor 1 (internationalization of the economy) accounts for almost 60%; Factor 2 (FC openness to foreign banking) provides a further 14%; Factor 3 (profitability of domestic banking) contributes 11%; and Factor 4 (creditworthiness) explains 7%.

We can now construct factor scores for each FC, and rank the FCs accordingly, for each of the four factors – see Table 15.3. Each FC thus has a different ranking in terms of the internationalization of the domestic economy, openness to foreign banking, the profitability of domestic banking, and creditworthiness. Tokyo, for example, ranks first in terms of internationalization, second in terms of the profitability of domestic bank-

Table 15.3 Rankings of twelve Asia Pacific financial centres on the basis of factor scores, 1992

Factor 1 (Internationalization)			Factor 2 (Openness)			Factor 3 (Profitability)			Factor 4 (Creditworthiness)		
Rank		Score	Rank		Score	Rank		Score	Rank		Score
1	Tokyo	+2.87	1	Hong Kong	+1.74	1	Manila	+2.08	1	Taipei	+2.01
2	Hong Kong	+0.65	2	Manila	+1.73	2	Tokyo	+1.07	2	Manila	+1.15
3	Singapore	+0.11	3	Singapore	+1.13	3	Seoul	+0.65	3	Bangkok	+0.82
4	Taipei	+0.05	4	Jakarta	+0.09	4	Wellington	+0.20	4	Shanghai	+0.65
5	Seoul	+0.05	5	Sydney	-0.22	5	Shanghai	+0.11	5	Tokyo	+0.27
6	Sydney	-0.23	6	K Lumpur	-0.29	6	Sydney	+0.07	6	Hong Kong	-0.11
7	K Lumpur	-0.40	7	Bangkok	-0.36	7	K Lumpur	-0.13	7	Sydney	-0.43
8	Jakarta	-0.45	8	Tokyo	-0.37	8	Singapore	-0.27	8	Wellington	-0.56
9	Bangkok	-0.47	9	Seoul	-0.54	9	Jakarta	-0.38	9	K Lumpur	-0.65
10	Shanghai	-0.49	10	Shanghai	-0.81	10	Bangkok	-0.47	10	Singapore	-0.78
11	Wellington	-0.70	11	Taipei	-0.83	11	Taipei	-1.07	11	Jakarta	-0.92
12	Manila	-0.98	12	Wellington	-1.28	12	Hong Kong	-1.86	12	Seoul	-1.43

ing, fifth in terms of creditworthiness, but only eighth in terms of openness to foreign banking. These rankings reflect the high costs associated with Tokyo, and the Japanese Government's traditional policies of protectionism and tight regulation.

Hong Kong and Singapore have similar rankings in terms of all four factors: high rankings for internationalization and for openness to foreign banking; low rankings for profitability and creditworthiness. Manila ranks last in terms of internationalization, but either first or second in terms of the other three factors. This reflects the Philippine Government's efforts at financial reform through the 1980s.

Taipei ranks fourth in terms of internationalization, and first in terms of creditworthiness. However, it falls to eleventh place in terms of both openness to foreign banking, and the profitability of domestic banking. These rankings are not surprising. Notwithstanding the recent rapid growth of the economy, the Taiwanese Government has for many years adopted a protectionist policy towards its financial institutions. The banking industry has been monopolized by a few inefficient state-run banks, and few foreign financial institutions have been allowed to open branches in Taipei. No new banks had been established for decades before, on 26 July 1991, the Taiwanese Government issued fifteen new banking licenses after overwhelming pressure from the private sector. Furthermore Taiwan has a long history of foreign exchange control: foreign exchange could not be held privately until the gradual liberalization of the late 1980s, and the Central Bank of China accumulated huge reserves.

THE PROSPECTS FOR TAIPEI

So what then are the prospects for Taipei to develop as a major Financial Centre, to rival Tokyo, Hong Kong and Singapore, in the 1990s? The analysis above suggests that the Taiwanese Government needs to address the following:

(a) the further promotion of the internationalization of the financial sector;
(b) the liberalization of the entry and activities of foreign banks in Taipei;
(c) an improvement in the efficiency of the domestic banking industry.

With regard to the further internationalization of the financial sector, the most significant shortfall for Taipei is in terms of the levels of foreign financial assets (FFA) and liabilities (FFL). The 1992 figures for Taipei are only ~5% of the corresponding figures for Singapore, ~3% of the figures for Hong Kong, and less even than the figures for Seoul and Shanghai.[10] The FFL in Sydney are four times higher than in Taipei, as a result of a series of successful financial reforms and liberalization measures in the 1980s.[11] In the past, Taiwan had a serious shortage of foreign exchange reserves, and this led the government to introduce the policy that all reserves had to be held by the Central Bank. The ever-increasing current account surpluses in the late 1980s generated inflationary pressures which made this policy unsustainable, and a number of deregulation measures have been introduced since 1987. For example, the forward foreign exchange market was opened to enable exporters and importers to hedge better against foreign exchange risk, and payments from imports were permitted to be freely converted into foreign currencies without limitation. Capital movement was liberalized, with the ceilings raised on outward remittances to US$1 million per transaction (US$5 million annually) for both firms and individuals. However, further liberalization of capital movements and of the foreign exchange regulations will be necessary before foreign financial institutions will want to bring further business to Taipei.

Furthermore, the rules regarding the entry and activities of foreign banks within Taipei need to be relaxed. Even now, the number of branches of foreign financial institutions grows slowly, and these branches do not enjoy national treatment. Foreign banks bring financial expertise and special ties with overseas business partners to which domestic banks do not otherwise have access. They also enhance competition by offering local savers and borrowers a greater choice of financial services. And, as Choi *et al.* (1986: 53) suggest, the agglomeration of financial institutions may lead to the development of an interbank market where foreign exchange and money market trading provide an activity in themselves.

Finally, action needs to be taken to improve the efficiency of the domestic banking industry. On the one hand, the scale of the money and capital markets should be enlarged through privatization of the inefficient state-run banks. On the other hand, markets for new financial instruments (e.g. options, futures, swaps) should be developed.[12] There are, of course, difficulties and dangers associated with the above programme, particularly if the various measures are introduced too quickly and without due consideration of their full effects on the domestic economy. Perhaps a greater threat to the prospects of Taipei, however, comes from competition from the other emerging FCs. What odds, for instance, against Shanghai becoming a major Financial Centre within the next ten years?

NOTES

1 'Developing Taiwan R.O.C. as a Regional Operation Centre.'
2 Kindleberger (1974: 6).
3 Choi, Tschoegl and Yu (1986: 52).
4 Tokyo is a serious omission from the classification. Furthermore, Hong Kong and Singapore can no longer really be described as underdeveloped countries.
5 See also Reed (1989: 250–1).
6 Reed (1981). See also Reed (1980).
7 Data on the first five variables were available and usable from 1900 onwards, but data on the final four variables were only available from 1955 onwards. Four additional FCs (Bahrain, Lisbon, Nagoya and Panama City) are included in 1980.

8 It is not clear in Reed (1989) how many other FCs, if any, are considered, or to what year the data relate.
9 For an excellent explanation of both techniques, see chapters 2 and 3 of Norusis (1993).
10 In comparison, the trade figures show Taipei, Hong Kong, Singapore and Shanghai with very similar levels of exports and imports.
11 The size of Sydney's foreign exchange futures market is much larger than Tokyo, Hong Kong or Singapore, and such a market does not even exist in Taipei and other FCs in the Asia Pacific region.
12 The value of shares traded on the Taipei Stock Exchange is exceptionally high (×3 the value in Hong Kong; ×10 the value in Singapore), but this is due to speculation.

BIBLIOGRAPHY

Abraham, J-P., Bervaes, N., Guinotte, A. and Lacroix, Y. (1993) *The Competitiveness of European International Financial Centres*, Bangor: Institute of European Finance.
Choi, S-R., Tschoegl, A.E. and Yu, C-M. (1986) 'Banks and the World's Major Financial Centers, 1970–1980', *Weltwirtschaftliches Archiv*, 122(1): 48–64.
Dufey, G. and Giddy, I.H. (1978) *The International Money Market*, Englewood Cliffs: Prentice-Hall.
Goldberg, M.A., Helsey, R. and Levi, M.D. (1989) 'The Prerequisities for an International Financial Center', in Y.S. Park and M. Essayyad (eds) *International Banking and Financial Centers*, Boston: Kluwer, pp. 49–63.
Gorostiaga, X. (1984) *The Role of International Financial Centers in Underdeveloped Countries*, New York: St Martin's Press.
Johnson, H.G. (1976) 'Panama as a Regional Financial Center', *Economic Development and Cultural Change*, 24(2) January: 261–86.
Kindleberger, C.P. (1974) *The Formation of Financial Centers: a Study in Comparative Economic History*, Princeton Studies in International Finance no. 36, Princeton: Princeton University Press.
Nadler, M. *et al.* (1955) *The Money Market and its Institutions*, New York: Roland Press.
Norusis, M.J. (1993) *Professional Statistics, release 6.0*, Chicago: SPSS Inc.
Park, Y.S. (1989) 'Introduction to International Financial Centers: their Origin and Recent Development', in Y.S. Park and M. Essayyad (eds) *International Banking and Financial Centers*, Boston: Kluwer, pp. 3–9.
Park, Y.S. and Essayyad, M. (eds) (1989) *International Banking and Financial Centers*, Boston: Kluwer.
Reed, H.C. (1980) 'The Ascent of Tokyo as an International Financial Center', *Journal of International Business Studies*, 11(3): 19–35.
—— (1981) *The Pre-eminence of International Financial Centers*, New York: Praeger.
—— (1989) 'Financial Center Hegemony, Interest Rates, and the Global Political Economy', in Y.S. Park and M. Essayyad (eds) *International Banking and Financial Centers*, Boston: Kluwer, pp. 247–68.

APPENDIX 15.1: DATA SOURCES

(i) FFA = Foreign Financial Assets of domestic deposit banks (US$ billion).

Sources: IMF, *International Financial Statistics Yearbook 1993*.
Economic Research Department, Central Bank of China, *Financial Statistics Monthly (June 1994)*.

(ii) FFL = Foreign Financial Liabilities of domestic deposit banks (US$ billion).

Sources: as for FFA.

(iii) LBH = The number of Large internationally active Banks Head-quartered in the FC.

Source: *The Banker's Almanac and Yearbook 1993*.

(iv) FBO = The number of large internationally active Foreign Banks with Offices in the FC.

Source: as for LBH.

(v) BANK = The number of domestic Banks ranked in the World Top 1,000.

Source: *Banker's Magazine (July 1993)*.

(vi) CAR = Capital/Asset Ratio of the large internationally active banks headquartered in the FC. (Average of 3 banks in each country, except if only 1 or 2 banks listed in World Top 1,000.)

Source: as for BANK.

(vii) PCR = Profit/Capital Ratio of the large internationally active banks headquartered in the FC. (Average of 3 banks in each country, except if only 1 or 2 banks listed in World Top 1,000.)

Source: as for BANK.

(viii) RAR = Return/Asset Ratio of the large internationally active banks headquartered in the FC. (Average of 3 banks in each country, except if only 1 or 2 banks listed in World Top 1,000.)

Source: as for BANK.

(ix) SHARE = Total value of Shares traded in the FCs Stock Exchange (£ million, annual total).

Sources: London Stock Exchange, *Stock Exchange Official Yearbook 1993–1994*.
Economist Intelligence Unit, *China Hand*.
Datastream.

(x) CAP = Market Capitalization in the FCs Stock Exchange (£ million, end year).

Sources: as for SHARE.

(xi) COMP = The number of domestic Companies listed on the FCs Stock Exchange (end year).

Sources: as for SHARE.

(xii) FOREX = Foreign Exchange Reserves of the country (US$ million).

Sources: as for FFA.

(xiii) EXPORT = Exports from the country (annual total) (US$ billion).
Source: IMF, *International Financial Statistics Yearbook 1993*.
(xiv) IMPORT = Imports to the country of the FC (annual total) (US$ billion).
Source: as for EXPORT.

16 The European Union and East Asia: Prospects for future economic co-operation

Roger Strange

INTRODUCTION

It is a measure of the recent economic success of many of the East Asian countries that the European Commission speaks of working towards a 'partnership of equals' in its 1994 document on future EU strategy for the region (Commission of the European Communities 1994: 1–2). But whereas the European Union is a distinct institutional entity with a sizeable bureaucracy and common policies on both economic and security issues,[1] East Asia has no such clearcut identity. Indeed, no universally acceptable definition even exists for the region, and no one organization speaks for the countries therein. In large part, this reflects the fact that the countries within the region are not only culturally diverse, but also differ markedly in their size, level of economic development, and political orientation.

Table 16.1 provides some illustrative statistics for Japan; the four 'Tigers' (i.e., Singapore, Hong Kong, Taiwan and the Republic of Korea); the three 'Dragons' (i.e., Indonesia, Malaysia, and Thailand); Brunei; the People's Republic of China (PRC); various low-income countries (Cambodia, Laos, the Philippines, Vietnam and Myanmar); and the United States, Canada, Australia and New Zealand (all members of APEC). In terms of population, the East Asian region is dominated by the PRC; in terms of GNP, by Japan. Japan generates 70 per cent of the GNP, but only accounts for 7 per cent of the population. The PRC accounts for 64 per cent of the population, but only generates 10 per cent of the GNP. The seven ASEAN countries (Brunei, Indonesia, Malaysia, Philippines, Singapore, Thailand, and Vietnam) have a combined population of over 400 million. Taiwan and South Korea are the largest of the 'Four Tigers', but average living standards are highest in Hong Kong and Singapore.

The disappointing economic performance of many European nations over the past thirty years is both well known and extensively analysed. In contrast, the reasons for the recent economic success of many East Asian economies are still the subject of heated debate, not only as a matter of historical inquiry but also with a view to establishing a potential model for other developing countries. Furthermore, while the European economies

Table 16.1 Illustrative statistics for various East Asian countries, 1994

Country	GNP per capita (US$)	GNP (US$m)	Popn (m)
Japan	34,630	4,321,136	124.8
Singapore	23,360	65,842	2.8
Hong Kong	21,650	126,286	5.8
Taiwan	10,479	244,200	21.0
South Korea	8,220	366,484	44.6
Four Tigers	10,820	802,812	74.2
Malaysia	3,520	68,674	19.5
Thailand	2,210	129,864	58.7
Indonesia	880	167,632	189.9
Three Dragons	1,366	366,170	268.1
Brunei	14,240	3,975	0.3
China	530	630,202	1190.9
Cambodia	200	1,800	10.0
Lao PDR	320	1,496	4.7
Myanmar	128	5,706	45.6
Philippines	960	63,311	66.2
Vietnam	190	13,775	72.5
EAST ASIA	3,344	6,210,383	1857.3
United States	25,860	6,737,367	260.5
Canada	19,570	569,949	29.1
Australia	17,980	320,475	17.8
New Zealand	13,190	46,578	3.5

Source: The World Bank Atlas 1996.

have sought their salvation in greater regional integration through the creation of the Single European Market (SEM) and subsequently the establishment of the European Union, the Asian economies have for the most part eschewed the formation of any formal trading blocs. Nevertheless, regional initiatives have intensified within East Asia in recent years with potential consequences for EU trade and investment.

The structure of the chapter is as follows. First, the influential study by the World Bank on the East Asian 'miracle' will be summarized, and some of the most potent criticisms of its conclusions highlighted. Second, the history of the various initiatives on cooperation within the region are reviewed, with particular emphasis given to the development of the Asia-Pacific Economic Cooperation (APEC) forum and its future prospects. Finally, the likely evolution of the EU–East Asia relationship is considered.

THE EAST ASIAN MIRACLE

Numerous authors have attempted to specify the key to the East Asian 'miracle'. One of the most influential studies was the 1993 report by the World Bank (World Bank: 1993). Although the conclusions have not met with universal acceptance, the report does provide perhaps the most comprehensive analysis yet attempted of the economic performance of Japan, the 'Four Tigers' and the three 'Dragons' over the period 1960 to 1990.

According to the Bank team, the essence of the miracle in these eight 'high-performing Asian economies' (HPAEs) was very high rates of private investment, high and rising endowments of human capital, and improved productivity. Two-thirds of the growth was attributed to the superior accumulation of human and physical capital; the remainder was due to superior productivity performance.

But how had this superiority been achieved? Cultural characteristics and geographical proximity were both discounted: the lack of economic success in Myanmar and the Philippines was cited as evidence. The answer was sound public policy – 'getting the fundamentals right' – supplemented, at times, by careful policy intervention. The team emphasized the different extent of government involvement in the eight countries, the wide range of instruments used, and the fact that the combinations of policies used varied across economies and over time. Furthermore, they stressed that pragmatic flexibility in the pursuit of their objectives – the capacity and willingness to change policies – was as much a hallmark of the HPAEs as any single policy instrument. The team found some evidence of effective policy intervention but concluded that sector-specific industrial policies (e.g., import protection, capital subsidies, low tariffs on imported capital goods) had had little effect on either the sectoral structure of industry or on rates of productivity change.

Rather the overall conclusion was that the rapid growth in the HPAEs had been a function of:

- Responsible macroeconomic management and stable macroeconomic performance, providing the essential framework for private investment. Creation of infrastructure complementary to private investment.
- Strong, prudential regulation and supervision of the financial system, combined with policies to make the banking system more accessible to small and rural savers. The resultant high savings contributed to the high levels of investment.
- Educational policies which first provided universal primary education, then increased the availability of secondary education, and later supported post-secondary education focused on technical skills. Broad technically inclined human capital bases were thus created, as were more equitable income distributions.
- Acquisition of advanced foreign technology through FDI and/or licensing and other means. The team noted that all eight countries had welcomed

technology transfer in the form of licenses, capital goods imports and foreign training, but that Japan, Korea, and to a lesser extent Taiwan, had restricted FDI.

- Mild financial repression (i.e. holding interest rates below market-clearing levels) and directed credit favoured borrowers (mostly firms) at the expense of savers (mostly households).

- Establishment of pro-export regimes, which encouraged the expansion of the countries' most productive industries and which facilitated access to international best-practice technologies through imports. All eight countries (except Hong Kong) had begun with a period of import substitution, and a strong bias against exports, but each eventually adopted export-push strategies. In the cases of Japan, Korea and Taiwan, this involved the provision of export credits, duty-free imports for exporters and their suppliers, export targets, tax incentives, and protection of the domestic market. In the cases of Indonesia, Thailand, and Malaysia, export promotion was provided through export credit and supporting institutions, general market incentives, and encouragement of FDI.

The Bank team noted that policy interventions such as industrial promotion, financial repression and export subsidies all involve costs, but suggested that the HPAE governments (unlike many others) had kept these costs within well-defined limits and hence the resulting price distortions had been mild.

As regards the next generation of developing economies, the team not only ruled out selective industrial promotion as a sensible strategy, but also suggested that financial repression, export subsidies and directed-credit programmes were no longer feasible in the 1990s.[2] In addition to the fundamental policies cited above, they recommended the creation of free trade environments for exporters, the provision of finance and support services for small and medium-size exporters, improvements to the trade-related aspects of the civil service, aggressive courting of export-oriented foreign direct investment, and the focusing of infrastructural investment in areas that encouraged exports. Many of these policies, they suggested, had been part of the success of Indonesia, Malaysia and Thailand, and it was these three countries that provided the appropriate model for the future.

The Bank's assessment of the less-than-miraculous reasons for the success of the East Asian countries has attracted criticism from various directions. Three in particular merit comment. A first line of criticism has focused on the conclusion that sector-specific industrial policies had been largely ineffectual in promoting economic growth.[3] Noting in particular the history of state intervention in Japan, Korea and Taiwan, the Bank concluded that industrial policy had had little effect and that the industrial structures in these countries had essentially evolved as would be expected given factor-based comparative advantage and changing factor endowments. The governments had intervened, but only to produce market-conforming results. In contrast, critics have argued that the governments successfully anticipated changes in comparative advantage and actively promoted the required changes in their economies' industrial structures.

The historical debate will no doubt continue and will probably never be resolved,[4] but what seems undeniable is that the role of the state in industrial policy in Japan, Korea and Taiwan has weakened considerably in the 1980s and 1990s, and that the governments in the other five countries have in general been rather less interventionist. This links to the second line of criticism which takes issue with the Bank's conclusion that the 'interventionist' model of the three North-east Asian countries is no longer capable of replication in the 1990s. Certainly many governments of developing countries still show considerable interest in the interventionist model, but it is also true that the three South-east Asian countries (Indonesia, Malaysia and Thailand) have adopted quite different policies (UNCTAD 1994: 72–6). Why are these three countries ignoring the apparently successful model of their northern neighbours? Do they have special circumstances or factor endowments which make the interventionist model inappropriate? Or is it, as the Bank suggest, that the world has changed and what might have worked in the 1950s and 1960s is unworkable in an era of global markets and footloose capital? Even if progress has been slow and disappointing, successive GATT Rounds have led to substantial reductions in tariff and non-tariff barriers to trade in all the lucrative markets of the developed economies and have reduced the scope for activist trade policy measures. Advances in information technology and communications have facilitated the international expansion and co-ordination of multinational enterprises. The liberalization and integration of global financial markets have reduced the efficacy of a range of monetary interventions, whilst also providing new opportunities for capital sourcing. And last, but not least, technology has become more advanced and more tacit, with implications for the feasibility of its transfer other than through the medium of FDI.

This latter point has received less attention than it deserves. The World Bank team emphasized the role of foreign technology in all eight HPAEs, and noted the different mechanisms adopted for its transfer in each. But the ability of countries to gain access to, and then to exploit, foreign technology depends crucially upon the mode of transfer. The experience of many countries (including China) in the 1980s and 1990s suggests that licensing and other arm's length methods of transfer are no longer appropriate for more advanced technology, and that foreign companies require majority ownership (and control) of their subsidiaries in order to countenance such transfer. This leads on to questions about the wisdom of encouraging substantial inflows of FDI, and how the potential long-term costs of FDI might be minimized (and the potential benefits maximized).

A final line of criticism concerns the lack of weight given by the Bank team to cultural determinants of growth. The Bank's neoclassical framework simply cannot capture the influence of the distinctive Asian business relationships, networks and value systems. Yet it is also true that these characteristics vary across the HPAEs, and they alone cannot provide a satisfactory explanation for the East Asian miracle. After all, economic success eluded these countries for many years prior to the recent past. It is also not clear, for example, whether informal Chinese business networks are either more or less efficient overall than the more market-oriented transactions to which Western firms are accustomed. In some ways and in certain circumstances the former are more efficient; in other ways and other circumstances the latter. But even within the neoclassical framework, cultural attitudes towards savings and education, for example, should not be neglected in explanations of the high rates of saving and human capital formation. It is one thing to make the banking system more accessible; it is another whether the population is minded to take advantage. As the proverb says, you can lead a horse to water but you cannot make it drink.

REGIONALISM IN EAST ASIA

Regional initiatives within the Asia Pacific region are not a new phenomenon. Three early non-governmental institutions are usually cited as forerunners of the contemporary initiatives (Woods 1991). As long ago as 1965, two Japanese economists proposed the creation of a Pacific Free Trade Area (PAFTA) patterned after the European Economic Community (EEC). PAFTA was to comprise five advanced countries – Japan, Australia, New Zealand, Canada, and the United States – as full members, while associate membership would be granted to the developing countries in the region. Discriminatory tariffs and other trade measures against non-members were envisaged, and it was conceived as a counterpart and a counterweight to the EEC. The PAFTA idea was subsequently taken up by the Japanese Government and gave rise to a 1968 conference on Pacific Trade and Development (PAFTAD). Although the trade bloc idea was not subsequently pursued, an ongoing PAFTAD conference series has examined a range of Asia-Pacific economic issues.

Concomitant with the above, a group of businessmen formed the Pacific Basin Economic Council (PBEC) in April 1967 as an organization to promote international business cooperation. Annual meetings have since been held to review economic and commercial conditions. The third group, the Pacific Economic Cooperation Conference (PECC), was established in September 1980 with a rather wider membership drawn not only from industry but also from government and academia. The PECC held annual meetings thereafter and brought together delegates from all the future principal members of APEC.[5] Beeson (1995: 3) notes that PECC was something of an extension of both PAFTAD and PBEC, and that it provided the foundations on which APEC could subsequently be built. Two important PECC achievements were the development of Pacific support for the

Uruguay Round of GATT negotiations, and the fostering of economic dialogue between China, Taiwan and Hong Kong.

At the governmental level, the Association of South-east Asian Nations (ASEAN) was established in August 1967 to facilitate the economic, social and cultural cooperation and development of its six members. The founding members were Thailand, Malaysia, Singapore, Indonesia, Brunei, and the Philippines who have a combined population (see Table 16.1) in excess of 330 million – i.e. slightly fewer than the fifteen-nation European Union, rather more than the United States, and two-and-a-half times more than Japan. Vietnam (population = 72.5 million) became a member in July 1995. Notwithstanding various attempts to reduce intra-ASEAN trade barriers, notably the 1992 establishment of the ASEAN Free Trade Area (AFTA), ASEAN's most enduring role has been as a regional spokesman on security matters. In July 1994, the ASEAN Regional Forum (ARF) was set up,[6] with the aim of establishing a security system for the Asia Pacific region. The ARF membership includes not only the six ASEAN countries, but also most of the other countries in East Asia (except North Korea), the United States, Russia, and the European Union.

Japan's interest in Pacific 'co-operation' goes back to the 'infamous Greater East Asia Co-prosperity Scheme (GEACS), the grand design for regional integration under the yoke of Imperial Japan . . . Concern has always been expressed however, whenever Japan makes a proposal for Pacific co-operation, that it might be a revival of the notorious Co-prosperity Sphere'.[7] In more recent times, a Pacific Basin Co-operation Study Group was established by the Prime Minister in March 1979. Another study group released a report in 1987 noting the threat posed by the creation of exclusive trading blocs, and urging the formation of a loose economic framework embracing the nations of Asia and North America. The 1988 White Paper from the Ministry of International Trade and Industry (MITI) went further and proposed the creation of an OECD-type organization.

> Rather too transparently, MITI indicated that the purpose of economic co-operation the Pacific would be to facilitate continued economic growth in Japan. In MITI's conception, agriculture would conveniently be excluded from the agenda of co-operation. Membership of the Japanese Asia Pacific Organization (APO) would definitely include the USA, Canada, and Hong Kong, but not the PRC or Taiwan . . . Japan's hidden agenda, which was not so carefully hidden, was its own continued economic restructuring.[8]

The proposal to establish APEC is normally traced to a January 1989 speech by the then Prime Minister of Australia, Bob Hawke. Beeson notes, however, that MITI has subsequently claimed credit for the idea and that Australia may have been allowed to promote the proposal so as to avoid the concerns noted above (Beeson 1995: 17). Certainly Japan has been an enthusiastic participant from the start, and has been at pains throughout not to offend the sensitivities of its Asian neighbours.

The first APEC meeting of ministerial-level representatives took place in Canberra, 5–7 November 1989, and the initial membership was the six ASEAN countries, together with the United States, Canada, Japan, South Korea, Australia and New Zealand. Australia had initially opposed the inclusion of Canada and the United States, and there were marked differences in enthusiasm for the APEC idea among the ASEAN members with Indonesia, in particular, concerned about loss of ASEAN influence. It is also interesting to note the countries excluded from the preliminary meeting: the socialist economies of the PRC, Vietnam, and the former Soviet Union, the market economies of Hong Kong and Taiwan, Mexico, the Pacific countries of Central and South America, and India.

Japan and the United States had both argued that Hong Kong should be included as it was a major influence on regional production, trade, and finance. But the political nature of the 'Three Chinas problem' meant that entry for both Hong Kong and Taiwan was deferred until the 1991 APEC conference in Seoul when the PRC, Hong Kong and Chinese Taipei (as Taiwan is officially known in APEC) were simultaneously admitted. Mexico and Papua New Guinea joined in 1993, Chile in 1994, and several other countries have expressed interest but a moratorium on new members was extended for three years after the 1993 meetings in Seattle. The membership at the 1995 meetings in Osaka thus numbered eighteen countries which together accounted for over 40 per cent of the world's population and almost 60 per cent of world GDP.

The declared objectives of APEC as set out at the Canberra conference were:[9]

- to try and present a united voice at the Uruguay Round of GATT negotiations;
- to set up working parties to find ways of increasing regional trade, investment, and technology transfer between rich and poor countries;
- to set up new data systems on trade, investment flows and commercial opportunities in the region.

Furthermore, it was agreed that APEC would not be a formal inter-governmental institution, but rather a non-formal process of consultation. No secretariat was established, and preparations for subsequent meetings were to be made informally by senior officials from each nation.

The Canberra conference was followed by subsequent Ministerial Meetings in Singapore (1990), Seoul (1991) and Bangkok (1992). Each provided a forum for dialogue, but achieved little by way of tangible results and attracted little attention.[10] However, a watershed came with the installation of the Clinton administration in January 1993, and with the subsequent increased appreciation of the potential role of APEC for the promotion of US regional interests.

On 7 July 1994, President Clinton gave a lecture at Waseda University in Tokyo in which he put forward his idea for a New Pacific Community, and proposed that the APEC leaders should hold a summit after the APEC Ministerial Meetings in Seattle that November. Furukawa notes that:

The ASEAN countries, ever wary of superpower leadership and domination, responded negatively to the proposal. When the US explained that the summit would be an informal venue for the candid exchange of views, however, the ASEAN countries acquiesced – with the exception of Malaysian Prime Minister Mahathir Mohamad, who rejected the idea throughout and did not attend. In order to win over the ASEAN countries, the US promised that, since the summit was informal, there would be no negotiations, declarations, or press conferences. Negotiations were held at the Seattle Summit, however, resulting in the acceptance of American demands which had been rejected in the Ministerial Meeting. Further, when the east Asian countries objected to declaring the formation of an Asia-Pacific Economic Community on the grounds that this aimed at achieving something on the model of the European Community (EC), the US remained insistent on the use of the word 'community', finally succeeding in inserting it uncapitalized.'[11]

The Seattle summit on Blake Island established a precedent, and there have been subsequent 'Economic Leaders' Meetings' in Bogor, Indonesia (1994) and Osaka, Japan (1995).

Concern about the evolution of APEC into a formal trade grouping which would promote US dominance in the Asia Pacific region had prompted Dr Mahathir's absence from the Seattle summit, and was also the basis for his 1991 proposal to create an East Asian Economic Group (EAEG) to provide the Asian nations with a collective voice on issues relating to the SEM and NAFTA. The membership was to be restricted to Asian nations, to the exclusion of the North American countries, Australia and New Zealand, and Japan's participation was deemed crucial to its success. The proposal drew strong criticism, particularly from the United States, and was later altered to make the group into an East Asian Economic Caucus (EAEC) within APEC.[12]

If the Seattle summit raised the status of the APEC forum, then the meetings the following year in Indonesia provided it with a real sense of direction and purpose. The Economic Leaders' Meeting was held at Bogor in the summer villa of the former Dutch Governors and gave rise to a commitment to free and open trade and investment in the region. The Bogor Declaration (APEC 1994) announced:

1 With respect to our objective of enhancing trade and investment in Asia-Pacific, we agree to adopt the long-term goal of free and open trade and investment in Asia-Pacific.

This goal will be pursued promptly by further reducing barriers to trade and investment and promoting the free flow of goods, services, and capital among our economies. We will achieve this goal in a GATT-consistent manner and believe our actions will be a powerful impetus for further liberalization at the multilateral level to which we remain fully committed.

2 We further agree to announce our commitment to complete the achievement of our goal of free and open trade and investment in Asia-Pacific no later than the year 2020.

The pace of implementation will take into account the differing levels of economic development among APEC economies, with the industrialized economies achieving the goal of free and open trade and investment no later than the year 2010 and developing economies no later than the year 2020.

3 We wish to emphasis our strong opposition to the creation of an inward-looking trading bloc that would divert from the pursuit of global free trade.

We are determined to pursue free and open trade and investment in Asia-Pacific in a manner that will encourage and strengthen trade and investment liberalization in the world as a whole. Thus, the outcome of trade and investment liberalization in Asia-Pacific will not only be the actual reduction of barriers among APEC economies but also between APEC economies and non-APEC economies.

In this respect, we will give particular attention to our trade with non-APEC developing countries to ensure that they will also benefit from our trade and investment liberalization, in conformity with GATT/WTO provisions.

The Bogor Declaration provided a vision for APEC, but was notably short on specifics except for the target dates – and even these were taken by many members to be negotiable. The task of providing a detailed proposals was deferred for clarification prior to, and adoption at, the Osaka Ministerial Meeting in November 1995.

The immediate reaction to the Osaka meetings was that they had been a great success and that the Japanese Government had provided effective leadership in resolving differences between the member economies. In their Declaration, the APEC Leaders formally adopted an Action Agenda which set out the blueprint for future progress towards the goals set out at Bogor. The Action Agenda established nine guiding principles as the basis for trade and investment liberalization and facilitation:

- Comprehensiveness: all impediments to free and open trade and investment within APEC should be addressed.
- WTO Consistency: all measures taken under the APEC Action Agenda should be consistent with WTO agreements and principles.
- Comparability: all APEC economies will endeavour to ensure the overall comparability of their liberalization and facilitation programmes.

- Non-Discrimination: all APEC economies will endeavour not to discriminate between and among themselves in the process of liberalization and facilitation of trade and investment.
- Transparency: each APEC economy should ensure the transparency of its respective laws, regulations and administrative procedures that affect the flows of goods, services, and capital among its fellow members.
- Standstill: each APEC economy will endeavour to refrain from measures which increase levels of protection.
- Simultaneous start, continuous process and differentiated timetables: all APEC economies will begin the process of liberalization, facilitation and cooperation with its fellow members simultaneously and without delay.
- Flexibility: each APEC economy shall have flexibility in the speed and scope of the liberalization and facilitation process taking into account their diverse circumstances.
- Cooperation: economic and technical cooperation contributing to liberalization and facilitation will be pursued.

On the basis of these principles, the Leaders committed their countries to the preparation of individual 'concrete and substantive' Action Plans with both short- and medium-term timeframes. The Action Plans[13] were to be submitted to the 1996 Ministerial Meeting in the Philippines, and were to be implemented from January 1997 and subject to annual review at subsequent Ministerial Meetings. Furthermore, each APEC member proposed a package of Initial Actions as a 'down payment' to demonstrate its commitment to the process of liberalization. These Initial Actions mainly comprised early implementation of WTO tariff reductions and improvements in administrative procedures.

The general consensus on most of the packages of Initial Actions was that most countries had offered little more than they had previously agreed under the Uruguay Round though some measures were to be implemented ahead of schedule. Even China's dramatic announcement that it would cut tariffs on 4,000 items, eliminate import quotas and licenses on 170 products, and reduce the overall level of protection by 30 per cent should be considered in the light of rampant customs tax evasion and the cancellation of import-tax exemptions for foreign-invested companies[14] Japan pledged to reduce tariffs on 697 industrial items two years earlier than the WTO schedule and to implement 50 deregulation measures to ease foreign access to the Japanese market. But notwithstanding its confirmation of cuts in preferential tariffs on 55 agriculture and fishery products from April 1995, there was little indication of any marked Japanese willingness to liberalize its agricultural sector.

The Action Agenda also identified thirteen specific areas for economic and technical cooperation, viz: human resources development; science and technology exchange; improved access for small and medium enterprises;

infrastructure improvement; energy forecasting; transportation; telecommunications and information; tourism; creation of a trade and investment database; trade promotion; marine resources conservation; fisheries conservation; and agricultural technology. Finally, the Declaration acknowledged the potential problems associated with rapid economic and population growth in the region, and noted that increased food and energy demand and environmental issues should be part of the long-term APEC agenda.

Behind the lofty principles and the affirmations of common resolve, however, lie a range of sensitive issues over which APEC members have fundamental differences of opinion. It is these differences and how – indeed whether – they may be resolved or accommodated that will determine the future direction of the APEC process.

The first issue relates to the ongoing debate about the modality of decision-making within APEC. In the Senior Officials' Meetings prior to Osaka, the United States and Australia had suggested that members should negotiate 'concessions' as in the GATT/WTO, and that all would be legally bound to implement the agreements under the threat of legal sanctions. The counter-proposal from Japan was that members should submit their own programmes and implement them unilaterally. This process of 'concerted unilateral liberalization' would be supplemented by peer pressure alone. The Japanese proposal was eventually adopted for the Osaka meetings, and much emphasis was placed *ex post* on how this 'Asian' way had contributed to the successful outcome.[15] A more sceptical view would be that the consensual approach was perhaps the most realistic way of building on the momentum of the Bogor Declaration given the vastly different circumstances of the APEC members, but that the true test of the 'Asian' way and the effectiveness of peer pressure will come at future meetings when explicit targets come to be debated. Dr Fred Bergsten, the US representative and Chairman of the now-abolished Eminent Persons Group, was quoted as saying that the United States would lose interest in APEC if the consensual approach failed to deliver its trade policy objectives.

A second area where there is lack of agreement is over the precise interpretations of some of the guiding principles upon which the Action Agenda is based, and here the choice of wording is often revealing. The most contentious principle is likely to be flexibility, and how much discretion each member has in the speed and scope of its liberalization process. There is already debate over how binding, or otherwise, are the deadlines for the achievement of free and open trade. The US and Australian position is that free and open trade means the abolition of all trade restrictions by the appointed dates. But Malaysia for one, and also some of the other developing economies, are adamant that they will only reduce their tariffs as and when they feel able to do so. However, the industrialized countries are unlikely to commit themselves to free trade by the year 2010 unless they are certain that the developing economies will follow suit by the year 2020.

In addition, there are likely to be fierce arguments over the methods and the pace of liberalization. In initial drafts of the Action Agenda, Japan had called for 'different treatment for sensitive sectors in the liberalization process' but this requirement had been replaced by the principle of flexibility in the final Declaration. Agriculture is a sensitive sector not only in Japan but also in South Korea, Taiwan and China, yet liberalization of domestic agricultural markets is high on the wish lists of both the United States and Australia.

The application of the non-discrimination principle was the source of disagreement between the United States and China, with the latter claiming it should thus receive automatic Most-Favoured-Nation status which the former was reluctant to concede. The Action Agenda wording thus notes that each APEC member will 'endeavour to apply' the principle to the other members, but specifies no deadlines.

A third issue concerns the desirability of APEC funding development cooperation. Some of the developing countries are wary of development cooperation as implying an inappropriate donor-recipient relationship. The United States, on the other hand, initially opposed Japan's Partners for Progress (PFP) initiative because it feared that Japan would use the development fund to dominate the Asian market. The PFP initiative envisages developing countries implementing the cooperation programmes themselves rather than the programmes being managed by the industrialized countries.

Fourth, there are questions about enlargement of the APEC membership. Possible future members might include Vietnam (now in ASEAN), India and even Russia together with a range of smaller countries in both Asia and Latin America. Any further widening of APEC could only exacerbate the difficulties of obtaining consensus on important issues and of deepening the extent of cooperation.

Fifth, and perhaps most importantly, there is no clear and common vision about the future role of APEC. Thusfar it has existed as a forum for dialogue on economic matters and can claim the not inconsequential successes of having brought not only the United States, Japan and China to the same table, but also the three Chinas (even if the President of Taiwan is not yet invited to the Economic Leaders' Meetings). It seems highly unlikely that APEC will evolve as a regional trading bloc, still less as an integrated unit like the European Union. One does not need to believe the rhetoric about commitment to 'open regionalism' to realise that the diverse economic circumstances of the countries do not favour common tariffs etc. It is also unlikely that APEC will evolve a strong bureaucracy notwithstanding the Osaka agreement to double the size of the Singapore-based APEC Secretariat from its current staff of twenty-eight (cf. more than 20,000 for the European Union). Indeed it is interesting to note that the uncapitalized 'community' of the Seattle Declaration had been diluted to a 'spirit of community' at Bogor, and further to a 'sense of community' in the Osaka Declaration.

APEC can, however, make an important contribution in at least six ways:

- As a mechanism for speeding up the implementation of, and ensuring adherence to, WTO agreements in the Asia Pacific region.
- As a coherent voice at the WTO in favour of greater liberalization of trade and investment worldwide.
- As a mechanism for promoting the effective multilateral dispersion of development funding in the Asia Pacific region.
- As a facilitator of China's integration into the world economy and of its eventual admission to the WTO. It has been suggested that China's dramatic package of Initial Actions at Osaka was a face-saving way of introducing measures required for its WTO entry without being seen to bow directly to international pressure.
- As a wider forum for reducing tensions in the US–Japan relationship.
- As a means of dissipating Asian fears of US and Japanese leadership (hegemony?), whilst still keeping both countries engaged economically in the Asia-Pacific region. This is particularly important at a time when the United States is re-evaluating its security relationship with the region.

The above list emphasizes the enabling roles that APEC can play, but it is notable for two omissions. First, there is no mention of the explicit deadlines of the Bogor Declaration, and it is likely that these will be downplayed (cf. the reappraisal of the concept of community) at successive annual meetings through calls on the principle of flexibility.[16] It is interesting to note that there was little opportunity for delegations to discuss the draft text of the Bogor Declaration (Furukawa 1995: 14–15), and it is to be hoped that its issuance and the subsequent raised expectations will not hinder meaningful APEC progress in the future. Second, no potential role is yet foreseen for APEC as a forum for the discussion of regional security issues. This is not to deny that there are many pressing security issues in the region (e.g. the territorial dispute over the oil-rich Spratly Islands, tensions between China and Taiwan, the substantial increases in many countries' military budgets) or to suggest that ARF is an appropriate body for their resolution, but the same forces which impel APEC to remain as a loose grouping of nations also drastically reduce its potential effectiveness as a power broker.

CONCLUDING REMARKS

What do East Asian growth and the development of APEC mean for the European businessman? First, the increased spending power in the Asian countries have created potentially lucrative new markets, with consequent implications for European exports and direct investment. Second, the low wage costs (often coupled with less strict environmental standards) and/or high productivity in many Asian countries have made them potent competitors in world (including European) markets. Third, increased European contact and involvement within the East Asian region have brought both recognition and appreciation of the distinctive business systems and management styles of the countries therein. This has raised questions about the applicability of Western concepts and methods to the Asian environment, and about the possible superiority (and transferability) of certain Asian concepts and methods to the West. Fourth, the discussion of the East Asian 'miracle' has highlighted the probable development paths which other East and South Asian countries will adopt in the future. It is salutary to note that the eight HPAEs have a combined population of less than 500 million, whilst China and India together have more than 2 billion. Fifth, the ongoing APEC process should be welcomed not just for the tangible results it brings in terms of trade and investment liberalization,[17] but also because it contributes towards a stable and predictable business environment in the Asia-Pacific region. Even if APEC as now constituted falls by the wayside, not only history but also contemporary commercial logic would suggest that something very similar would emerge as a replacement.

A final comment relates to how the EU–East Asia relationship is likely to evolve. The short answer is very quickly, and driven by private commercial imperatives rather than official governmental initiatives. The relationship will involve trade and investment flows in both directions (cf. the recent increases in Korean and Taiwanese FDI in Europe) as well as increasing numbers of non-equity linkages and strategic alliances. Furthermore, the relationship will involve not only inter-regional, but also intra-regional competition. For instance, Choi *et al.* suggest that European firms might profitably seek strategic alliances with firms from Korea, Taiwan, Hong Kong and Singapore in their efforts to compete effectively with their Japan counterparts. Not only would firms from the 'Four Tigers' have greater knowledge of Asian markets, but they might also be able to provide more detailed information on Japanese business practices (Choi, Lee and Lynskey 1995: 25–6). From an European point of view, the most worrying aspect is the lack of general awareness of both the scale and scope of the challenges involved – particularly when compared to the greater level of Asian awareness. It is to be hoped that this volume may, in some small way, help to remedy this deficiency.

NOTES

1 Notwithstanding often heated differences of opinion between the Member States.
2 Financial repression would require the closure of domestic financial markets to the outside world. Export subsidies and direct export credit are not consistent with WTO principles, and would invite retaliation from trading partners.
3 See Smith (1995) for an excellent discussion of the debate about the use of industrial policy in East Asia. Also Kang (1995).

4 As the World Bank acknowledge, there is a 'central methodological problem. Since we chose the HPAEs for their unusually rapid growth, we know already that their interventions did not significantly inhibit growth. But it is very difficult to establish statistical links between growth and a specific intervention and even more difficult to establish causality. Because we cannot know what would have happened in the absence of a specific policy, it is difficult to test whether interventions increased growth rates. Other economies attempted similar interventions without success, and on average they used them more pervasively than in the HPAEs. Because the HPAEs differed from less successful economies both in their closer adherence to policy fundamentals and in the manner in which they implemented interventions, it is virtually impossible to measure the relative impact of fundamentals and interventions on HPAE growth. Thus, in attempting to distinguish interventions that contributed to growth from those that were either growth-neutral or harmful to growth, we cannot offer a rigorous counterfactual scenario.' (World Bank 1993: 6)

5 The eighteen members in 1991 were the six ASEAN countries, Australia, New Zealand, Canada, the United States, China, Japan, South Korea, Taiwan, Hong Kong, Chile, Peru and Mexico (Low 1991: 382).

6 As an extension of the annual ASEAN Post Ministerial Conference. See Commission of the European Communities (1994: 9).

7 Chiba (1989: 44).

8 Day and Herbig (1995: 15).

9 *Far Eastern Economic Review*, vol. 146, no. 46 (16 November 1989) p. 10.

10 A permanent APEC Secretariat was established in Singapore in January 1993. The work of APEC has also been supported by ten working groups, and various temorary advisory bodies such as the Eminent Persons Group and the Pacific Business Forum. The Eminent Persons Group was established in 1992 to provide an independent long-term vision for APEC, and was composed of academics and former government officials from the APEC economies. It published three reports, but was abolished at the Osaka meeting. The Pacific Business Forum was established in 1993 to gather opinion from the business sector: its status was upgraded at Osaka into a permanent body called the APEC Business Advisory Council whose remit was to put forward specific proposals on ways to facilitate private business.

11 Furukawa (1995: 13–14).

12 *Far Eastern Economic Review*, vol. 156, no. 46 (18 November 1993) p. 17.

13 Actions are required in fifteen specific areas: tariffs, non-tariff measures, services, investment, standards and conformance, customs procedures, intellectual property rights, competition policy, government procurement, deregulation, rules of origin, dispute mediation, mobility of business people, implementation of the Uruguay Round outcomes, and information gathering to assist the liberalization process.

14 *The Asian Wall Street Journal* (20 November 1995) p. 12.

15 Much of the comment *ex ante* was on the weak nature of Japan's leadership!

16 Note also the abolition of the Eminent Persons Group which had been instrumental in recommending the deadlines included in the Bogor Declaration.

17 APEC may not only bring about trade and investment liberalization in the Asia-Pacific region, but may also prompt the European Union to consider favourably the idea of a trans-Atlantic free trade area with NAFTA!

BIBLIOGRAPHY

APEC (1994) *APEC Economic Leaders' Declaration of Common Resolve*, Bogor, Indonesia: November.

APEC (1995) *APEC Economic Leaders' Declaration of Action*, Osaka, Japan: November.

Beeson, Mark (1995) 'Australia, APEC, and the Politics of Regional Economic Integration', *Asia Pacific Business Review*, 2(1), Autumn: 1–19.

Chiba, Akira (1989) 'Pacific Co-operation and China', *The Pacific Review* 2(1): 44–56.

Choi, Chong Ju, Soo Hee Lee and Michael J. Lynskey (1995) 'Europe's Asian Opportunities: Learning from the USA and Japan', *European Business Review* 95(2): 24–7.

Commission of the European Communities (1994) 'Towards a New Asia Strategy', COM(94) 314 final, Luxembourg: Office for Official Publications of the European Communities.

Day, Ken and Paul Herbig (1995) 'Outgrowth of ASEAN, a Common Market of the Pacific: Lessons to be Learned from the European Experience', *European Business Review* 95(2): 12–23.

Furukawa, Eiichi (1995) 'APEC Meetings: From Bogor to Osaka', *Kansai Forum* 3(21), August/September: 10–21.

Kang, David C. (1995) 'South Korean and Taiwanese Development and the New Institutional Economics', *International Organization* 49(3), Summer: 555–87.

Low, Linda (1991) 'The East Asian Economic Grouping', *The Pacific Review* 4(4): 375–82.

Smith, Heather (1995) 'Industry Policy in East Asia', *Asian-Pacific Economic Literature* 9(1), May: 17–39.

UNCTAD (1994) *World Investment Report 1994: Transnational Corporations, Employment and the Workplace*, Geneva: United Nations.

Woods, Lawrence T. (1991) 'Non-governmental Organizations and Pacific Cooperation: Back to the Future?' *The Pacific Review* 4(4): 312–21.

World Bank, (1993) *The East Asian Miracle: Economic Growth and Public Policy*, New York: Oxford University Press.

Index